T0181233

Lecture Notes in Computer Science 13888

Founding Editors

Gerhard Goos
Juris Hartmanis

Editorial Board Members

The series Lecture Notes in Computer Science (LNCS), including its subseries Lecture Notes in Artificial Intelligence (LNAI) and Lecture Notes in Bioinformatics (LNBI), has established itself as a medium for the publication of new developments in computer science and information technology research, teaching, and education.

LNCS enjoys close cooperation with the computer science R & D community, the series counts many renowned academics among its volume editors and paper authors, and collaborates with prestigious societies. Its mission is to serve this international community by providing an invaluable service, mainly focused on the publication of conference and workshop proceedings and postproceedings. LNCS commenced publication in 1973.

Kai Rannenberg · Prokopios Drogkaris ·
Cédric Lauradoux

Editors

Privacy Technologies and Policy

11th Annual Privacy Forum, APF 2023
Lyon, France, June 1–2, 2023
Proceedings

 Springer

Editors
Kai Rannenberg
Goethe University Frankfurt
Frankfurt, Germany

Prokopios Drogkaris
European Union Agency for Cybersecurity
Athens, Greece

Cédric Lauradoux
Inria Centre - Université Grenoble Alpes
Montbonnot-Saint-Martin, France

ISSN 0302-9743 ISSN 1611-3349 (electronic)
Lecture Notes in Computer Science
ISBN 978-3-031-61088-2 ISBN 978-3-031-61089-9 (eBook)
https://doi.org/10.1007/978-3-031-61089-9

This Springer imprint is published by the registered company Springer Nature Switzerland AG
The registered company address is: Gewerbestrasse 11, 6330 Cham, Switzerland

If disposing of this product, please recycle the paper.

Preface

I had the privilege of being general chair of the Annual Privacy Forum (APF 2023) in Lyon, France. I would like to thank all the participants, whether they are authors of the contributions in this volume, guest speakers, panelists or simple participants. This conference would not have been possible without the support of ENISA, Inria and the University of Lyon 2. I would like to thank also all those who did not attend the conference but who contributed greatly with their reviews or by their proposed contributions. APF would not be such a unique forum between computer scientists, legal scholars and data supervisory authorities without the contributions of Prokopios Drogkaris and Kai Rannenberg. These conference proceedings will allow those who were not present in person at the event to find a trace of the fascinating discussions which took place.

November 2023

Cédric Lauradoux

Organization

General Chair

Cédric Lauradoux   Université Grenoble Alpes, Inria

Program Committee Chairs

Kai Rannenberg	Goethe University Frankfurt
Prokopios Drogkaris	ENISA
Cédric Lauradoux	Université Grenoble Alpes, Inria

Program Committee

Pedro Adão	University of Lisbon
Roman Bieda	Kozminski University
Athena Bourka	ENISA
Giuseppe D'Acquisto	Italian Data Protection Authority, Italy
Debajyoti Das	Katholieke Universiteit Leuven
José M. Del Álamo	Universidad Politécnica de Madrid
Matteo Dell'Amico	University of Genoa
Vasiliki Diamantopoulou	University of the Aegean
Piotr Drobek	Polish Data Protection Authority
Petros Efstathopoulos	Norton Research Group
Ana Ferreira	ENISA
Simone Fischer-Hübner	Karlstad University
Marta Fydrych-Gasowska	mBank
Olga Gkotsopoulou	Vrije Universiteit Brussel
Javier Gomez	ENISA
Nils Gruschka	University of Oslo
Kristina Irion	University of Amsterdam
Meiko Jensen	Karlstad University
Christos Kalloniatis	University of the Aegean
Irene Kamara	Vrije Universiteit Brussel
Agnieszka Gryszczyńska	Cardinal Stefan Wyszynski University in Warsaw (UKSW)

Sokratis Katsikas	Norwegian University of Science and Technology, Norway
Nicholas Kolokotronis	University of Peloponnese
Konstantinos Limniotis	Hellenic Data Protection Authority
Luigi Lo Iacono	Hochschule Bonn-Rhein-Sieg University
Nikolas Molyndris	Decentriq
Maria Owczarek	Personal Data Protection Office (UODO)
Davy Preuveneers	Katholieke Universiteit Leuven
Delphine Reinhardt	University of Göttingen
Cristiana Santos	Utrecht University
Erich Schweighofer	University of Vienna
Jan Tolsdorf	Georg-August-Universität Göttingen, Germany
Tom Van Cutsem	Katholieke Universiteit Leuven
Griet Verhenneman	Ghent University
Jan Willemson	Cybernetica

Additional Reviewers

Katerina Mavroeidi
Alexandre Lodie
Victor Morel
Argyri Pattakou
Aikaterini-Georgia Mavroeidi

Contents

x   Contents

Emerging Technologies and Protection of Personal Data

A Universal Data Model for Data Sharing Under the European Data Strategy

Malte Hansen[1]([✉]) [ID], Nils Gruschka[1] [ID], and Meiko Jensen[2] [ID]

[1] Department of Informatics, University of Oslo, Oslo, Norway
{maltehan,nilsgrus}@ifi.uio.no
[2] Karlstad University, Karlstad, Sweden
meiko.jensen@kau.se

Abstract. The current European data strategy foresees a novel ecosystem of data sharing and data trading among public and private sector organizations in the EU member states. The focus is on enabling and fostering data sharing among the stakeholders while maintaining compliance with existing EU and national data protection legislation, such as the European General Data Protection Regulation (GDPR).

However, managing data sharing in such a compliant manner requires additional metadata to be exchanged amongst the actors in this ecosystem. Therefore, this paper proposes a novel data model for managing data sharing activities. This model takes current and planned regulations (e.g., the Data Governance Act) and the resulting data ecosystem architectures (e.g. data intermediaries) into account and is applicable to different actions that are necessary for compliant data exchange, like data subject rights requests or intellectual property enforcement.

Keywords: data sharing · data model · European data strategy · Data Governance Act · GDPR

1 Introduction

The well-known quote "Data is the new gold!" is more than a decade old, but illustrates nowadays more than ever the value of data and data exchange for commercial enterprises as well as for the public sector. However, when not handled in compliance with legislation, especially data protection regulations, data sharing can violate the rights and freedom of individuals, which led to a second expression: "Data is the new uranium!". On the other hand, the fear of high fines for violation of data protection regulations can lead to a complete blockade of any data exchange. In light of this dilemma, the goal of the European data strategy is to enable data sharing while complying with EU and national legislation, such as the European General Data Protection Regulation (GDPR) [1].

Consequently, it becomes necessary for data controllers, data processors, data intermediaries, and other actors in this ecosystem to address these legal requirements in their data sharing agreements and platforms. More specifically, they

K. Rannenberg et al. (Eds.): APF 2023, LNCS 13888, pp. 3–19, 2024.
https://doi.org/10.1007/978-3-031-61089-9_1

need to provide means for managing federated data sharing scenarios—involving multiple actors—in such a way that legal compliance is maintained, especially concerning GDPR obligations like purpose binding and data subject rights (cf. Art. 5, 15ff. GDPR [1]). This requires standardized interactions among data sharing actors in a decentralized, federated manner.

This paper proposes a novel data model for managing data sharing activities in such a pan-European data ecosystem. Based on the roles defined in the respective legislation, we analyze the needs for interaction and metadata exchange, and we derive a universal data model that can generically be utilized for managing data sharing interactions in a compositional, decentrally organized, legally compliant manner. The model can serve multiple purposes, such as data subject rights enforcement, data breach notification, intellectual property rights enforcement, and many more.

The paper is organized as follows. In the next section, we provide the legal and policy background for this work, based on the novel European legislation and data strategy. Section 3 then summarizes the state of the art in research on these topics. In Sect. 4, we define the proposed universal data model, providing its requirements and core technical aspects. The subsequent section illustrates the use of this data model in practice, based on an example scenario from the logistics domain. In Sect. 6, we discuss different areas of application of the data model, and the paper concludes with a discussion of relevant properties and open issues in Sects. 7 and 8, respectively.

2   Background

In this section, we briefly present the European data strategy [2] and its relevant regulations, which lead to a demand for an optimized data model for data sharing in the European market.

2.1   The European Data Strategy

Data has been identified as an essential resource by the European Commission, able to foster economic growth, research, and societal progress if used appropriately. This led to the commission's proposal of a common European data strategy [2]. The EU data strategy aims to create a single market for data, connecting public and private actors across multiple sectors. In this market, data is intended to flow freely for the benefit of all involved parties, facilitating access and re-use of data, hence optimizing data use. A set of European regulations were proposed to build the framework for this data ecosystem, fostering the elaboration of practical and clear rules for the access and use of data, while guaranteeing compliance with existing privacy and data protection legislation like the GDPR. These combined efforts shall strengthen the position of the EU as an attractive competitor in the global data economy, offering a fair, secure, and dynamic environment for data flows. To achieve these proclaimed goals, the

European Commission has proposed several new European regulations, including the Data Governance Act [3] (DGA), Data Act [4], Digital Services Act [5], and Digital Markets Act [6].

2.2   The Data Governance Act and Data Intermediaries

The European Data Governance Act (DGA) [3], which will come into force in September 2023, acts as a central cornerstone in the European data strategy. It aims to increase data availability and facilitate the reuse of data across the European market. To achieve this, common European data spaces are to be built, including actors from both public and private entities, that allow for sharing and reuse of data across multiple sectors. A key role in this new environment will fall upon the so-called Data Intermediaries (DI). DIs are designed to act as a mediator between different Data Controllers (DC), either storing or requesting data sets. Defined as a benevolent actor in the DGA, a DI should not have a commercial interest in using the data it obtains by itself. Rather, a DI's main duty is to fulfill requests for data issued by other actors, aggregating applicable data sets from their data sources, and distributing them to the requesting organizations in a secure and privacy-preserving way. In these data sharing scenarios, they will aid in enforcing data subject rights, as well as compliance with other relevant obligations of the GDPR and applicable European laws and regulations.

An open issue leading up to the official enforcement of the DGA is how the interaction between the DIs and the other actors, most importantly DCs and Data Subjects (DS), will be realized in detail. The pooling and distribution of data sets of personal data across different European countries, actors, and sectors, while also offering easy enforcement of data subject rights and transparency, requires a common baseline for all involved parties, such as a standardized collaboration protocol for mutual interaction. This leads to the demand for a universal data model for data sharing under the European data strategy. This model can then later be leveraged to design and optimize processes and help the DGA fulfill its role and obligations assigned in the DGA and reach the goals of the European data strategy.

2.3   Digital Markets Act and Market Fairness

A key element in the European Data Strategy is the empowerment of innovative small-size market actors. The data strategy addresses multiple current stumbling stones for data sharing, such as the tendency of device manufacturers and market platform operators to hoard data obtained from their customers for themselves, rather than making them accessible to other market actors. Here, the Data Act and the Digital Markets Act define several conditions under which the collection and sharing of data may even become mandatory by law.

As one example, the Digital Markets Act obliges huge digital market platform operators, the so-called *gatekeepers* (like social media giants, cloud service providers, and global scale service providers), to make the data they collect on their digital platforms accessible to other, less powerful market actors in a fair an appropriate way (as long as several specific conditions are met). However, at the very same time, these gatekeepers remain the primary contact point for DSs trying to exercise their data subject rights. Hence, it becomes inevitable for these gatekeepers to keep track of all data sharing transactions they perform. Thus, gatekeepers require a standardized data sharing communication protocol with their data sharing partners, in order to implement this legal obligation. Here, the proposed universal data model for data sharing may play a key role.

3   Related Work

P3P [7] is a legacy framework for privacy preferences that has since seen many adaptions (e.g. [8–10]). Ulbricht and Pallas [11] developed a language to address consent requirements that came with the GDPR. Becher and Gerl [12] introduce a privacy preference language with the aim to provide privacy language compatibility via privacy interfaces. A prominent approach for applying privacy policies are sticky policies [13]. Iyilade and Vassileva introduce a policy language for data sharing [14]. An overview of additional privacy-related policy languages can be seen in [15].

For modeling data sharing agreements (DSA) specifically, some previous approaches exist. Swarup et al. present a language for DSAs that declares obligations and constraints in the form of "distributed temporal logic" that defines data flows and data storage [16,17]. CNL4DSA [18] is another example of a DSA language that focuses on increased user-friendliness. CNL4DSA later acts as a basis for a DSA lifecycle management framework [19]. However, all these contributions focus on the execution and management of privacy policies and DSAs, rather than their role in the data sharing process, and do not yet consider the obligations that came with the GDPR.

Additionally, there is research on the application of the GDPR in the context of various processes that impact data sharing. privacyTracker [20] introduces a framework that allows for a reliable construction of a data trail. Insynd [21] unifies privacy-preserving transparency and logging. Our previous work [22] discusses how to annotate data in face of the GDPR. LPL [23] is a privacy language that defines expressions for privacy properties in the context of the GDPR. TILT [24] is a language for transparency information in a machine-readable format based on requirements from the GDPR. In previous work [25] we presented a data model for the execution of right-of-access requests specifically. In the data model proposed below, we will combine these aspects and put them into the context of data sharing of the European data strategy.

Further, ENISA has released a report on how to engineer personal data sharing [26], specifying the interactions between DI and DS or DC, respectively, which serves as a guideline for the model.

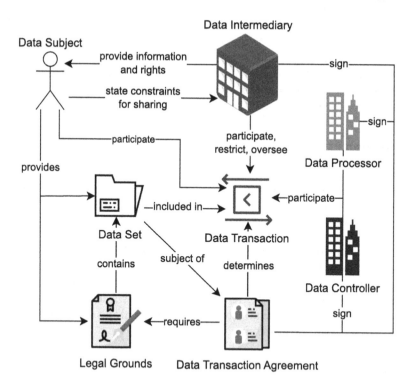

Fig. 1. Overview of interactions between relevant actors and resources in Data Model

4 Data Model

The goal of the proposed data model is to provide a format for data sharing in compliance with the EU data strategy and EU data regulations, potentially serving as a standardization. A participant in a data sharing scenario is obliged to prove compliance with these regulations, fulfill requests for DS rights, and report privacy breach notifications. Currently, the information that an actor can provide is restricted to their own involvement, which makes it also very difficult to audit these processes from the outside. Especially for the intended role of DIs and gatekeepers, this is very impractical. This data model aims to offset these deficiencies by providing the required metadata. While the model will focus on personal data transactions and the role of the DI, it will also be applicable to non-personal data use cases, such as intellectual property rights. As depicted in Fig. 1 the model will revolve around data transactions. A data transaction is defined as an exchange of a data set between two actors that is regulated by a data transactions agreement (DTA) We define a DTA as a generalization for agreements for the exchange or collection of data between two parties, such as data sharing or data-use agreements. An actor participating in a data transaction can be a DS, DC, data processor, or DI. The DI can additionally serve as a controlling instance for these transactions and aid the DS in the execution of their rights. As the scope of all relevant actors and applications in the EU data strategy is quite wide, we have to focus on the most relevant factors in this work. Hence, the model will not address the conditions, obligations, and execution of the underlying DTA. Rather, we will introduce a wrapper for data transfers that provides the necessary information to respect compliance with EU regulations, promotes transparency, and facilitates the execution of DS rights.

4.1   Requirements

This leads us to the requirements for the data model. First, it needs to depict a traceable data flow, allowing us to see the sources and destinations of data. The data sharing scenario demands a class for the data transaction and the underlying agreement, describing the conditions for the data transaction. For the transaction, agreement, and data trail the involved actors and their respective roles, as senders or recipients, as well as the data sets that are being exchanged, have to be included. Additionally, the model must be able to display several constraints given by the GDPR. Collection and processing of personal data under the GDPR require a purpose [1, Art. 5(2)], as well as a legal ground [1, Art. 6], e.g. consent. Further, special categories of personal data, e.g. health data, underlie stricter rules for processing [1, Art. 9].

4.2   Classes and Attributes

An overview of all classes and attributes can be seen in Fig. 2. One attribute all classes share is the identifier. Generally, the ids depend on a known context. This means, that two actors who engage in a data transaction know or negotiate the shared local id, e.g. for the DTA. For the legal ground, purpose, and category classes standardization across the EU data market is recommendable, which will be discussed in Sect. 7. The attributes in all the classes are limited to the strictly necessary ones. If the context of a scenario requires additional attributes they can be added to the existing model on demand.

The data set class describes the properties of the underlying data that it is wrapping. The exact method of wrapping is not covered in this work, as it is not essential in the data sharing process. Different solutions are possible, e.g. as a reference or embedded in the document. The best option depends on the scenario. The data set class contains references to the categories, legal grounds, and DSs of the underlying data. A data set can contain more than one of each of these fields, e.g. aggregation of data can lead to multiple DSs or categories of data in a single data set instance. Also, the data subject field can be empty to consider the scenario of non-personal data. The creation and retention date fields exist to serve as control instances for compliance with the time frame of legal grounds and DTAs. Lastly, the source field refers to the data transformation or transaction that was used to obtain the data set. Over this reference, the sources and destinations of a data set can be depicted, which is required for a Right of Access request [1, Art. 15(1)(c)+(g)].

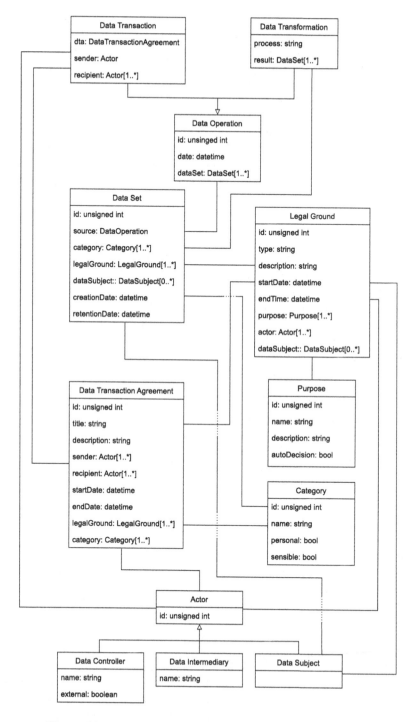

Fig. 2. Classes and attributes in the data sharing data model

The data operation class is a generalization of data transactions and data transformations. Each operation contains a timestamp and a list of the data sets included in the operation. A data transformation is any processing of a data set, where you take a data set and change its properties to generate a new data set. While a data transformation has to be considered as a possible source for a data set, it is not relevant to the data sharing scenario. Therefore, the field describing the process is kept general as a string. Instances of the data transaction class are the realization of any data sharing process. They include the underlying DTA, as well as the involved actors. A transformation always contains one actor that sends the transaction and one or more actors who receive it. This can be leveraged to create a data trail. An actor is the generalization of either a DS, DC, or DI. A DC instance can describe a data processor as well. If a distinction is required at a later point, the model can be expanded. The external attribute of the DC can be used to identify data transactions that leave the EU.

DTAs include a title and a description. The sender and recipient attributes define which actors are allowed to act as the sending or receiving party in any data transaction under this DTA respectively. The start and end dates define the time frame in which the DTA can be used as a basis for a data transaction. Additionally, it is defined which legal grounds and categories can be leveraged in the transaction. These can then be compared with the corresponding fields in the data sets, which are attached to the transaction, to verify compliance.

The legal ground contains a description and time frame as well. Further, the type can be defined, e.g. consent, contract, or legal obligations. It also covers which actors are allowed to act upon this legal ground and the data of which DSs they are allowed to process in this case. Additionally, a legal ground must contain at least one purpose for the processing of data. The purposes are modeled in their own class, including a field for marking the existence of automated decision-making in it. Lastly, the category class describes the category of data that is contained in a data set. It can be distinguished between non-personal, personal, and sensible personal data.

5   Illustrating Example

In order to give a better overview of the application of the proposed data model, this section describes an example of a common data exchange scenario between DCs and DIs, as is shown in Fig. 3.

Our DC, *City C Bus*, is a private bus company operating several bus lines in City C, State Z. *City C Bus* considers introducing new bus lines inside of City C, giving commuters a direct connection between the central station and the new business parks popping up on the outskirts of City C. To get an overview of potential customers, *City C Bus* wants to analyze mobility data sets for train, bus, and car commuters in the region. For this purpose, they contact *State Z Commute*, a DI responsible for mobility in State Z. *City C Bus* requests the following data sets: Mobility data for individuals for workdays between 06:00 and 18:00, including passenger ID, starting location, destination, vehicle, start

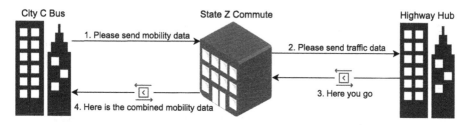

Fig. 3. Overview of the scenario for a data request of City C Bus to the DI State Z Commute

time, end time, and information about ticket subscription for public transport. While the exact content of a data set is not relevant to the data sharing process, it is important to note, that it contains personal data in the form of personal identifiers and location data. *State Z Commute* has access to the public transport data in State Z itself. For the highway traffic data, they depend on *Highway Hub*, an independent DC, as a data source.

In a general flow of a data request to a DI by a DC, depicted in Fig. 4, the DC, in this case, *City C Bus*, sends the request to the DI, *State Z Commute*. The DI then checks if the requested data can be sent from their own data store or if they require additional data from one of their data sources. A data source can be another DI, a DC, or a DS. For our scenario, this results in the following possible sequence of events:

First, the DI *State Z Commute* receives the request from *City C Bus*. *State Z Commute* checks its own data store for the requested data. To get a complete data set, they send a request for the highway traffic data to their data source *Highway Hub*. The response from *Highway Hub* now contains the first data transaction, as seen in Listing 1.1. The format of the data sets in this scenario is JSON. Additionally, ids have been replaced with clear names in most instances for the sake of readability. In the data transaction instance, we can see the timestamp, attached data sets, sender, and recipient of the transaction. Further, the basis for the data transaction, the DTA (see Listing 1.2) is included. It shows us who is allowed to send and receive data sets between the involved actors and defines the properties of the data sets that can be sent, namely the time frame, legal ground, and categories of data. We can now use this information to confirm the legitimacy of the data transaction by comparing the information in the DTA with the values in the data transaction instance and the attached data sets. To assert the correct usage of the DTA, you can compare the date, sender, and recipient fields in the data transaction and DTA instances. For compliance of the sent data sets with the DTAs a comparison between the date, legal ground, and category fields in the involved DTA and data set instances is possible. By doing so we can see that everything is legitimate in this transaction.

After receiving the transaction with the highway traffic data from its data source, *Highway Hub*, the DI, *State Z Commute*, aggregates the data set with the mobility data from their own data store. This can be modeled as a data

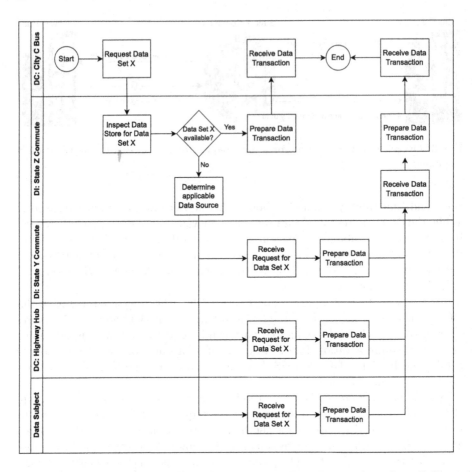

Fig. 4. Simplified flow of events for a data request to Data Intermediary State Z Commute by Data Controller City C Bus

transformation. They then send the complete data to *City C Bus* and complete the request. The resulting data transaction, see Listing 1.3, uses the same DTA, as seen in Listing 1.2, since the agreement covers all three involved actors. However, if we audit the legitimacy of this data transaction now, we can see that *State Z Commute* committed a mistake. The sender and recipients defined in the agreement only allow for a data flow from the DCs, *City C Bus* and *Highway Hub*, to the DI, *State Z Commute*. Therefore, the selection of this DTA for this data transaction was not valid and compliance was breached.

6   Application Areas

As seen in the scenario described above, the model can be applied to the exchange of data between different DCs and DIs that have an agreement to properly define

Listing 1.1. Data Transaction between *Highway Hub* and *State Z Commute*

```
1  {
2    "id": 30091,
3    "date": "2023-02-01 13:27:53",
4    "dataSet": [15454, 15455],
5    "dta": [Z State traffic route utilization agreement],
6    "sender": Highway Hub,
7    "recipient": [State Z Commute]
8  }
```

Listing 1.2. Data transaction agreement between the actors in State Z

```
1  {
2    "id": 7,
3    "title": "Z State traffic route utilization agreement",
4    "description": "Formal agreement on the exchange of
          route utilization data between operators of public
          traffic routes in Z State and Z State Commute for
          the fulfillment of legal obligations",
5    "sender": [City C Bus, Highway Hub],
6    "recipient": [State Z Commute],
7    "startDate": "2019-01-01 00:00:00",
8    "endDate": "9999-12-31 23:59:59",
9    "legalGround": [Requirement to share route utilization
          with competent authority],
10   "category": [location, public transport id]
11 }
```

their data transactions. Alternatively, the model can also be applied to data transactions with DSs. For example, the collection of personal data from a DS can be realized in the same way as the transaction in the scenario. Here, the DTA could be a terms of service document instead. In this way, the intended roles of the DIs and gatekeepers in the EU data strategy can be fulfilled with this data model.

As shown in the scenario, validating the legitimacy of data transactions can be done automatically, for example with pre-defined queries. This opens the path for preventive and detective measures against compliance breaches as well. Scanning incoming data sets against said queries can prevent potential breaches. Consequently, compliance with European regulations should improve across the whole European data market. Additionally, for DIs in particular this is a very potent tool to facilitate the distribution and re-use of data sets.

Another use case for the proposed data model is the improved ease of implementation for DS rights and transparency. DS rights are rights to enact control about one's personal data granted to European citizens by the GDPR [1, Chapter

Listing 1.3. Data Transaction between *State Z Commute* and *City C Bus*

```
1  {
2    "id": 30158,
3    "date": "2023-02-02 21:43:18",
4    "dataSet": [15454, 15455],
5    "dta": [Z State traffic route utilization agreement],
6    "sender": State Z Commute,
7    "recipient": [City C Bus]
8  }
```

3]. Examples include the Right of Access, Right to Erasure, or Right to Data Portability. As an example, a DI could create a data trail for a DS by processing the different sources and destinations of their data transactions, potentially supplementing them by requesting additional information about data transactions for the same data sets from their data sources. This data trail has a lot of possible applications. For example, it can be leveraged to fulfill a request for the deletion of personal data by a DS. In the context of data altruism, this can also be applied to the withdrawal of consent. It can further be used for privacy breach notifications. As the implementation of these DS rights in companies is often lackluster, the concept of Data Subject Rights as a Service (DSRaaS) has been introduced (cf. e.g. [27]). The goal of DSRaaS is to introduce a service provider for DS rights that acts as a bridge between the DSs and DCs, removing obstacles in both the implementation and execution of DS rights. With their goal of aiding in the enforcement of DS rights, DIs are a natural fit for the role of a DSRaaS provider. For the execution of this role, an appropriate data model is required. As the proposed data model fulfills the requirements for this purpose, it builds an important cornerstone in the realization of the DSRaaS architecture.

While the depicted scenario handles a transaction of personal data, it can be applied to non-personal data as well, by leaving the DS field in a data set instance empty or pointing to the rights holder in case of intellectual property rights scenarios instead. A prime example of a use case for non-personal data would be the enforcement of intellectual property rights [28].

7 Discussion and Open Issues

The data model assumes that data sets of non-personal data contain a category, legal ground, and therefore purpose as well. While adding this information to non-personal data is not required by law, it has its use cases, as can be seen in the previously discussed case of intellectual property rights. Further, in cases of mixed personal and non-personal data, or cases where data is incorrectly classified as non-personal data, the addition of this information can serve as a tool to guarantee or correct compliance. To fill out this information default values can be applied. For example, the framework for free flow of non-personal data

[29] serves as a prime example of possible legal grounds. Adding this classification to data would additionally facilitate possible measurements of the success of this framework in the future. This does not imply that the data model must be used for every data set, regardless of conditions.

Another important aspect is how the model manages changes to any of its elements. In the proposed model, changes to an instance of any of its classes are restricted, meaning that each change is a new instance of said class, meaning that e.g. changing the actors that are allowed to act as a sender of data in a DTA, would create a new document of this DTA. This is done to be able to verify under which conditions a data sharing scenario occurred. If, for example, a DTA is adjusted at a later point in time, it is important to still be able to see the version under which the transaction happened to investigate any potential compliance breaches. While this greatly improves the long-term verification of compliance, it creates additional data, which contradicts the principle of data minimization [1, Art. 5(1)(c)]. Therefore, to keep the additional data to a minimum, changes that do not alter the nature of the data sharing process, such as a rephrasing of a description, should not generate a new instance of an element.

Another observation of relevance must be made with respect to the relation of the proposed universal data model to the data minimization principle of the GDPR. Obviously, introducing a detailed tracking mechanism of data sharing interactions as proposed here introduces a large amount of additional data, metadata, to be precise, with respect to ongoing data processing. This may be perceived as being in contrast to the data minimization principle of the GDPR. For instance, Recital 57 states that it should not be mandatory for data controllers to store additional personal information (like the data transactions proposed here) for the sole purpose of complying with the data subject rights obligations. However, it is necessary to understand that this recital does not prohibit the collection of such metadata either. Further, data subject rights and data breach notifications are a mandatory part of the GDPR's legal obligations, hence justifying the storage of metadata of data processing activities in general. When it comes to anonymization, where all links to any data subjects are removed from the data, the resulting anonymous data obviously no longer requires tracking of its processing for implementing GDPR obligations, hence the proposed data transactions are no longer—and should no longer be—created for such anonymized data. For all other cases, where the link to any DS is still explicitly and intentionally part of the personal data, keeping track of its processing entities remains required and mandated by the GDPR. The same holds true for cases where other legal grounds apply.

An important question is how the data model would perform in partial dissemination, as it is not realistic that every DI and DC immediately adopt the proposed model. If we reflect upon the exemplary scenario shown above, we can now imagine that one DC, e.g. Highway Hub, did not adopt the model. This means, that the data the DI, *State Z Commute*, receives from the DC does not contain the information attached to the normally referenced data transaction agreement class. However, as the data transaction agreement between the two parties does exist anyways, the DI can still adapt this agreement according to the model and add the information on their own. This means that for the DI the use cases of the model still exist. However, the ability to build a data trail would be limited in this scenario. As the data flow can only reliably be traced between actors that have adopted the data model, the data trail would stop after reaching the DC here.

As mentioned in Sect. 4.2, the categories of data, as well as the legal grounds and purposes for data processing, would greatly profit from standardization across the European data market, and possibly further beyond. This would greatly increase the comprehensibility of these elements, especially for non-specialists. Consent, as a legal ground, specifically profits from this, as a common baseline would facilitate consent management, especially in distributed systems. Further, standardized processes for the handling of data with specific properties, e.g. data raised for the purpose of advertising, could be introduced, promising a strong tool for auditing and compliance as well.

The question of how to create identifiers for DSs has to be examined closely as well. While a local id works great in a specific context, another solution has to be found when the problem is applied to a larger scope. If a DS, for example, withdraws its consent for the sharing of its personal data and wants all recipients of this data to delete it, the data might have traveled between multiple contexts. The id must remain traceable throughout these contexts to fulfill this request for deletion. This id then also must be designed in a way that allows for a maximum degree of anonymity and does not reveal any information to a third party that would have otherwise not been able to retract this information.

8   Conclusion

Data exchange and sharing is and will be an important cornerstone of both the European and global data market. Currently, these data exchanges are very hard to track reliably, which makes it difficult to verify compliance and exert DS rights. The data model we have developed aims to resolve this by introducing an approach centered around data transactions and data transaction agreements to attach the relevant metadata in data sharing scenarios. A data transaction references the metadata of data sets that are subject of the data sharing scenario, the actors that act as sender and recipients, and a reference to the underlying data transaction agreement between the involved actors. The data transaction agreement then further defines the conditions of the data transaction.

We demonstrated an exemplary application of this model in an illustrating scenario, featuring a common data sharing scenario under the DGA, a request for data to a DI by a DC. As shown in the example, by comparing the data in the data transaction, data transaction agreement, and the attached data sets, compliance can easily be verified, possibly in an automated process. Additionally, a data trail can be built based on the model that can be leveraged for further use cases, such as data breach notifications, DS right enforcement, and consent management. While the model focuses on the application for personal data, it can also be used in non-personal data scenarios, e.g. for managing intellectual property rights.

The proposed model can serve a useful role in the development of other open issues, such as the standardization of legal grounds, purposes and categorization of personal data, and the development of privacy-preserving identifiers for DSs. While a complete adoption in the European data market would help, not only in the progression of these issues, but also in improving compliance and DS right enforcement in data sharing scenarios within all of Europe, the model can fulfill most of its use cases in a partial dissemination as well. To achieve these improvements, a standardization of the data sharing process based on this model would therefore be a valuable consideration.

Acknowledgements. The contribution of M. Jensen was partly funded by the Swedish Knowledge Foundation (KK-Stiftelsen) as part of the TRUEdig project.

References

1. European Parliament and Council. Regulation (EU) 2016/679 of the European Parliament and of the Council of 27 April 2016 on the protection of natural persons with regard to the processing of personal data and on the free movement of such data, and repealing Directive 95/46/EC (General Data Protection Regulation) (Text with EEA relevance), 4 May 2016. http://data.europa.eu/eli/reg/2016/679/oj/eng. Accessed 24 Apr 2018
2. European Commission. European data strategy – Making the EU a role model for a society empowered by data (2022). https://ec.europa.eu/info/strategy/priorities-2019-2024/europe-fit-digital-age/european-data-strategy_en
3. Proposal for a Regulation of the European Parliament and of the Council on European data governance (Data Governance Act). COM/2020/767 final
4. Proposal for a Regulation of the European Parliament and of the Council on harmonised rules on fair access to and use of data (Data Act). SEC(2022) 81 final - SWD(2022) 34 final - SWD(2022) 35 final
5. Regulation (EU) 2022/2065 of the European Parliament and of the Council of 19 October 2022 on a Single Market For Digital Services and amending Directive 2000/31/EC (Digital Services Act)
6. Regulation (EU) 2022/1925 of the European Parliament and of the Council on contestable and fair markets in the digital sector and amending Directives (EU) 2019/1937 and (EU) 2020/1828 (Digital Markets Act)
7. Cranor, L.F.: P3P: making privacy policies more useful. IEEE Secur. Priv. **1**(6), 50–55 (2003). https://doi.org/10.1109/MSECP.2003.1253568
8. Agrawal, R., et al.: An XPath-based preference language for P3P. In: Proceedings of the 12th International Conference on World Wide Web, pp. 629–639 (2003)
9. Yu, T., Li, N., Antón, A.I.: A formal semantics for P3P. In: Proceedings of the 2004 Workshop on Secure Web Service, pp. 1–8 (2004)
10. Li, N., Yu, T., Anton, A.: A semantics based approach to privacy languages. Comput. Syst. Sci. Eng. **21**(5), 339 (2006)

11. Ulbricht, M.R., Pallas, F.: YaPPL - a lightweight privacy preference language for legally sufficient and automated consent provision in IoT scenarios. In: Garcia-Alfaro, J., Herrera-Joancomartí, J., Livraga, G., Rios, R. (eds.) DPM CBT 2018. LNCS, vol. 11025, pp. 329–344. Springer, Cham (2018). https://doi.org/10.1007/978-3-030-00305-0_23
12. Becher, S., Gerl, A.: ConTra preference language: privacy preference unification via privacy interfaces. Sensors **22**(14), 5428 (2022)
13. Pearson, S., Casassa-Mont, M.: Sticky policies: an approach for managing privacy across multiple parties. Computer **44**(9), 60–68 (2011)
14. Iyilade, J., Vassileva, J.: P2U: a privacy policy specification language for secondary data sharing and usage. In: 2014 IEEE Security and Privacy Workshops, pp. 18–22, May 2014. https://doi.org/10.1109/SPW.2014.12
15. Kasem-Madani, S., Meier, M.: Security and privacy policy languages: a survey, categorization and gap identification. arXiv preprint arXiv:1512.00201 (2015)
16. Swarup, V., Seligman, L., Rosenthal, A.: A data sharing agreement framework. In: Bagchi, A., Atluri, V. (eds.) ICISS 2006. LNCS, vol. 4332, pp. 22–36. Springer, Heidelberg (2006). https://doi.org/10.1007/11961635_2
17. Swamp, V., Seligman, L., Rosenthal, A.: Specifying data sharing agreements. In: Seventh IEEE International Workshop on Policies for Distributed Systems and Networks (POLICY 2006), pp. 4-pp. IEEE (2006)
18. Matteucci, I., Petrocchi, M., Sbodio, M.L.: CNL4DSA: a controlled natural language for data sharing agreements. In: Proceedings of the 2010 ACM Symposium on Applied Computing, pp. 616–620. Sierre Switzerland: ACM (2010). ISBN: 978-1-60558-639-7. https://doi.org/10.1145/1774088.1774218. https://dl.acm.org/doi/10.1145/1774088.1774218. Accessed 16 Jan 2023
19. Ruiz, J.F., et al.: A lifecycle for data sharing agreements: how it works out. In: Schiffner, S., et al. (eds.) APF 2016. LNCS, vol. 9857, pp. 3–20. Springer, Cham (2016). https://doi.org/10.1007/978-3-319-44760-5_1
20. Gjermundrød, H., Dionysiou, I., Costa, K.: privacyTracker: a privacy-by-design GDPR-compliant framework with verifiable data traceability controls. In: Casteleyn, S., Dolog, P., Pautasso, C. (eds.) ICWE 2016. LNCS, vol. 9881, pp. 3–15. Springer, Cham (2016). https://doi.org/10.1007/978-3-319-46963-8_1
21. Peeters, R., Pulls, T.: Insynd: improved privacy-preserving transparency logging. In: Askoxylakis, I., et al. (eds.) ESORICS 2016. LNCS, vol. 9879, pp. 121–139. Springer, Cham (2016). https://doi.org/10.1007/978-3-319-45741-3_7
22. Jensen, M., Kapila, S., Gruschka, N.: Towards aligning GDPR compliance with software development: a research agenda. In: ICISSP, pp. 389–396 (2019)
23. Gerl, A., et al.: LPL, towards a GDPR-compliant privacy language: formal definition and usage. In: Hameurlain, A., Wagner, R. (eds.) Transactions on Large-Scale Data and Knowledge-Centered Systems XXXVII. LNCS, vol. 10940, pp. 41–80. Springer, Heidelberg (2018). https://doi.org/10.1007/978-3-662-57932-9_2
24. Grünewald, E., Pallas, F.: TILT: a GDPR-aligned transparency information language and toolkit for practical privacy engineering. In: Proceedings of the 2021 ACM Conference on Fairness, Accountability, and Transparency. FAccT 2021, pp. 636–646. Association for Computing Machinery, New York (2021). ISBN: 978-1-4503-8309-7. https://doi.org/10.1145/3442188.3445925. Accessed 30 Nov 2022
25. Hansen, M., Jensen, M.: A generic data model for implementing right of access requests. In: Gryszczyńska, A., et al. (eds.) APF 2022. LNCS, vol. 13279, pp. 3–22. Springer, Cham (2022). https://doi.org/10.1007/978-3-031-07315-1_1
26. Engineering Personal Data Sharing. ENISA. https://www.enisa.europa.eu/publications/engineering-personal-data-sharing. Accessed 16 Feb 2023

27. Hansen, M., Gruschka, N., Jensen, M.: Introducing the concept of data subject rights as a service under the GDPR. In: Schiffner, S., Ziegler, S., Jensen, M. (eds.) DPLICIT 2023, pp. 17–31. Springer, Cham (2023). https://doi.org/10.1007/978-3-031-44939-0_2
28. European Commission. Enforcement of intellectual property rights. https://single-market-economy.ec.europa.eu/industry/strategy/intellectual-property/enforcement-intellectual-property-rights_en. Accessed 08 Feb 2023
29. Regulation (EU) 2018/1807 of the European Parliament and of the Council of 14 November 2018 on a framework for the free flow of non-personal data in the European Union (Text with EEA relevance.) Legislative Body: EP, CONSIL (2018). http://data.europa.eu/eli/reg/2018/1807/oj/eng. Accessed 14 Feb 2023

A Decision-Making Process to Implement the 'Right to Be Forgotten' in Machine Learning

Katie Hawkins[✉] [iD], Nora Alhuwaish[✉] [iD], Sana Belguith[iD], Asma Vranaki[iD], and Andrew Charlesworth[iD]

University of Bristol, Bristol, UK
{katie.hawkins,hw19625,sana.belguith,asma.vranaki,
a.j.charlesworth}@bristol.ac.uk

Abstract. The unprecedented scale at which personal data is used to train machine learning (ML) models is a motivation to examine the ways in which it can be erased when implementing the GDPR's 'right to be forgotten'. The existing literature investigating this right focus on a purely technical or legal approach, lacking the collaboration required for this interdisciplinary space. Recent works has identified there is no one solution to erasure in ML and this must therefore be decided on a case-by-case basis. However, there is an absence of guidance for controllers to follow when personal data must be erased in ML. In this paper we develop a novel, decision-making flow that encompasses the necessary considerations for a controller. Addressing, in particular, the interdisciplinary considerations relevant to the EU GDPR and data protection scholarship, as well as concepts from computer science and its application in industry. This results in several optimal solutions for the controller and data subject, differing with levels of erasure. To validate the proposed decision-making flow a real case study is discussed throughout the paper. The paper highlights the need for a clearer framework when personal data must be erased in ML; empowering the regulator, controller and data subject.

Keywords: Right to be Forgotten · GDPR · Erasure · Machine Learning · Machine Unlearning · Decision-Making

1 Introduction

In 2017, a company known as Clearview AI created a database that now has more than 30 billion facial images scraped from online accessible sources, including social media networks and videos extracted from online platforms [1]. Facial images are considered as biometric data,[1] and are particularly sensitive, due to the link to a person's physical identity and its unique way to identify someone. The vast majority of people whose images were scraped and processed were unaware of Clearview AI's methodology [2]. Several complaints were made by data subjects, defined as natural persons that had

---

[1] GDPR Article 4(14) defines biometric data as "personal data resulting from specific technical processing relating to the physical, physiological or behavioural characteristics of a natural person, which allow or confirm the unique identification of that natural person".

K. Rannenberg et al. (Eds.): APF 2023, LNCS 13888, pp. 20–38, 2024.
https://doi.org/10.1007/978-3-031-61089-9_2

their images processed by the company [3, 4]. After numerous investigations in various countries in the EU, such as France [2], it was found that Clearview AI was in breach of the General Data Protection Regulation (GDPR) [3]. This regulation aims to ensure the protection of natural persons' fundamental rights and freedoms, and sets rules for the free movement of personal data [5]. The GDPR grants data subjects several rights, including an important and novel right; the right to erasure, otherwise known as the 'right to be forgotten' (RTBF) articulated in Art.17 GDPR. The RTBF is defined as the data subject's right to obtain erasure of personal data related to the data subject without undue delay, on six grounds, explained in Sect. 3.1. In this case, Clearview is defined as the controller, where the company determines the purposes and means of processing personal data [6]. This controller's processing of personal data, breached various elements of the GDPR including processing without a legal basis and failure to take into account data subjects' rights, such as the right to erasure [2]. Clearview AI was given formal notice to cease the collection and use of personal data in the absence of a legal basis and to comply with erasure requests within a period of two months [2].

This is not a unique case, there are several other cases where a controller has been ordered to erase personal data from their facial recognition systems [7]. These systems take advantage of Machine Learning (ML) – training models on a large database of images, that provide the capability to identify faces of known individuals, comparing faces, and detecting similar faces in a database [8]. Following on from these examples, the question regarding erasure arises: how should controllers erase personal data that has already been deployed in ML models?

Answering this question is significantly challenging due to the complexities of ML, which does not retain data in raw format, but rather embeds the data throughout the system, as part of the development of the model [9]. The erasure problem for ML models, as expressed by Dang, is similar to asking a person to forget a single lesson from an entire educational background [9]. Numerous studies have shown that some ML models tended to 'memorise' data on which they had been trained [10, 11]. This memorisation may lead to a 'leak' of those data, and in some cases, result in re-identification of data subjects [11, 12]. This is a privacy attack known as membership inference [13]. The attacks have been applied on many supervised models and generative models [11].

The RTBF has captured the attention of many researchers due to its importance in strengthening data protection rights [14] and the challenges of practically implementing its requirements [15]. Both legal and technical literature have attempted to overcome this challenge, but not without several limitations that have inhibited the effective application in ML [16, 17]. This results in multiple problems; firstly, researchers have argued that certain ML models could be classified as personal data under EU's GDPR [11, 12]. The GDPR adopts a wide definition of personal data, as any information related to an identified or identifiable natural person – going beyond name or phone numbers to include dynamic IP addresses, browser fingerprints or smart meter readings. This wide approach is also adopted by the Court of Justice of the EU (CJEU) [18].

Secondly, this creates problems from the perspective of the data subject. If the ML model is classified as personal data but erasure is too complex, it negates the ability of the data subject to exercise this right. This could breach individuals' fundamental rights to privacy and data protection in Articles 7 and 8 of the Charter of Fundamental Human Rights [19], as well as the RTBF in Article 17 GDPR [3].

Thirdly, public reports from controllers such as Google have shown an increase in requests to delist content under European privacy law [20]. Erasure requests are likely to continue to increase as the creation of new privacy attacks are able to successfully identify data subjects [11]. Therefore, there is a need for developing erasure techniques to efficiently deal with large volumes of requests as well as ensuring personal data is erased from the ML model currently in operation.

A final problem is the flexible interpretation of the RTBF from a legal perspective, noted by the European Union Agency for Cybersecurity (ENISA) [21]; the deliberate generality and extensiveness of the RTBF results in "a range of interpretations appropriate for many different situations". This may allow controllers to have more than one suitable approach for erasure, but it is not clear what the approaches are or how those approaches can be determined from a technical perspective.

1.1 Paper Contributions

This paper focuses on bridging the gap between the legal and technical literature for the RTBF in ML models. In particular, the paper is the first to integrate the multidisciplinary problem space of the EU GDPR and data protection scholarship, with concepts from computer science and industry application. In doing so, the authors create a novel decision-making flow that provides a practical outcome for the controller to implement the RTBF in ML models. The decision flow identifies the relevant decision, outlines the necessary legal and technical considerations and assesses alternative resolutions. This supports the need for a clearer framework when personal data must be erased in ML; empowering the regulator, controller and data subject.

1.2 Paper Structure

The rest of this paper is organised as follows: Sect. 2 provides an overview of the basic concepts related to ML, followed by a literature review. Section 3 demonstrates the decision-making flow alongside a discussion of GDPR's requirements for the RTBF, followed by the erasure techniques. The paper concludes with a summary of the discussion and a proposal for future works.

2 Background

2.1 Machine Learning

To gain a grasp of the challenges and this paper's recommendations, a brief introduction to the field of ML is necessary. ML is a set of techniques that allow computers to learn by creating or using algorithms based on data [22]. Most of the literature refers to ML models, this represents the output of a ML algorithm that is run on some data. ML varies in complexity due to the variety of options available, including the data processing methods, algorithm types and objectives. For simplicity here, the development of a trained ML model is split into two phases: (1) Training and Validation Phase, and (2) Deployment and Monitoring Phase.

Within the first phase, an objective for the model is defined, for example, the ability to identify and classify an image as a dog or cat. It then proceeds with selecting an algorithm, as well as gathering and preparing data. The prepared data will be used to train, test and validate the model. For the purpose of enforcing the RTBF, the assumption is that personal data has been collected and processed within this phase. In the second phase, the model has been created and now deployed for use on new unseen data, hence 'learning'. The deployed model continues to be maintained and its performance monitored.

2.2 Literature Review

The literature review aims to demonstrate the inspiration for the authors' proposed decision-making flow. The literature can be categorized into three categories. First, legal literature that considers the RTBF. Second, literature that considers the application of the RTBF in ML, including the proposed technical solutions. Finally, literature that considers both the legal requirements and technical solutions.

After the GDPR's explicit protection of the RTBF, numerous regulatory guidelines and academic papers have been published to explain the right [23–27]. However, understanding how the RTBF is to be adequately implemented in ML practices remains inconclusive. There are three types of legal literature on the RTBF that are considered significant for this paper. The first type is the literature that discusses the RTBF's scope, grounds, exemptions and the need to balance the RTBF with other rights and interests [28]. Such literature provides the basis for the authors to understand and identify the legal requirements for implementing the RTBF, which frames the first part of the proposed decision-making flow, explained below. However, the majority of this literature lacks consideration of the technical development and application of ML which could significantly impact practical interpretation of the RTBF. The second type of legal literature focuses solely on the implementation of the RTBF in the search engine field, as well as analysing critical cases that mainly addressed its implementation in relation to Google, notably the CJEU decision on *Google Spain* [29] or *Google vs CNIL and GC and Others* [30], since this is the most common practice of the right [31–35]. The CJEU's flexible and subjective interpretation of the right in its jurisprudence leads the authors to construct an adaptive holistic approach to implementing the RTBF. However, the *Google Spain* case was pre-GDPR and much current jurisprudence in the CJEU or Member States' Courts and EU DPA guidance addresses particular scenarios like delisting requests received by search engines [24, 27]. So there are limits to how much extrapolation can be employed given the differing contexts. The third type of legal literature focuses on the barriers and challenges to applying the RTBF, and either criticises the vagueness of the legal requirements for implementing the right, or expresses the technical difficulty and impracticality of applying the right [16, 36, 37]. These challenges inspired the authors to construct a decision-making flow that could aid in overcoming these challenges.

In the context of the technical literature within the RTBF, the majority focus on a range of techniques to determine *how* to erase training data from models. The objective is to determine how a controller can remove training data from the established knowledge of a deployed ML model in phase 2. The field of research is known as machine unlearning, proposed by Cao and Yang [38]. The current state-of-the-art attempts to produce machine unlearning solutions that overcome challenges relevant to the practical deployment, for example, reducing the computational efficiency, cost and skills required [39]. Limitations usually arise in the applicability of machine unlearning solutions, as proposals lack a broad scope for ML models. It is crucial that these limitations are presented to a controller, as this will determine the appropriate erasure technique. Therefore, the technical considerations of each erasure technique, including the applicability, is discussed in Sect. 3.2. A further limitation is the absence of legal analysis within the proposed techniques.

In the decision-making literature, there has been no attempt to create a decision-based process relevant to the RTBF in ML. Therefore, the final part of the literature review focuses on the literature that involves both a legal and technical discussion. One of the first papers to highlight the interdisciplinary gap was published in 2018, arguing that the current privacy regulation is not fit to handle the challenges of AI [17]. It provides a technical and legal discussion of the problem space and calls for further research to investigate the balance between the RTBF and a ML model's need to remember information used to train it. However, it limits the technical solutions to differential privacy and data minimisation. These techniques are preventative measures, as it assumes the model has not yet been trained. It also lacks the capability for exact erasure, and remains prone to privacy attacks [40]. Another study investigates the RTBF and its implementation in ML [9]. They review the definitions of the RTBF in several major legal documents, and its application in practice. It highlights similar questions relating to the level of erasure and the techniques required, but limits its discussion to a brief analysis. The paper argues that differential privacy can be considered as the framework to define the RTBF, whilst machine unlearning is a usable technique to practice the RTBF. However, the paper lacks the required analysis and understanding of the RTBF requirements and other GDPR provisions related to the RTBF, such as the RTBF's grounds and exemptions. In another paper, the types of techniques for erasure are expanded from differential privacy, and include influence functions and machine unlearning [41]. The majority of research within this field concludes with the need for more interdisciplinary researchers to identify other technologies that can be used, as well as discuss the wider problem space for both the legal and technical fields [16, 17, 41, 42]. Other interdisciplinary papers on the topic focus on classifying models as personal data [12]. For example, Veale, Binns and Edwards' paper explains model inversion and membership inference attacks, and how the GDPR is likely to classify models as personal data. It then describes selected consequences for data subjects' rights to have access to new information, erasure and objection. Although the paper limits the legal considerations to the applicability of personal data in ML, it helps to shape the understanding of personal data and privacy harm in ML models. This interpretation is incorporated into the considerations when deciding on the level of erasure within the authors' decision-making process.

3 Decision-Making Flow

Figure 1 presents the first decision-making flow for implementing the RTBF in ML. Produced by the authors, it aims to illustrate (at a high-level) the steps and decisions once a RTBF is requested. The following section walks through the flow in greater detail.

Section 3.1 discusses the initial legal steps in the flow, including the level of erasure, grounds and exemptions. Section 3.2 then considers the lower level of the flow, where erasure techniques must be applied.

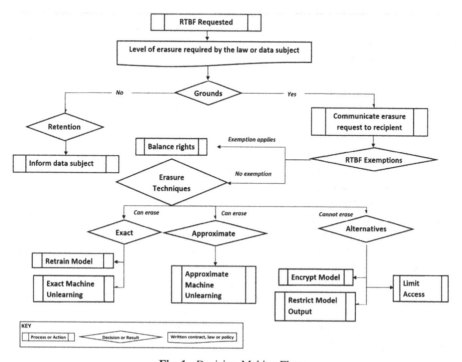

Fig. 1. Decision-Making Flow

3.1 Legal Requirements for Implementing the RTBF

There are multiple layers of legal requirements that should be considered in order to implement the RTBF. This section analyses the legal requirements for the RTBF and argues that each legal requirement should be considered and assessed in a decision-making flow in order to implement it in ML.

Level of Erasure Required by the Law or Data Subject. As can be seen in Fig. 1, the legal requirements that the controller should consider in the RTBF decision-making flow start with identifying the required level of erasure. The erasure level is determined by two factors: the context of the data subject's request and the law. The GDPR does not specify how the controller should receive and understand a data subject's request, which leaves it to the controller to inform the data subject of the differences between erasure levels and manage such requests accordingly [43]. Controllers should be absolutely clear with data subjects about what is meant by erasure and what actually happens to their personal data once the controller has erased it [44]. The controller can require data subjects to state the exact data points they want to be removed (e.g., remove a name or address) [44]. In that way, the controller should be able to identify the level of erasure requested by the data subject [43]. Regardless of the technical possibility of erasure levels in ML systems, the data subject can either request limited erasure where the personal data is removed from a specific level of the system, such as the user interface, or request complete erasure that removes personal data from the whole system. If the data subject requests complete erasure, to what extent does the GDPR require the controller to erase the data in complicated systems such as ML?

The GDPR does not clarify the extent of erasure required. Both the CJEU and national courts have interpreted the RTBF as limited erasure by, for example, restricting access [45] or removing the link between personal data and search results associated with the data subject's name [29, 30]. The European Data Protection Board (EDPB) [46], the body responsible for ensuring the consistent application of the GDPR throughout the EU, has published guidelines on interpreting the RTBF [24]. Yet, the guidelines focus only on delisting requests submitted by data subjects in search engines and assert that the delisting request does not result in the personal data being completely erased, as the requested personal data is not erased from either their source (the website) or the search engine's index [24]. Personal data can remain publicly available and accessible, but no longer be linked to the results of searching on the data subject's name [24]. The guidelines do, however, emphasise that search engine providers are not exempt from the duty to fully erase in exceptional cases. Unfortunately, the guidelines do not provide further information about these exceptional cases, they only provide an example. Therefore, it appears, erasure can be interpreted as limited (without the personal data being completely erased, as is the case with a delisting request) or complete erasure (in some exceptional cases). Interpreting erasure in ML based on the analogy of delisting in search engines is challenging. Unlike search engines, the desired and required impact of erasure in ML is not to remove the data from the public. Another difference is that ML processing does not contradict the right to freedom of expression or use of personal data for journalistic purposes, which may require making personal data available at a certain level. Rather it may contradict other interests, such as the controller's legitimate interest or legal obligations. In addition, the function of search engines is dissimilar to ML, which is often both more complex and difficult to understand and explain.

Local Data Protection Authorities (DPA), independent public authorities that supervise, investigate and have corrective powers to the application of the GDPR, provide expert advice on GDPR issues, and handle complaints lodged against violations of the GDPR and the relevant national laws [47], have published guidelines. For example, the French regulator's AI compliance guidelines assume that personal data can be present in all life cycles of AI including training data, deployment data and data in the model; therefore, data subjects' rights will apply across all these cycles [48]. It is important to note that the ML phases may differ from AI phases explained by the guidelines. This is because ML is just a subset of AI and that AI has much broader application. Thus, this paper adopts the ML phases outlined in Sect. 2.1.

Even if the RTBF applies to all phases and throughout the life cycles of the ML system, it is still questionable whether the law requires an exact or approximate degree of erasure from the deployed model, as it can be technically difficult to guarantee 100 percent erasure. The GDPR neither requires complete erasure nor prevents it. However, the legislation appears to strengthen the RTBF, encouraging controllers to devise various techniques that help meet the objective of the GDPR in protecting fundamental rights, for two main reasons. First, the difficulty and impracticality of complete erasure must have been envisaged by the multidisciplinary experts who participated in drafting the GDPR. This is evident in the proposal for the GDPR, which allowed restriction instead of erasure when technically difficult to erase personal data, and limited this exemption to systems that were designed before the application of the GDPR [49]. This paragraph was omitted in the final version of the GDPR, which may indicate that technical difficulties to erase are no longer considered a reasonable excuse for restricting personal data instead of erasure [50]. In addition, erasure may differ from one type of data to another. For example, in the case of images by "blurring the picture with no retroactive ability to recover the personal data that the picture previously contained, the personal data are considered erased in accordance with GDPR" [51]. Additionally, local DPAs have the discretion to assess the need for erasure on a case-by-case basis as a result of the normative evaluation, which places the controller in a flexible position where it may be required to refuse the erasure, implement complete, limited, or approximate erasure based on data type, level of harm, the grounds and exemptions of the RTBF, as discussed below.

Grounds. The second legal requirement that should be considered by the controller in the RTBF decision-making flow is establishing a ground for the erasure request. The RTBF is not an absolute right, and the erasure request should be established on one of six grounds specified in Article 17(1) GDPR. These different grounds partially overlap [52]. Three of the grounds assume the lack of a legal basis for processing: when the personal data are no longer necessary for the purpose of collection and processing (subparagraph (a)), data subject withdraws consent, and there is no other ground for processing (subparagraph (b)), or the controller processes personal data unlawfully (subparagraph (d)). The latter ground, which can be seen as a general clause, is clarified by Recital 65 in which it is stated that the RTBF can be invoked by a data subject where the processing does not comply with the GDPR. The fourth ground is based on Article 21, the invocation of the right to object when processing is necessary for public interest or in the exercise of official authority vested in the controller in point (e) and on legitimate interest in point (f) of Article 6(1) where there are no other overriding interests, or when the objection is based on direct marketing (subparagraph (c)). The fifth ground is when processing personal data of a child in relation to the offer of information society services based on the child's consent. In this situation, the data has to be erased upon simple request. Recital 65 clarifies that the data subject should be able to exercise the RTBF notwithstanding the fact that they no longer are a child. It is emphasised that the RTBF is relevant in particular where the data subject has given his/her consent as a child and is not completely aware of the risks involved by the processing, and later wants to erase that personal data (subparagraph (e)). Finally, (subparagraph (f)) requires the controller to erase personal data when this is mandated under EU or Member State law.

As illustrated in Fig. 1, the erasure request requires a decision that it is either accepted as establishing a ground or be refused. The controller will need to internally assess whether or not the purpose of processing was, and is still, necessary, and identify the legal base for the personal data collection. If the initial legal base is consent, then this cannot be changed to another legal base if the data subject withdraws his/her consent.

The controller should have a clear understanding of all the GDPR requirements in order to determine whether the personal data is lawfully processed. The controller also needs to take the data subject's age into consideration. In the Clearview AI example, the most applicable reason for the application of the RTBF is unlawful processing. This is because Clearview AI violated several GDPR requirements; processed personal data without a legal basis, and not adequately informing data subjects about, or facilitating the exercise of, their rights to access and erasure [53].

If it has been decided that the personal data in question provides grounds for erasure, the controller must take reasonable steps to inform other controllers of the data subject's request, such as when personal data has been made public (for example by broadcasting) [54]. These steps must include technical measures which take into account available technology and implementation cost. In addition, the controller should, to the extent possible, notify anyone to whom the personal data has previously been disclosed according to Article 19 GDPR. The controller must inform the data subject about those recipients if the data subject requests it.

Alternatively, if the erasure request fails to establish that any of the aforementioned grounds are applicable, the controller can retain the personal data and must inform the data subject of the decision without unduly delay, which was specified as a period of a month, in accordance with Article 12 of the GDPR.

Exemptions. Even when one of the above grounds applies, the controller must make sure that no exemption applies to the personal data before erasing the personal data. In the GDPR, the controller is obliged to refuse the erasure request if the processing is necessary for one or more of the following. First, exercising the right of freedom of expression and information (subparagraph (a)). Second, complying with a legal obligation under the EU or national laws that the controller is subject to, for the performance of a task carried out in the public interest or in the exercise of official authority (subparagraph (b)). Third, cases in which the processing of special categories of personal data is necessary for public health in certain grounds provided for in Article 9 GDPR (subparagraph (c)). The same holds true when processing is necessary for archiving purposes in the public interest, scientific or historical research purposes or for statistical purposes in accordance with Article 89(1) GDPR (subparagraph (d)). This exemption can be invoked insofar as the RTBF is likely to render impossible or seriously impair achieving the objectives of the processing. The final exemption can be invoked when processing is necessary for the establishment, exercise or defense of legal claims (subparagraph (e)).

In the Clearview AI example, the first exemption is unlikely to be relevant. Although the RTBF in ML may contradict other fundamental rights or public interests, it rarely contradicts the right to freedom of expression and information, as it is the case in search engines. It does not seem, from the company's function, that it has legal obligations to retain personal data in, for example, taxation or labour requirements. Clearview AI processing might be necessary for the performance of a task carried out in the public interest or in the exercise of official authority, as the company offers its services to law enforcement authorities in order to help identify perpetrators or victims of crime, so the second exemption may apply. Clearview AI is using people's images, which are considered a special category of the personal data in the GDPR, but it seems that the company does not need the personal data for reasons of public interest in public health, which renders that third exemption as inapplicable. The fourth exemption applies to Clearview AI when the processing is necessary for scientific research or statistical purposes. Similarly, when processing is necessary for exercise or defense of legal claims.

The way the GDPR articulates the exemptions creates three main considerations when applying the RTBF in ML. First, the GDPR shifts the responsibility of balancing the right to privacy and data protection and other rights from the government to the controller [31]. In other words, controllers are required to determine whether the data subject's rights outweigh, for example, other rights, interests or the legal requirements. The EU and national courts' interpretation of balancing has been inconsistent and based on a case-by-case approach [55]. The courts sometimes order erasure [56], or require restricted access [45], or refuse the erasure request and allow the controller to retain the personal data [57]. The criteria for conducting such balancing are subjective, and available guidelines are mainly relevant to search engines and, as such, are inadequate to be implemented in ML [24].

Second, a problem may arise when controllers, instead of undertaking a long and subjective assessment of the exemptions and balancing of the RTBF against other public interests, automatically erase personal data upon a RTBF request. This would lead to 'over-erasure' out of an abundance of caution to avoid financial penalties [58]. However, the choice to favour the RTBF may be hypervigilant, and the controller is obliged to consider the exemptions, especially when the RTBF contradicts other fundamental rights or legal requirements. Third, before erasing personal data based on the RTBF, the controller should be aware of all legal requirements from EU laws or national regulations that apply within the jurisdiction relevant to the controller.

There are many variables at play and each RTBF request will have to be evaluated individually. After assessing the applicability of the five exemptions, controllers have two tracks: either to invoke an exemption or not. In the first track, the controller should balance the RTBF with the interests in the applied exemptions. The result of the balance can be refusing the RTBF request and retaining personal data, erasing personal data or coming up with an alternative solution that balances the RTBF and other interests. Erasure and other alternatives are discussed in the next section. The second track is the way when there is no exemption to be considered and the controller must erase the personal data.

3.2 Machine Learning Techniques for Erasure

At this point within the decision-making flow, the controller is required to erase the data subject's personal data. Thus, the discussion moves to the ways in which data can be erased from the ML model.

Before considering the techniques for erasure, it is crucial to understand that personal data can be contained at numerous points within ML phases. As mentioned in Sect. 2, within the training and validation phase, personal data can be collected and used within the training dataset. This is not the case in all models, where personal data is not used or personal data is removed during pre-processing. For the purposes of the RTBF, this paper assumes some form of personal data is held within the training dataset and possibly in ML models after it has been deployed [59].

Exact Erasure. Exact erasure techniques focus on the challenging case where personal data is involved in the ML model itself. The goal is to identify the exact same deployed model as if the user data was never part of the training dataset. For exact erasure, it is assumed that simply erasing the data subject's data from the training dataset (independent of the trained model) is insufficient. It is the strictest requirement for removal as the requested data must be removed from the deployed model (phase 2) and the training dataset (phase 1). This complete and thorough erasure is most often what is desired by data subjects [39], but can be the most challenging to implement.

Although the controller may not be able to determine whether or not personal data can be inferred from the model, exact erasure is necessary when the Data Protection Authority (DPA) or the data subject present evidence that their personal data could be inferred from the deployed model [48]. This links back to the notion of privacy harms, where data subjects may use research on inference attacks as evidence to illustrate the unanticipated use of personal data. Thus, the data subject will likely have to apply or prove such attacks to the ML model in question to sufficiently support the plausibility of re-identification of their personal data. Some may argue that neither the DPAs nor the data subjects have the technical capabilities to provide such evidence, however, recent publications could aid data subjects (and potentially adversaries) to determine whether their data was used to train a ML model [60]. Whilst the publication is only applicable to text-generation models, increased RTBF requests could in turn generate an industry for gathering such evidence for the data subject. Other technical research has investigated the quality of privacy protection and the detection of privacy violations (e.g. RTBF), where the authors suggest these as ways to verify possible misuse of the data in ML [61].

Thus, this scenario is relevant in cases where other removal methods are insufficient, and the data subject has proven evidence of personal data inference. This is likely to be a growing future scenario that could be adopted as more exact erasure techniques are identified and endorsed by industry.

Techniques. The first and naïve approach to erasing a data subject's data from many basic ML models is to completely retrain the deployed model on the remaining training dataset. This approach requires the controller to retrain the model from scratch after every erasure request. This retraining carries significant energy, time, labour and costs [12]. The controller must consider the likelihood of a request and whether the computational time and effort to retrain is the best solution. For most controllers, this would not be a viable option. This impractical approach motivates academics to research efficient ways for models to "unlearn" the requested data from their existing deployed model.

The second approach is to apply exact unlearning methods. This proposed solution allows the system to 'unlearn' a piece of data without having to retrain the entire model and the associated relationships between data [62]. Thus, it is more efficient and practical from the controller's perspective than the previous option, especially where complete erasure is necessary for more than one RTBF request. This area of research is still active and there is no endorsed technique, nor a technique applicable to every ML model, and researchers have stated it is likely impossible to have a technique that would be able to fit such criteria [17]. Currently, there are only two methods relevant to exact unlearning. The first method provided a general definition for an unlearning algorithm in a general case, i.e. without being specific to a particular training dataset [63]. The paper then proposes an unlearning algorithm that is more efficient than retraining from scratch. The limitation is the applicability, as it can only be applied to controllers required to erase data in clustering problems, specifically k-means clustering. Possibly the best progress for model-applicability was published in 2021, where the authors proposed a framework that is applicable to any unlearning algorithm but designed to achieve the largest improvements for deep neural networks [64]. It partitions the deployed model into smaller sub-models, removing the need to retrain the entire model and instead retrain a sub-model that contains the personal data requested for erasure.

Before applying exact unlearning techniques, controllers may need to consider the capability of the controller. For example, the unlearning solution published in 2021 [64] will still require technical expertise to ensure the framework can be successfully tailored to the controller's deployed model. It is also dependent on the type of erasure request, this proposal only considers the type where certain items are removed from the training data, it does not include class removal, for example, where image removal is required. As the goal for exact erasure is to identify the exact same deployment model as if the user data was never part of the training dataset, controllers may question how the removal of personal data might affect the performance of the deployed model. It is hard to predict how erased points will change the model [65], but research in unlearning has looked at how many data subject requests can be performed before degrading the accuracy of the deployed model [66]. The current state-of-the-art claims it could handle a higher batch of unlearning requests than the estimated unlearning requests anticipated by Google [64]. Also, the controller may have to consider the architecture of their ML system, as the ease of erasure will depend on the way in which the model is deployed, including whether the model is outsourced. In this case, some controllers may not be able to erase data from or even understand the outsourced ML model.

It is important to note that exact erasure is not always the best solution for the data subject. For example, exact erasure does not imply complete privacy of the individual [63], as it could be possible to re-identify the data subject that had their data erased (in the rare case where someone has access to both the old and new model).

Ultimately, there is an extremely long way to go to reach any endorsement or use of exact unlearning in practice, and therefore remains a great opportunity to produce more exact unlearning approaches that can be realistically adopted.

Approximate Erasure. At the same point within the decision-making diagram as exact erasure, approximate erasure is another approach to erase data from the deployed model. The difference is that it relaxes the strict requirements of exact erasure to make the problem computationally manageable [62]. This results in a range of techniques that do not guarantee all the data subjects' personal data has been removed, rather, providing a statistical bound as to its ability to remove the requested data from the existing deployed model. The goal of approximate unlearning is to approximate the model parameters one would obtain by exact unlearning [67].

Approximate erasure may be deemed necessary when the controller is unable to retrain the model from scratch and the exact unlearning techniques are not applicable or computationally expensive. Due to the limited techniques for exact unlearning and current lack of endorsement in industry, this is a likely scenario.

Techniques. The techniques considered for approximate erasure include any technique that replaces/removes the majority of data that identifies the data subject. For approximate unlearning, most of the approaches either perform less computationally expensive actions on the parameters or modify the architecture [39]. As the requirements are more relaxed, there are more solutions applicable to a range of ML models, generating roughly 40 proposed solutions. As with exact unlearning, there is no one endorsed method, and the techniques differ on the erasure request and ML model used by the controller. The following approximate unlearning techniques have been chosen due to their wider applicability to ML models and efficiency of unlearning.

In one approach, the authors propose a differentially private unlearning mechanism for streaming data removal requests [68]. It is the first paper that examines the provision of deletion guarantees with the motivation that users may wish to erase their data exactly because of what deployed models reveal about them. This motivation for removal is likely to increase as new membership attacks re-identify data subjects from the deployed model. This is a suitable legal justification, requiring revocation under the "unlawful processing" grounds explained above. Another proposed solution for approximate erasure uses a certified removal technique applied to linear models [69]. This also takes advantage of differential privacy's objective, stating that the model after removal is indistinguishable from a model that never trained on the removed data. This unlearning solution is mostly applicable to deep neural networks in the image domain. Another relevant to classification models looks at approximate unlearning for the specific setting of class-wide erasure requests, for example facial recognition [42].

Similar to the considerations in exact erasure, it is difficult to determine how the techniques can be applied, and there is an assumption in the literature that the controller has the relevant expertise to be able to apply such methods. As the techniques exist currently, there is no evidence that these have been applied to industry. The majority of the paper's proposals do use example data sets as part of its evaluation, but the effectiveness for industry is not yet clear.

Some academics argue that approximation techniques are more beneficial for the privacy of the data subject: the techniques for approximate unlearning, such as differential privacy, do not focus on data erasure but attempt to make data private or non-identifiable. As approximate unlearning techniques do not erase all the requested personal data, the data subject may want some form of verification that the unlearning technique has been applied. The controller is obliged according to Article 12 GDPR to inform the data subject of the controller's decision on the request. Although there are no direct requirements for the verification of erased data points, it is worth mentioning that one of the main principles of the GDPR is accountability, which means that the controller is the one responsible for complying with the law and being able to demonstrate compliance. Controllers may demonstrate compliance by stating whether the erasure request is implemented or not, without providing details of how the system functions. This undetailed notice to the data subject may be a result of wishing to protect the trade secret and intellectual property in the system. Either way, whether the erasure is proved or not, the controller remains responsible for any breach or non-compliance. That means if the controller was not considering a technical approach that applies the required erasure, the controller may face the risk of being held non-compliant. Therefore, the technical literature does focus on providing theoretical guarantees alongside their proposed unlearning techniques [39]. It would be advantageous for controllers to have the ability to efficiently and confidently confirm to data subjects their requested removal was successful. There are various ways to verify erasure, including measuring erasure via applying privacy attacks [70], information leakage [71] or apply cryptography with verifiable proof [72].

Alternatives. As research in machine unlearning is still evolving, it is likely that controllers may struggle to adopt the exact and approximate unlearning measures discussed above. Therefore, the decision-making flow considers that some controllers cannot erase the data and alternative approaches must be applied. This is based on the assumption that the chosen technique is adequate to meet the requirements of the data subject and the law. This is because the alternatives do not erase the subject's personal data in the ML model, but they do attempt to decrease the privacy harms associated with ML. Alternatives may be necessary where data cannot be erased, for example, if the erasure of data will destroy the model or result in unfounded complexities, especially where third parties are involved.

Techniques. One of the possible alternatives is restricting the model output to prevent privacy harms against the deployed model. This could be relevant where the data subject has provided sufficient evidence of re-identification of the deployed model. For example, mitigation strategies have been proposed to prevent membership inference attacks against ML models if the data cannot be erased [13]. This includes limiting the model's predictions to top k classes and decreasing the precision of the prediction. This approach reduces the work required for the controller but in turn reduces the accuracy of the model's output.

Encrypting the ML model is another technique used to protect the confidentiality of the model output, without affecting the performance. Homomorphic encryption has been proposed on the gradients [73]. The scheme can prevent information leakage to the honest-but-curious cloud server, focusing on controllers using collaborative deep learning. A simpler technique is to erase or restrict access to the training dataset only. Restricting access could include storing encrypted copies of the training data. This was a practical interpretation by ENISA under the RTBF [21].

It is important to note that the RTBF and the right to restriction are different rights in the GDPR. Article 18 grants data subjects the right to restrict the processing of their personal data in specific circumstances different from the RTBF grounds [74]. As clarified by Recital 67 GDPR, restriction of processing can include temporarily moving the selected personal data to another processing system; making the selected dataset unavailable to users, or temporarily removing published data from a web page [75]. However, restriction can be imposed as a result of balancing different rights or interests, as stated in the CJEU judgement in the *Camera di Commercio* case, to balance the data subject's right to erasure and legal obligations [45]. Similar to restriction, in backup systems, it can be impractical to erase data because of the technical difficulty or security requirement [36]. In those cases, the UK DPA, the Information Commissioner (ICO), for example, directs controllers to explain this clearly to the data subject and not to use the backup data for any other purposes; to put the requested data 'beyond use', publicly and privately [26].

For some controllers, the alternatives could be the only viable option to implement, especially as the machine unlearning techniques are still in their infancy. The techniques are less costly in terms of time and computation. However, this may also raise the concern that controllers will use these alternatives as an 'easier' way of complying with the data subject's erasure request. Thus, these techniques must only be used where the controller has provided sufficient evidence that it is unable to use erasure techniques.

4   Conclusion

This paper is the first to investigate a wider scope of the problem space for the RTBF in ML, and in turn hopes to aid both regulators and controllers for future cases. It illustrates that implementing the RTBF is not a matter of mere erasure of personal data or refusal of the erasure request, rather it is about establishing a decision-making process that begins by identifying the required level of erasure, establishing a ground for erasure, balancing the right requested against other rights and interests, and then deciding the most appropriate technique in a case-by-case approach.

In the case of Clearview AI, the decision-making flow demonstrates that erasure is required, but the level of erasure was not mentioned. Firstly, if Clearview AI was to only erase the training database of the facial images, independently to the deployed model, the level of erasure would not be sufficient; the deployed model would still be able to detect the erased images as the biometric template that has been trained on has not changed. Although erasing the whole model is not what the GDPR nor its guidance directly require, it is likely a scenario that may be requested by the Data Protection Authority (DPA) or courts. Thus, the decision-flow would find that exact erasure is necessary. Instead, Clearview AI did not address the formal notice and the French DPA imposed a penalty of 20 million euros [2]. Similar fines and erasure orders were imposed by the competent authority in the UK, Italy, Greece, Australia and the US [76–79]. For future erasure requests, and to avoid future fines, Clearview AI (and other controllers) must allow the use of efficient unlearning techniques, weighing up the considerations (both legally and technically) to decide the best approach.

In summary, this work sheds light on critical decision-making challenges that warrant further investigation. Specifically, greater interdisciplinary research exploring how personal data can be inferred from the output of the ML model will underscore the need for more stringent erasure techniques. In addition, the authors recommend testing the proposed solution on both hypothetical and real-world scenarios to solidify its validity and feasibility. This could also involve considering other complex ML applications such as federated learning, repurposing, transfer learning and one-shot learning. Overall, addressing these challenges will contribute to the development of efficient and easy to apply erasure techniques that prioritise the privacy of the data subject.

Acknowledgements. Nora Alhuwaish is a PhD student sponsored by Kind Saud University. Katie Hawkins is a PhD student sponsored by the EPSRC Centre for Doctoral Training in Cyber Security.

References

1. Clearview AI | Facial Recognition. https://www.clearview.ai. Accessed 31 Jan 2023
2. Facial recognition: 20 million euros penalty against CLEARVIEW AI | CNIL. https://www.cnil.fr/en/facial-recognition-20-million-euros-penalty-against-clearview-ai. Accessed 19 Jan 2023
3. Regulation (EU) 2016/679 of the European Parliament and of the Council of 27 April 2016 on the protection of natural persons with regard to the processing of personal data and on the free movement of such data, and repealing Directive 95/46/EC (General Data Protection Regulation). Hereinafter [The GDPR]. Official Journal of the European Union L119, pp. 1–88, May 2016. http://eur-lex.europa.eu/legal-content/EN/TXT/?uri=OJ:L:2016:119:TOC. Accessed 11 Sep 2022
4. GDPR, Article 4(1)
5. GDPR, Article 1
6. GDPR, Article 4(7)
7. Mann, M., Smith, M.: Automated facial recognition technology: recent developments and approaches to oversight. Univ. New South Wales Law J. **40**, 121–145 (2017). https://doi.org/10.3316/ielapa.771179858194317
8. Ugail, H.: Chapter 6 - Deep face recognition using full and partial face images. In: Davies, E.R. Turk, M.A. (eds.) Advanced Methods and Deep Learning in Computer Vision, pp. 221–241. Academic Press (2022). https://doi.org/10.1016/B978-0-12-822109-9.00015-1
9. Dang, Q.-V.: Right to be forgotten in the age of machine learning. In: Antipova, T. (ed.) Advances in Digital Science, pp. 403–411. Springer, Cham (2021). https://doi.org/10.1007/978-3-030-71782-7_35
10. Hartley, J., Tsaftaris, S.A.: Measuring Unintended memorisation of unique private features in neural networks. http://arxiv.org/abs/2202.08099 (2022). https://doi.org/10.48550/arXiv.2202.08099
11. Rigaki, M., Garcia, S.: A survey of privacy attacks in machine learning. http://arxiv.org/abs/2007.07646 (2021). https://doi.org/10.48550/arXiv.2007.07646
12. Veale, M., Binns, R., Edwards, L.: Algorithms that remember: model inversion attacks and data protection law. Philos. Trans. R. Soc. A Math. Phys. Eng. Sci. **376**, 20180083 (2018)
13. Shokri, R., Stronati, M., Song, C., Shmatikov, V.: Membership inference attacks against machine learning models. arXiv arXiv:1610.05820 (2017). https://doi.org/10.48550/arXiv.1610.05820
14. Edwards, L., Veale, M.: Slave to the Algorithm? Why a "Right to an Explanation" Is Probably Not the Remedy You Are Looking For. Social Science Research Network, Rochester, NY (2017). https://doi.org/10.2139/ssrn.2972855
15. Szeghalmi, V.: Difficulties regarding the right to be forgotten in the case law of the strasbourg court. Athens J. Law **4**, 255–270 (2018). https://doi.org/10.30958/ajl.4-3-4
16. Fabbrini, F., Celeste, E.: The right to be forgotten in the digital age: the challenges of data protection beyond borders. German Law Journal. **21**, 55–65 (2020). https://doi.org/10.1017/glj.2020.14
17. Villaronga, E.F., Kieseberg, P., Li, T.: Humans forget, machines remember: artificial intelligence and the right to be forgotten. Comput. Law Secur. Rev. **34**, 304–313 (2018). https://doi.org/10.1016/j.clsr.2017.08.007
18. Case C-434/16 Peter Nowak v Data Protection Commissioner [2017] THE COURT (Second Chamber) ECLI:EU:C:2017:994
19. Charter of Fundamental Rights of the European Union. https://eur-lex.europa.eu/EN/legal-content/summary/charter-of-fundamental-rights-of-the-european-union.html. Accessed 06 Feb 2023

20. Requests to delist content under European privacy law – Google transparency report. https://transparencyreport.google.com/eu-privacy/overview?hl=en_GB. Accessed 27 Jan 2023

21. The right to be forgotten - between expectations and practice. https://www.enisa.europa.eu/publications/the-right-to-be-forgotten. Accessed 19 Jan 2023

22. Alzubi, J., Nayyar, A., Kumar, A.: Machine learning from theory to algorithms: an overview. J. Phys. Conf. Ser. **1142**, 012012 (2018). https://doi.org/10.1088/1742-6596/1142/1/012012

23. Ausloos, J.: The Right to Erasure in EU Data Protection Law. OUP Oxford, Oxford, New York (2020)

24. Guidelines 5/2019 on the criteria of the Right to be Forgotten in the search engines cases under the GDPR (part 1) | European Data Protection Board, V.2 Adopted on 7 July 2020. https://edpb.europa.eu/our-work-tools/our-documents/guidelines/guidelines-52019-criteria-right-be-forgotten-search-engines_en (2022)

25. Do we always have to delete personal data if a person asks? https://ec.europa.eu/info/law/law-topic/data-protection/reform/rules-business-and-organisations/dealing-citizens/do-we-always-have-delete-personal-data-if-person-asks_en. Accessed 07 Dec 2022

26. Right to erasure. https://ico.org.uk/for-organisations/guide-to-data-protection/guide-to-the-general-data-protection-regulation-gdpr/individual-rights/right-to-erasure/. Accessed 12 Nov 2022

27. The right to de-listing in questions | CNIL. https://www.cnil.fr/en/right-de-listing-questions. Accessed 28 Nov 2022

28. Kuner, C., et al.: The EU General Data Protection Regulation (GDPR): A Commentary (2020). https://doi.org/10.1093/oso/9780198826491.002.0001

29. Google Spain SL and Google Inc v Agencia Española de Protección de Datos (AEPD) and Mario Costeja González (2014)

30. Case C-136/17, GC and Others v Commission nationale de l'informatique et des libertés (CNIL), judgment of 24 September 2019 (Grand Chamber) (ECLI:EU:C:2019:773)

31. Tzanou, M.: The unexpected consequences of the EU right to be forgotten: internet search engines as fundamental rights adjudicators. https://papers.ssrn.com/abstract=3277348 (2018)

32. Verschaeve, S.: Going dark or living forever: the right to be forgotten, search engines and press archives. https://papers.ssrn.com/abstract=3669865 (2020). https://doi.org/10.2139/ssrn.3669865

33. Klinefelter, A., Wrigley, S.: Google LLC v. CNIL: The location-based limits of the EU right to erasure and lessons for U.S. privacy law. https://papers.ssrn.com/abstract=3844968 (2021)

34. Globocnik, J.: The right to be forgotten is taking shape: CJEU judgments in GC and others (C-136/17) and Google v CNIL (C-507/17). GRUR Int. **69**, 380–388 (2020). https://doi.org/10.1093/grurint/ikaa002

35. Razmetaeva, Y.: The right to be forgotten in the European perspective. TalTech J. Eur. Stud. **10**, 58–76 (2020). https://doi.org/10.1515/bjes-2020-0004

36. Politou, E., Alepis, E., Virvou, M., Patsakis, C.: The "Right to be Forgotten" in the GDPR: implementation challenges and potential solutions. In: Politou, E., Alepis, E., Virvou, M., Patsakis, C. (eds.) Privacy and Data Protection Challenges in the Distributed Era, pp. 41–68. Springer, Cham (2022). https://doi.org/10.1007/978-3-030-85443-0_4

37. Yoo, C.S.: The overlooked systemic impact of the right to be forgotten: lessons from adverse selection, moral hazard, and ban the box. https://papers.ssrn.com/abstract=4124596 (2022)

38. Cao, Y., Yang, J.: Towards making systems forget with machine unlearning. In: 2015 IEEE Symposium on Security and Privacy, pp. 463–480 (2015). https://doi.org/10.1109/SP.2015.35

39. Nguyen, T.T., Huynh, T.T., Nguyen, P.L., Liew, A.W.-C., Yin, H., Nguyen, Q.V.H.: A survey of machine unlearning. http://arxiv.org/abs/2209.02299 (2022). https://doi.org/10.48550/arXiv.2209.02299

40. Protivash, P., Durrell, J., Ding, Z., Zhang, D., Kifer, D.: Reconstruction attacks on aggressive relaxations of differential privacy. http://arxiv.org/abs/2209.03905 (2022)

41. Shintre, S., Roundy, K.A., Dhaliwal, J.: Making machine learning forget. In: Naldi, M., Italiano, G.F., Rannenberg, K., Medina, M., Bourka, A. (eds.) Privacy Technologies and Policy, pp. 72–83. Springer, Cham (2019). https://doi.org/10.1007/978-3-030-21752-5_6

42. Baumhauer, T., Schöttle, P., Zeppelzauer, M.: Machine unlearning: linear filtration for logit-based classifiers. Mach. Learn. **111**, 3203–3226 (2022). https://doi.org/10.1007/s10994-022-06178-9

43. Gutmann, A., Warner, M.: Fight to be forgotten: exploring the efficacy of data erasure in popular operating systems. In: Naldi, M., Italiano, G.F., Rannenberg, K., Medina, M., Bourka, A. (eds.) Privacy Technologies and Policy, pp. 45–58. Springer, Cham (2019). https://doi.org/10.1007/978-3-030-21752-5_4

44. Deleting personal data. https://ico.org.uk/media/for-organisations/documents/1475/deleting_personal_data.pd

45. Case C-398/15: Request for a preliminary ruling from the Corte suprema di cassazione (Italy) lodged on 23 July 2015 — Camera di Commercio, Industria, Artigianato e Agricoltura di Lecce v Salvatore Manni (2015)

46. GDPR, Article 70(1)(a) to (y)

47. GDPR, Article 51 to 59

48. AI: ensuring GDPR compliance | CNIL. https://www.cnil.fr/en/ai-ensuring-gdpr-compliance. Accessed 05 Dec 2022

49. Council of the European Union, Proposal for a Regulation of the European Parliament and of the Council on the Protection of Individuals with Regard to the Processing of Personal Data and on the Free Movement of Such Data (General Data Protection Regulation), revised and consolidated draft, Interinstitutional File: 2012/0011 (COD)

50. P7_TA(2014)0212 Protection of individuals with regard to the processing of personal data (2014)

51. Guidelines 3/2019 on processing of personal data through video devices | European Data Protection Board. https://edpb.europa.eu/our-work-tools/our-documents/guidelines/guidelines-32019-processing-personal-data-through-video_en. Accessed 14 Jan 2023

52. Kranenborg, H.: Article 17 Right to erasure ('right to be forgotten'). In: The EU General Data Protection Regulation (GDPR). Oxford University Press (2020). https://doi.org/10.1093/oso/9780198826491.003.0049

53. Facial recognition: the CNIL orders CLEARVIEW AI to stop reusing photographs available on the Internet | CNIL. https://www.cnil.fr/en/facial-recognition-cnil-orders-clearview-ai-stop-reusing-photographs-available-internet. Accessed 05 Dec 2022

54. GDPR, Article 17(2)

55. Frantziou, E.: Further developments in the right to be forgotten: the European Court of justice's judgment in case C-131/12, Google Spain, SL, Google Inc v Agencia Espanola de Proteccion de Datos. Hum. Rights Law Rev. **14**, 761–777 (2014). https://doi.org/10.1093/hrlr/ngu033

56. Google LLC. v. Audiencia nacional (Spanish). https://globalfreedomofexpression.columbia.edu/cases/google-llc-v-audiencia-nacional. Accessed 02 Feb 2023

57. NT1 v Google LLC, NT2 v Google LLC EWHC 799 (QB) (UK) (2018)

58. Kelly, M., Satola, D.: The right to be forgotten. Univ. Ill. Law Rev. **2017**, 1–64 (2017)

59. How do we ensure individual rights in our AI systems? https://ico.org.uk/for-organisations/guide-to-data-protection/key-dp-themes/guidance-on-ai-and-data-protection/how-do-we-ensure-individual-rights-in-our-ai-systems/. Accessed 27 Jan 2023

60. Song, C., Shmatikov, V.: Auditing data provenance in text-generation models. http://arxiv.org/abs/1811.00513 (2019). https://doi.org/10.48550/arXiv.1811.00513

61. Pyrgelis, A., Troncoso, C., De Cristofaro, E.: Knock knock, who's there? Membership inference on aggregate location data. http://arxiv.org/abs/1708.06145 (2017). https://doi.org/10.48550/arXiv.1708.06145

62. Izzo, Z., Smart, M., Chaudhuri, K., Zou, J.: Approximate Data Deletion from Machine Learning Models: Algorithms and Evaluations. arXiv:2002.10077 (2020)
63. Ginart, A., Guan, M., Valiant, G., Zou, J.Y.: Making AI forget you: data deletion in machine learning. 14 arXiv:1907.05012 (2019)
64. Bourtoule, L., et al.: Machine unlearning. arXiv:1912.03817 [cs]. (2020)
65. Sarker, I.H.: Machine learning: algorithms, real-world applications and research directions. SN Comput. Sci. **2**, 160 (2021). https://doi.org/10.1007/s42979-021-00592-x
66. Ullah, E., Mai, T., Rao, A., Rossi, R., Arora, R.: Machine unlearning via algorithmic stability. http://arxiv.org/abs/2102.13179 (2021). https://doi.org/10.48550/arXiv.2102.13179
67. Thudi, A., Jia, H., Shumailov, I., Papernot, N.: On the Necessity of Auditable Algorithmic Definitions for Machine Unlearning, http://arxiv.org/abs/2110.11891, (2022). https://doi.org/10.48550/arXiv.2110.11891
68. Gupta, V., Jung, C., Neel, S., Roth, A., Sharifi-Malvajerdi, S., Waites, C.: Adaptive machine unlearning. http://arxiv.org/abs/2106.04378 (2021). https://doi.org/10.48550/arXiv.2106.04378
69. Guo, C., Goldstein, T., Hannun, A., van der Maaten, L.: Certified data removal from machine learning models. arXiv:1911.03030 [cs, stat]. (2020)
70. Jagielski, M., et al.: Measuring forgetting of memorized training examples. http://arxiv.org/abs/2207.00099 (2022). https://doi.org/10.48550/arXiv.2207.00099
71. Goel, S., Prabhu, A., Kumaraguru, P.: Evaluating inexact unlearning requires revisiting forgetting. http://arxiv.org/abs/2201.06640 (2022). https://doi.org/10.48550/arXiv.2201.06640
72. Eisenhofer, T., Riepel, D., Chandrasekaran, V., Ghosh, E., Ohrimenko, O., Papernot, N.: Verifiable and provably secure machine unlearning. http://arxiv.org/abs/2210.09126 (2022). https://doi.org/10.48550/arXiv.2210.09126
73. Liu, B., Ding, M., Shaham, S., Rahayu, W., Farokhi, F., Lin, Z.: When machine learning meets privacy: a survey and outlook. http://arxiv.org/abs/2011.11819 (2020). https://doi.org/10.48550/arXiv.2011.11819
74. The GDPR, Article 18 - Right to restriction of processing (2019)
75. Vollmer, N.: Recital 67 EU General Data Protection Regulation (EU-GDPR). https://www.privacy-regulation.eu/en/recital-67-GDPR.htm. Accessed 02 Feb 2023
76. ICO fines facial recognition database company Clearview AI Inc more than £7.5m and orders UK data to be deleted. https://ico.org.uk/about-the-ico/media-centre/news-and-blogs/2022/05/ico-fines-facial-recognition-database-company-clearview-ai-inc/. Accessed 31 Jan 2023
77. Greek DPA imposes 20M euro fine on Clearview AI for unlawful processing of personal data. https://iapp.org/news/a/greek-dpa-imposes-20m-euro-fine-on-clearview-ai-for-unlawful-processing-of-personal-data/. Accessed 31 Jan 2023
78. Facial recognition: Italian SA fines Clearview AI EUR 20 million | European Data Protection Board. https://edpb.europa.eu/news/national-news/2022/facial-recognition-italian-sa-fines-clearview-ai-eur-20-million_en. Accessed 31 Jan 2023
79. Clearview AI breached Australians' privacy. https://www.oaic.gov.au/updates/news-and-media/clearview-ai-breached-australians-privacy. Accessed 31 Jan 2023

Data Protection Principles and Data Subject Rights

A Data Protection-Compliant Framework for Wi-Fi-Based Location Tracking (in Law Enforcement)

Stephanie von Maltzan$^{(\boxtimes)}$

Karlsruhe Institute of Technology, Karlsruhe, Germany
stephanie.maltzan@kit.edu

Abstract. Law enforcement agencies continue to deploy new surveillance, identification and tracking technologies that tend to intrude on privacy. These include Wi-Fi-based location tracking methods that take advantage of the fact that Wi-Fi enabled devices exchange data with each other even when they are not connected. At very short intervals, probe requests are sent to all surrounding devices. The contents of the data packets include the MAC addresses and preferred SSID lists, which can provide information about the daily behaviour of the users. The scenario to be considered is initially limited and, due to technical and legal complexity, narrowed down to the domestic domain and the privacy issues are discussed using the example of intrusion detection. In view of the difficulty of defining the perimeter, the spatial and temporal limitations depending on the personal data and, above all, the information obligations and opt-out solutions will be discussed.

Keywords: Wi-Fi-based location tracking · MAC address · data protection · privacy preserving data collection · information obligations

1 Introduction

The ever-changing pace of technology has left law enforcement officials with the task of finding legal ways to investigate and search for suspected criminal activity. As a result, law enforcement agencies as well as private companies continue to deploy new surveillance, identification and tracking technologies that tend to intrude on privacy [Big Brother Watch, 2018]. These include Wi-Fi-based location tracking methods which take advantage of the fact that Wi-Fi enabled devices exchange data with each other even when they are not connected. The contents of the packets include MAC addresses and preferred SSID lists, which can provide information about user's daily behavior [Sapiezynski et al., 2015]. This means that everyone leaves a trace every time they do not turn off the Wi-Fi connection. Using MAC addresses and SSID lists can be a valuable tool for law enforcement to begin their search to locate suspects. The development and use of information and advanced analytics to inform law enforcement could thus become a policing strategy or tactic. For this reason, such a detector could also be of interest for private use. Especially when it comes to solving burglaries in residential areas.

K. Rannenberg et al. (Eds.): APF 2023, LNCS 13888, pp. 41–56, 2024.
https://doi.org/10.1007/978-3-031-61089-9_3

The detection of a burglary at home is still an important task for the police, but one that has so far been difficult to solve. The police are still only able to solve a fraction of the crimes that are committed. Often there is nothing that even the police can do after a burglary has occurred. So far, there is a lack of sufficient technical approaches to support the police in their investigations. In Germany, less than 20% [Rudnicka, 2022] of the total number of burglaries reported are solved. Victims are often left with feelings of powerlessness, mistrust and fear that it could happen again [Beaton et al., 2000]. Although the legal situation in principle allows for the extensive use of technical means, there is a lack of targeted technical measures to support the police in their investigations. Many people consequently rely on intruder alarms. A number of expensive security mechanisms such as CCTV cameras and alarm systems have been developed to protect buildings. As a result, there is a need for a solution that is not only cost effective, but also universally applicable and practical. While most houses and apartments do not have alarm systems installed, almost every household has a Wi-Fi router which could be extended with the possibility of an alarm system. To the extent that it can be designed in a privacy-friendly way, the Wi-Fi Detector could meet this need.

The Wi-Fi detector uses the following principle: Mobile devices constantly transmit their location and identity as soon as they are switched on. The Wi-Fi routers can therefore also detect unknown mobile devices used by potential criminals giving every household with a Wi-Fi router the opportunity to retrofit a kind of alarm system.

From a privacy perspective, this detector could challenge the breadth of law enforcement's investigative techniques and create a blurred line between the responsible person to protect their property as well the user's right to privacy and the law enforcement's duty to apprehend criminals.

This paper aims to describe a privacy-friendly framework for Wi-Fi tracking and discusses how to design information obligations and opt-out possibilities. The scenario to be considered is initially limited and, due to technical and legal complexity, narrowed down to the domestic domain and the privacy issues are discussed using the example of intrusion detection. An interdisciplinary project[1] underpins the paper.

This work assumes a basic level of understanding of data protection.

2 Related Work

Crowd control, marketing and real-time monitoring of public space usage can all benefit from the information derived from Wi-Fi signals, as discussed by Ogawa [Ogawa et al., 2011]. The monitoring of user mobility via Wi-Fi has been the subject of much research in the technical literature [Kalogianni et al., 2015; Reichl et al., 2018; Soundararaj et al., 2020], however, the research tends to focus more on a statistical tracking in public spaces or on a general technical approach. In addition, there has been little research into the technical effort involved in the use of Wi-Fi to detect criminal activity. Similarly, MAC addresses have not been systematically considered as potential evidence in criminal prosecutions. It is also worth noting that the research that generally discusses Wi-Fi tracking does not adequately address privacy issues. The majority of papers - if they

---

[1] See https://itsec.cs.uni-bonn.de/wachmann/.

address these issues at all- focus on the technical aspects of privacy-preserving data collection.

Relevant to this work is also the work on privacy preserving techniques [Gebru, 2022] such as anonymisation and pseudonymisation. Finally, several works and guidelines [EDPB, 2020] on security and privacy of connected vehicles have been published at national and international level, which will be useful in terms of information obligations. These initiatives aim to complement existing data protection and privacy frameworks with sector-specific rules that could be applied to the Wi-Fi tracking scenario.

The aim of the project, which underpins this paper, is to transfer current technical research to a privacy-preserving reliable and low error spatial intrusion detection. In the legal context, the particular challenge is to create or ensure data protection compliant framework. This serves to acknowledge the trustworthiness of the system. Its use should not lead to mistrust of Wi-Fi networks or police authorities. Accordingly, acceptable use and public acceptance require not only privacy compliance at every stage of the system's development, but also in its use, especially in interaction with neighbours, visitors and the police. The focus here is on defining a perimeter in a privacy-friendly way, as well as on information obligations and opt-out possibilities for neighbours. So far these points have been ignored in literature.

3   System and Scenario for a Domestic Wi-Fi Detector

Residential intrusion is the central use case for the project. In this use case, the Wi-Fi detector is used by individuals in private, i.e. to protect private property. Wi-Fi routers are used in most homes, and homes, especially in remote locations, are lucrative targets for burglars. The system to be developed should, on the one hand, be able to distinguish between Wi-Fi-enabled devices inside the perimeter to be protected and those that are located outside the perimeter. On the other hand, it should be able to extract information from these devices that can be used for tracking purposes. An architecture[2] has been developed to enable the system to achieve these objectives.

Wi-Fi enabled devices do not only exchange data with each other when they are connected, but also when they are in a so-called non-associated state. Mobile Wi-Fi devices are constantly searching for Wi-Fi networks to connect to. With "Wi-Fi", it is possible to monitor all packets sent by other devices in the vicinity. When other devices send their own packets, the information contained in them and the transmission information can be evaluated. In particular, it is possible to extract CSI data and MAC addresses from all packets, and SSIDs from probe requests, using methods for extracting detectable data types.

MAC addresses serve as a unique identifier for a particular device while SSIDs are, in a nutshell, the names of Wi-Fi networks such as ("FRITZ!Box 7490" or "Home"). The mobile Wi-Fi device sends a list of SSIDs of networks to which it has already connected to all surrounding devices. This allows it to check whether a device to which it is already connected is in range. When a conventional connection is established between a mobile Wi-Fi device and a Wi-Fi router, the mobile Wi-Fi device sends a probe request to all

---

[2] Further information on the project and the consortia can be found at https://itsec.cs.uni-bonn. de/wachmann/.

surrounding Wi-Fi routers to establish a connection. This probe request is transmitted over the Wi-Fi connection. As an extension to conventional Wi-Fi routers, the Wi-Fi detector takes advantage of the network communication between mobile Wi-Fi devices and Wi-Fi routers. It uses the data received from the mobile Wi-Fi devices to determine their approximate location. The Wi-Fi detector initially goes beyond the conventional functionality of Wi-Fi routers by analysing the information received to determine the approximate location of all surrounding devices.

Typically, the mobile Wi-Fi devices send out probe requests at short intervals (approximately every 5 s) to all nearby Wi-Fi devices, which then respond depending on the connection options. Supported standards, data rates, frequencies, device MAC addresses and preferred SSID lists are included in the probe request data packets. The project seeks to capitalise on the fact that these devices continuously transmit their position and identity (via MAC address – even the Wi-Fi network data does not contain specific location information) to Wi-Fi networks and thus to the corresponding routers, and aims to enable Wi-Fi routers to automatically detect the mobile devices of intruders. The aim is to detect a device within the geographical area (predominantly the flat/house) to be protected, known as the perimeter, and monitor its Wi-Fi transmissions. But not every device unknown to the network is a direct indication of a criminal intruder. In addition, given the range of signal strength, any devices outside the flat/house may also be affected. This needs to be considered when personal data is involved.

The question of whether MAC addresses are personal data (the household exemption does not apply; in particular due to signal strength and the monitoring capabilities) has occasionally been raised in the literature. However, Data Protection authorities [ULD, 2019; Art. 29 Data Protection Working Party, 2017; Dutch Data Protection Authority, 2010; CNIL, 2011] agree that MAC addresses are personal data because of the inherent ability to uniquely singling out a person and indirectly assigning a MAC address to a natural person globally. This could be handled differently, as in Android version 10 MAC randomisation is enabled by default.[3] This affects around 68% of Android devices.[4] See Sect. 3.6 for a discussion of randomised MAC addresses and location data in regard to personal data. However, there are a number of approaches [Vanhoef et al, 2016; Fenske et al, 2021] to identifying devices that counteract randomisation. This work focuses more on specific and more problematic issues rather than a general discussion about personal data or controllership. In addition, it is possible to determine the typical locations of a data subject through the preferred SSID lists and thus to identify them, making the preferred SSID lists also personal data. In this respect, the use of the Wi-Fi detector could involve the processing of personal data. However, this is only likely to be the case if, in addition to evaluating the signal strengths and angles of radiation of the individual probe requests, the MAC addresses of the devices that are located in the perimeter are concerned. Therefore, the scope of the GDPR only applies if the Wi-Fi detector processes the MAC addresses and/or the list of SSIDs of the devices in question. As

[3] https://source.android.com/docs/core/connect/wifi-mac-randomization   (accessed   on 05.04.2023).
[4] https://www.androidpolice.com/android-13-platform-distribution-stats/   (accessed   on 05.04.2023).

described above, the application requires data processing of MAC addresses and lists of SSIDs.

A strong data protection framework is therefore of crucial importance. To this end, in addition to the implementation of pseudonymisation of all data collected, role concepts, access control, separate systems and processes, including storage and processing locations of pseudonyms and raw data, as well as further demarcations and modes within the defined perimeter have been developed (it is not possible to remove parts of the MAC addresses as they are processed further). Furthermore, the detector is designed in such a way that, on the one hand, there is no direct automatic transmission to the police in the event of suspicion (an unauthorised device is detected inside the perimeter) and, on the other hand, the data is only stored by the authorised person - e.g. after entering a time period - so that Art. 22 GDPR does not apply.

The focus here is on defining a perimeter in a privacy-friendly way, as well as on information obligations and opt-out possibilities for neighbours. Therefore, as part of the legal analysis, the following sections describe a way to develop a data protection compliant framework for domestic Wi-Fi-based location tracking.

3.1 Limitation of the Perimeter

The first step is to define the living area as a perimeter. For the purposes of legal analysis, this work will not focus on the precision and accuracy that can be achieved or the dependence on the transmitter strength and the signal path between the device and the router.

The perimeter should be limited to the private area and should not include public areas such as streets, pavements, etc. The range of the Wi-Fi detector should be limited to the immediate vicinity of the premises. For apartments, this means that only the immediate apartment and not areas outside the living area - such as stairwells, communal gardens, basements, etc. - can be covered by the perimeter. For detached houses, this means that only the area immediately surrounding the house can be covered by the perimeter. The owner, hereinafter the responsible person, of the router should be able to define or limit the area to be monitored on an individual basis. This should include the maximum signal range ($d^{maximum}$), the actual perimeter area ($d^{perimeter}$), an error area (d^{error}) and an area where detection is safe and privacy-preserving (d^{safe}):

$d^{maximum}$: Maximum signal range in which the router can still receive packets. Packets sent from devices within this range can be processed by the router.

$d^{perimeter}$: Perimeter in which a device should be detected as an intruder. The detection accuracy of the detector should be as close as possible to $d^{perimeter}$.

d^{safe}: Perimeter in which a device is safely detected as an intruder. Regardless of an error of the detection algorithm for localising a measurement, a localisation within d^{safe} means that the real position of the localised device is within the perimeter $d^{perimeter}$, i.e. a doubtless detection of an intruder.

d^{error}: Range within which a device can be located, taking into account the error deviation of the algorithm used. Within this range, it is possible for a device to be located inside the building even though it is actually located outside, and vice versa.

The second step is to develop the router's operating modes according to the perimeter in which a device is located. In passive mode, the router monitors for new devices without generating any packets itself. It estimates the position of the devices solely on the basis of the technical information contained in these packets. This mode initially detects all devices located within $d^{maximum}$. The active mode initiates actions that cause individual potentially suspicious devices to communicate more actively to help pinpoint those devices more accurately. It is triggered when a device is within the error range of the d^{error}. The position of the suspicious device is estimated based on all packets received from it. This mode ends when the suspect device has been safely detected outside the perimeter. The tracking mode extends the active mode, which triggers when the mobile device has been securely placed within the perimeter d^{safe}. The router initiates targeted actions to extract data from the suspect device. Depending on the mode and the perimeter different technical and/or personal data will be collected.

In terms of location accuracy, the above mentioned options should be combined: in the initial location tracking mode, neither a MAC address nor a SSID list should be collected by the Wi-Fi detector during the first probe request. The Wi-Fi detector should be limited to evaluating all received probe requests to determine if they are within the perimeter based on signal strength and beam angle - regardless of MAC address and SSID lists. Only hit/no-hit processing of non-personal data is performed in the first step. If this indicates that the mobile device may be in the location's error zone, the Wi-Fi detector remembers which frequencies and system standards the mobile Wi-Fi device supports in order to match the device's next probe request, regardless of personal data.

As soon as the next probe request confirms that the device is within the perimeter, the same data will be stored once again. If a third probe confirms that the device is in the perimeter, the device's MAC address is also stored and the additional communication required to pinpoint where the device is located is initiated. The accuracy of location increases exponentially with each probe request. As a result, from the third probe request onwards, there is a high probability that the device is actually inside the perimeter and therefore suspicious. Conversely, all stored data is immediately erased if one of the probe requests indicates that the device is not inside the perimeter. Similarly, if additional communication with the device shows it is not in the perimeter.

In summary, the first data processing step of the Wi-Fi detector that is relevant under the GDPR, beyond the typical functionality of a Wi-Fi router, is the more precise detection of the location of the mobile device. The MAC address of the mobile Wi-Fi device is taken into account and additional communication is triggered if there is a high probability that the mobile Wi-Fi device is within the perimeter, based on a total of three probe requests.

3.2 Limitation of the Duration of Data Collection and Storage

In order to ensure the principle of data minimisation with regard to the temporal scope of data collection, on the one hand, and to ensure that data collection only takes place on an event-related basis, on the other hand, data collection by the Wi-Fi detector should be temporarily restricted as follows.

On the one hand, event-independent data should only be stored encrypted for eight hours in a black box with access safeguards and controls. On the other hand, in the case of event-related data collection, the data should be retained for approximately two (up to five days) after the responsible person has typically become aware of the suspicious event that triggered the event-related data collection. The timeframe of eight hours and two up to five days provides a reasonable privacy-preserving way to determine an intrusion as well as report it to the police. In addition to other technical and organisational measures, access security and controls should be in place for event-related data storage.

In case of suspicion (see above Sect. 3.1) the Wi-Fi detector should store data from all devices within (and only) the d^{safe} perimeter for approximately eight hours. The data should be stored on a so-called Black Box, meaning that all collected data is immediately encrypted and stored in a software defined separate location. This is done in the form of a ring buffer that is continuously overwritten with new data. This ensures that only the last eight hours of data is stored. The suspicious data is stored independently of the black box memory and is not automatically overwritten after eight hours, but is stored until an authorised person's device re-enters the perimeter. The authorised person can then determine if an intrusion has occurred. At that point, as a second step, a period of two (up to five) days begins, after which the suspect's data is automatically erased. Within this period, the responsible person can again manually separate the data relevant to the suspicious case based on time stamps and store it separately for law enforcement. This data can be used after a complaint has been filed with the police by the authorised person. All access must be logged. This is to ensure control and transparency, as well as a privacy-friendly way to track devices and ensure privacy by default by forcing the authorised person to determine an intrusion according to the given settings.

3.3 Detection of Authorised and Unauthorised Devices

When setting up the Wi-Fi detector, one or more Wi-Fi devices belonging to the responsible person should be defined to enable event-related data collection. The aim is to have the Wi-Fi detector register whether the responsible person has left the perimeter. In this respect, the responsible person should define as authorised devices only those Wi-Fi devices that he or she normally carries with him or her when he or she leaves the perimeter. If more than one person has access to the living area - for example, in a household with several people, or if neighbours are watering the plants - then a device that they usually have with them should be defined as an authorised device (his/her own smartphone as well as those of their partners and, above all, of the children living there). If the Wi-Fi detector registers that none of these authorised devices are within the perimeter, then any unknown device that enters the perimeter is suspected of unauthorised intrusion and therefore of committing a criminal offence - probably in the form of (attempted) burglary.

Devices outside the perimeter are initially unsuspicious. Only an unauthorised device detected by the Wi-Fi router within the perimeter will raise suspicion. Therefore, the router collects and processes information about this device, which is processed by the router, as it could potentially be an intruder.

3.4 Lawfulness of Processing

The responsible person (resident and user of the detector) acts as a natural person on his/her own responsibility when using the Wi-Fi detector as described above and is therefore the controller [Art. 29 Data Protection Working Party, 2010; EDPS, 2019] with regard to the GDPR. In particular, he/she identifies the authorised devices (his/her own as well as those of their partners and, above all, the children living there), determines the perimeter, initiates the separate storage of data in case of possible intrusion and initiates the transmission of this separate data to the police.

The data processing is thus initiated by the responsible person. The what, whether, how and why of the data processing is therefore determined by the responsible person. In this context, the classification as controller does not strictly depend on the possession of the data and the physical control over the processing. It is therefore irrelevant whether she/he has access to pseudonymised data or to raw data.

The only relevant provision for the processing of data by the Wi-Fi detector is the legitimate interest pursuant to Art. 6 para. 1 lit. f GDPR. In this respect, the property of the responsible person is also regarded as a legitimate interest. In this context, both a preventive purpose - i.e. the securing of property - and a repressive purpose - i.e. the securing of evidence for the investigation and prosecution of criminal offences as well as for judicial assertion - may be pursued.

In addition, the data processing operations must also be necessary for the purpose that is being pursued. This means that the legitimate interests cannot be pursued just as effectively by other, less intensive means. For example, specific data processing is not necessary if its purpose can also be achieved by processing anonymised data or other privacy-by-design approaches. Accordingly, for the question of the lawfulness of data processing by dash cams, it is assumed [EDPB, 2019] that in any case, the permanent recording along the route is not necessary for the protection of interests, since technically only short-term, event-related storage is possible. For similar reasons, in the case of video surveillance of private driveways and/or entryways, for example, the principle of necessity may mean that video surveillance is only permissible on an occasional basis - for example, when the doorbell or a light barrier [DSK, 2020] is activated. In this respect, the infringement must be limited to the absolute minimum - in particular also through a privacy by design approach - which also follows from the principle of data minimisation according to Art. 5 para. 1 lit. c GDPR. Finally, the intensity of the intrusion of the data processing must be taken into account and mitigated by balancing the interests of the data subjects.

As mentioned above the Wi-Fi detector limits the collection of data in terms of space, time and personal data. The processing of personal data only takes place when the Wi-Fi location tracking determines, on the basis of the probe requests issued, that there is a high probability that an unknown device is located in the immediate vicinity of the dwelling and has been detected in the d^{safe} perimeter. With regard to the time limitation the data processing is limited to the necessary extent in that the storage, regardless of the reason, is only carried out for 8 h and is immediately deleted if the responsible person does not separate any data on the basis of timestamps during this period. In this case the Wi-Fi detector will only store the data required for this purpose until such time as the responsible person becomes aware of the suspicious event and can then separate the data. Furthermore, the data collection is limited to gathering information about the device and its behaviour in the perimeter, and it is technically ensured that no telecommunications data are collected. It should also be noted that this location data is limited to the very small spatial area of the perimeter, and thus to a private area. On the other hand, it is possible to collect a large amount of data about the devices and people involved. In principle, the locations where the person in question is usually found can be determined from the collected preferred SSID lists. In this respect, it is possible to derive information about the data subject that goes beyond the mere information that he or she was in the perimeter at a certain time. However, this circumstance is adequately addressed by the fact that unknown suspicious devices are only stored for a short period of 8 h. Only the event-related storage is longer, and even then only for a limited period of 2 to 5 days until the authorised person re-enters the perimeter. In addition, the risk of misuse is reduced by controlling data access and the pseudonymising or encrypting data, among others.

Another consideration is the hidden data collection of the Wi-Fi detector which the data subjects can probably only avoid by switching off all Wi-Fi connections of their mobile Wi-Fi device. This can be counteracted by informing the data subject about the data collection by the Wi-Fi detector and by limiting the data collection to a narrow geographical area. The possibility of an opt-out solution for certain devices is also technically developed. Finally, the risks associated with the processing of the data from the Wi-Fi detector must also be taken into account. For example, there is a risk of misuse of the Wi-Fi detector. However, this risk is addressed by the automatic storage and deletion concept described above, as well as by access controls and pseudonymised or encrypted data. In addition, the risks are addressed by limiting the physical perimeter. Admittedly, there is still a risk of misuse if the user defines the perimeter beyond the boundaries of the home. However, this could be addressed, depending on the technical possibilities, either by having the Wi-Fi detector automatically determine the perimeter and periodically check the incoming data and/or by giving the user a similar warning when setting up the Wi-Fi detector. Given the fact that, on the one hand, the Wi-Fi detector in question only processes personal data if there is a high probability that a device is located within the perimeter based on multiple probe requests, that this data processing must be adequately labelled and on the other hand that the data storage is very limited and that effective opt-out possibilities exist, there should be no overriding interests of the data subjects. In particular, it must be taken into account that although the purpose of the Wi-Fi detector pursued here is not the statistical counting of devices, the purposes of securing evidence and property pursued here are likely to be of particular importance.

Accordingly, there are no overriding interests of the data subjects in the use of the Wi-Fi detector proposed here. Both purposes - the preservation of evidence and the protection of property - are legitimate interests of the controller according to Art. 6 para 1 lit. f GDPR, which are given particular weight in the context of the balancing of interests to be carried out. In this respect, the planned use of the Wi-Fi detector in this case pursues legitimate interests.

Nevertheless, the opinion of the Art. 29 Data Protection Working Party on Wi-Fi tracking [Art. 29 Data Protection Working Party, 2017] must be taken into account. Nevertheless, this opinion considers Wi-Fi tracking in public and with the aim of measuring congestion/traffic flows, and typically not to identify specific suspects. It should be noted that this opinion is based on the following examples of Wi-Fi connections and connection requests from mobile devices used to analyse visitor flows and possibly their behaviour in shopping centres. Traffic congestion on motorways [Hamburgischen

Beauftragten für Datenschutz und Informationsfreiheit, 2016] or waiting times at security checkpoints can also be measured in this way. However, this opinion is a helpful guideline for tracking Wi-Fi in a privacy-friendly way.

The Art. 29 Working Party states in the above mentioned opinion that Wi-Fi tracking is permissible either with the consent of the data subject or if the personal data collected is immediately anonymised. However, it is also permissible under certain conditions if the purpose of the data collection does not allow it. However, for it to be permissible in the case of non-anonymised data, it is necessary that: "MAC addresses of visitors' devices inside of a specific location, such as a store, have to be anonymised immediately upon the collection, without any permanent storage of the MAC addresses, and in such a way that re-identifiability is technically excluded". In addition, not only the purpose of the data processing is limited to purely statistical counting but also the tracking is limited in space and time to what is strictly necessary for this purpose, as well as existing effective opt-out possibilities and the information requirements are met by means of sufficient notices.

In addition, the Art. 29 Working Party has stated that the consent of the data subject is a primary requirement for determining the location of devices, in particular over a longer period of time or over a wider geographical area (across several shops). However, in certain circumstances, the location of the data subject can be determined and tracked without his or her consent. This is the case, for example, with the collection of data in queues at security checkpoints. Nonetheless, the data collected must be deleted or anonymised immediately after passing through the security checkpoint. However, the obligation to provide information applies to all situations.

Therefore, in addition to the technical and organisational measures mentioned above, the data processing of the detector should take into account the information obligations as well as sufficient opt-out possibilities.

3.5 Information Obligations – A Legal Minefield

The principle of transparency means that personal data must be processed in good faith and in a manner that is comprehensible to the data subject. This principle is closely linked to the information obligations under Art. 13 and Art. 14 of the GDPR. These information obligations also form the basis for the exercise of data subjects' rights. The data subject can only exercise his or her rights if he or she is aware that his or her personal data are being processed. This work will focus on the possibilities that allow the data subject to exercise this right and not on the prerequisites of Art. 12 et seq. GDPR [EDPB, 2020].

The Art. 29 Data Protection Working Party [Art. 29 Data Protection Working Party, 2018] recommends in this respect that a balance should be struck between the burden of providing the information and the consequences for the data subject of not providing the information. Wi-Fi monitoring detects the signal that Wi-Fi enabled devices are constantly sending out as they search for a Wi-Fi access point. As the user is not actively involved in this process, he or she should be informed that this type of measurement is taking place. In view of the difficulty in defining the area of signal strength, the obligation to provide information outside one's own home (with the exception of information at the front door and information of neighbours in multiple dwellings) is difficult. Similar to the dashboard camera issue, the information requirements for the use of signal strength-based detectors are a legal minefield.

In its guideline [EDPB, 2019] the EDPB suggests the use of a layered approach, with the most important information displayed on a highly visible sign (e.g. a sticker on the outside of a vehicle in this specific case of dash-cams), alerting individuals to the fact that a detector is being used, and providing a means to obtain further information (e.g. using a QR code that individuals can scan with a smartphone and which links to an online privacy notice with the required information). Similarly, the UK Information Commissioner's Office's code of practice on video surveillance [Information Commissioner's Office, 2023] states that such signs should be clearly visible and appropriate, and should be more prominent where people are less likely to expect to be filmed.

The use of Wi-Fi detectors typically does not have a direct relationship with the people who may pass through the signal, making it more difficult to provide the necessary information to these people. When using a Wi-Fi detector there are no clearly identifiable areas where information can be provided by means of signs. Providing information by means of a sticker when, for example, a car passes by seems not only legally insufficient, but also absurd, especially considering the size of the sticker required to comply with the information requirements. Considering this standard in the light of the personal data processed by the detector, it could be that informing the data subjects is practically impossible or would involve an exorbitant effort. Nevertheless, Art. 11 GDPR is not applicable. This article concerns data processing for the identification of an individual, and not, as in this case, an information obligation to provide information on the basis of a data processing operation being carried out. This article is mainly applicable in cases of Art. 15 GDPR.

Therefore, it is crucial that data controllers comply with the information obligations imposed by the GDPR. As in the case of video surveillance, it may therefore be advisable to provide information about the data collection and transfer of data on road signs, using easily understandable icons and standardised messages via QR codes, so that data subjects can make an informed decision. An alternative hardly seems possible.

The low intensity of the intervention in the passive mode must also be taken into account here, as only a linking of the packets without personal data takes place. In addition, neighbours' devices connect to their own known access points, depending on the signal range. As long as the data subject is not in the perimeter, technical and organisational measures can be taken to protect the freedoms and interests of the data subject. Furthermore, the widespread information about the use of the Wi-Fi detector would be counterproductive or even impossible – although this is a weak argument and would only be made possible by the proposed far-reaching safeguards, in particular the renunciation of the collection of MAC addresses in public spaces. And, above all, it cannot be used as an argument for not complying with the obligation to provide information.

All the necessary information will be positioned prominently on the front door and in the hallway of an apartment building using stickers and/or QR codes in a layered [Art. 29 Data Protection Working Party, 2016] approach [EDPB, 2020]. At the same time, a technical concept should be developed on how to implement effective opt-out options for neighbours and visitors, which is described in the following paragraph. The public space, where no MAC addresses are collected, cannot be informed to this extent. In this respect, a balancing exercise has been carried out, in which the interests of the data subjects in being informed - this can be on the one hand the renunciation of the collection of MAC addresses and on the other hand other appropriate safeguards - have been considered less important than the interests of the controller in achieving the purpose of the data processing.

3.6 Opt-Out Possibilities

According to the previous legal classification of the detector, it is necessary to implement effective opt-out options for potential data subjects such as neighbours (and guests; the party mode can be used to turn off the tracking). The reason for this is in particular the right to object and in particular the above described legal assessment of the Art. 29 Working Party on Wi-Fi tracking. Opt-out measures have been developed to provide data subjects with further recourse, even if the responsible person has demonstrated that the rights of data subjects are not overridden as a result of the perimeter restriction and the tiered data processing.

So far, the following two different variants have been considered: Firstly, neighbours who do not want their data tracked can enter the MAC addresses of their devices into the Wi-Fi detector. This would create a list of MAC addresses whose data should not be collected. The Wi-Fi detector would then have to compare the data of all devices with MAC addresses from this list in a preliminary step before its actual data processing and immediately separate them out. This option can be referred to as MAC address opt-out. On the other hand, it may be technically possible to opt out of the neighbour's data on the basis of technical device data already used to assign multiple probe requests to the same device in combination with certain signal strengths and radiation angles as well as specific technical identification characteristics of the neighbour's devices. This possibility can be referred to as opting out of tracking data. In this way, the Wi-Fi detector could 'learn' the device data and signal strengths that it should not look at in the future.

The MAC address opt-out is already used in particular for commercial tracking in public spaces. Private providers of tracking services [DILAX; PrivacySIG] in public spaces offer the possibility to enter the MAC address of the device that does not want to be tracked on a website. When tracking in public spaces, the first step is to check whether one of the received probe requests originates from one of the MAC addresses listed in this way. These probe requests are then immediately stopped from being processed.

However, opt-out based on MAC addresses raises the following main privacy concerns.

First, it is problematic that in order for this opt-out to work, the MAC address must first be stored as personal data and matched in order to eliminate the corresponding data. In this respect, the processing of personal data relevant under data protection law (in this specific case, the storage of the MAC address) is basically required in order to exercise the right not to be affected by the data processing. The private tracking service providers counter this data protection problem by arguing that there is no other way to guarantee an effective opt-out and that this data processing must therefore be allowed. Furthermore, the effectiveness of this opt-out option is questionable due to the widespread use of MAC address randomisation. It is also problematic that Wi-Fi detectors and private tracking services can record not only the (randomised) MAC addresses of nearby devices, but also their approximate locations. This raises the question: Can personal data be derived from this location data, despite the randomisation of the MAC addresses? Given that MAC addresses do not constitute permanent identifiers. The reason for this is that it may be possible to identify individuals on the basis of this location data. For this reason, data from private location services [DILAX] is not collected if, for example, there are fewer than five devices in its radius, in order to avoid the possibility of establishing a personal connection. This is problematic for the Wi-Fi detector, as a similar exclusion is not possible here, as otherwise the purpose of the data processing (= preservation of evidence for criminal prosecution) cannot be guaranteed effectively enough. The question therefore arises as to the extent to which randomised MAC addresses in combination with location data and/or the specific technical characteristics of devices can be considered personal data. It should be noted that this assessment has to be made on a case-by-case basis. In principle, location data can be used to uniquely identify individual devices, but this depends on the scope and accuracy of the location data available and whether and how many other devices are being tracked at the same time. For example, in the context of location data that can be collected in mobile communications, it is assumed that a device can be uniquely identified if its location can be tracked over time [Spitz, 2009]. Similarly, in the case of Wi-Fi tracking, a device can be uniquely identified if, for example, there is only one device at a particular location or within the radius of the Wi-Fi detector. In addition, the project found that even apparently randomised devices had specific technical characteristics.

In this respect, the question of whether personal data are processed in the case of randomised MAC addresses depends on the specific case, since the identifiability of individuals always depends on the correlation of several pieces of information by the controller. However, due to the described risks of identification based on circumvention of MAC address randomisation and identification based on collected location data, it must be assumed that personal data are involved.

The advantage of the MAC address opt-out is that it is relatively easy to implement and is a very reliable way of preventing unwanted data collection, but only for non-randomised MAC addresses. On the other hand, it is problematic that it requires the storage of MAC addresses as a further processing operation relevant under data protection law.

In summary, the advantage of the MAC address opt-out is its ease of implementation and its basic effectiveness. On the other hand, its disadvantage lies in the fact that further processing of personal data relevant under data protection law takes place and that the MAC address opt-out is not sufficiently effective in the case of randomised MAC addresses.

Alternatively, the opt-out could be based on tracking data. Tracking data is primarily the data that the device sends as part of the probe requests, such as the supported frequency rates and technical standards. In principle, a device cannot be uniquely identified globally on the basis of this data. However, it is very likely that one of several devices in the vicinity of the Wi-Fi detector can be identified on the basis of this data. For example, several probe requests received by the Wi-Fi detector may be attributed to the same device, or they may be determined to be from different devices. The probability of detection increases as there are fewer devices in the vicinity of the Wi-Fi detector. If it is indeed possible – as it seems in this project – to make such an attribution or identification on the basis of the tracking data, then these data could also be used for the opt-out option considered here.

The opt-out should be implemented in particular for multi-family dwellings, where the close proximity of living areas increases the risk that neighbours will be affected by the data processing. This is particularly likely if the Wi-Fi detector is located close to a neighbour's living area, or close to common areas such as stairwells or basements. Therefore, depending on technical feasibility, it may be possible to implement an opt-out option for these particularly vulnerable areas based on the designated tracking data.

For example, the Wi-Fi detector could store or learn what tracking data is coming from neighbours' devices, and also store or learn that these should only be eliminated if the devices are within a certain spatial area - the perimeter d^{error}. On the one hand, this could provide an opt-out option for particularly affected neighbours without the need to store and compare directly identifiable personal data. On the other hand, the opt-out could be limited to those geographical areas where there is a correspondingly increased risk of data processing of uninvolved individuals, thus additionally ensuring that the Wi-Fi detector continues to provide an effective contribution to law enforcement.

As each of the two options presented has advantages and disadvantages, each of which will depend on the specific application of the Wi-Fi detector, a combination of the two options is recommended.

An anonymous opt-out option, without direct contact with the user of the Wi-Fi detector, would also be advisable. However, the question is whether and how this can be implemented in practice. For example, if a QR code is posted in the stairwell to enable the opt-out option, there is a risk that potential criminals will use it.

4   Conclusion

From a privacy perspective, Wi-Fi tracking can potentially challenge the breadth of law enforcement's investigative techniques and create a blurred line between a person's responsibility to protect their property, the user's right to privacy, and the law enforcement's duty to apprehend criminals. This work shows, nevertheless, that Wi-Fi tracking can be compliant if it is operated in a narrowly defined and delimited space. However, the issues raised by the range of the signal, particularly with regard to information requirements and possible opt-out solutions, are difficult to resolve and remain a legal minefield. Future work will show how the presented framework can be further improved and which privacy-enhancing solutions - especially with regard to information requirements and opt-out solutions - can be further developed. In particular, the focus will be on ensuring that tracking can be stopped immediately upon request and that the restricted perimeter can detect neighbouring devices without processing personal data.

References

Article 29-Data Protection Working Party: WP 169, Opinion 1/2010 on the concepts of "controller" and "processor" (2010)

Article 29 Data Protection Working Party: WP 247, Opinion on the proposed Regulation for the e-Privacy Regulation (2017)

Article 29 Data Protection Working Party: WP 252, Opinion 03/2017 on processing personal data in the context of Cooperative Intelligent Transport Systems (2017)

Article 29 Data Protection Working Party: WP260 rev.01, Guidelines on transparency under Regulation (2018)

Beaton, A., Cook, M., Kavanagh, M., Herrington, C.: The psychological impact of burglary. Psychology. Crime and Law, pp. 33–43 (2000)

Big Brother Watch: Home Affairs Select Committee: Policing for the Future Inquiry (2018)

Commission Nationale de l'Informatique et des Libertés, CNIL: decision n° 2011–035 (2011)

DILAX Intelcom GmbH. https://www.dilax.com/de/rechtlich/wifi-tracking-opt-out. Accessed 31 Jan 2023

Datenschutzkonferenz, DSK: Orientierungshilfe Videoüberwachung durch nicht-öffentliche Stellen (Guidance on Video Surveillance by Non-Public Bodies of the German Data Protection Conference) (2020). https://datenschutzkonferenz-online.de/media/oh/20200903_oh_v%C3%BC_dsk.pdf. Accessed 02 Feb 2023

Dutch Data Protection Authority: Investigation into the Collection of Wi-Fi Data by Google Using Street View Cars' (2010)

European Data Protection Board, EDPB: Guidelines 3/2019 on processing of personal data through video devices (2019)

European Data Protection Board, EDPB: Guidelines 1/2020 on processing personal data in the context of connected vehicles and mobility related applications (2020)

Fenske, E., Brown, D., Martin, J., Mayberry, T., Ryan, P., Rye, E.: Three years later: a study of mac address randomization in mobile devices and when it succeeds. In: Proceedings on Privacy Enhancing Technologies 2021.3, pp. 164–181 (2021)

Gebru, K.: A privacy-preserving scheme for passive monitoring of people's flows through Wi-Fi beacons. In: IEEE 19th Annual Consumer Communications & Networking Conference (CCNC), Las Vegas, NV, USA, pp. 421–424 (2022)

Information Commissioner's Office, ICO. https://ico.org.uk/for-organisations/guide-to-data-protection/key-dp-themes/guidance-on-video-surveillance-including-cctv/how-can-we-comply-with-the-data-protection-principles-when-using-surveillance-systems/. Accessed 31 Jan 2023

European Data Protection Supervisor, EDPS Guidelines. on the notions of "controller", "processor" and "joint controllership" under Regulation (EU) 2018/1725 (2019)

Hamburgischen Beauftragten für Datenschutz und Informationsfreiheit: 25. Tätigkeitsbericht 2014/2015. https://datenschutz-hamburg.de/assets/pdf/25._Taetigkeitsbericht_Datenschutz_2014-2015_HmbBfDI_01.pdf. Accessed 31 Jan 2023

Kalogianni, E., et al.: Passive Wi-Fi monitoring of the rhythm of the campus. In: AGILE International Conference on Geographic Information Science, Lisbon, pp. 1–4 (2015)

Ogawa, K., Verbree, E., Zlatanova, S., Kohtake, N., Okhami, Y.: Towards seamless indoor-outdoor applications: developing stakeholder-oriented location-based services. Geo-spatial Inf. Sci. 14(2), 109–118 (2011)

PrivacySIG, https://www.privacysig.org/opt-out.html. Accessed 02 Feb 2023

Reichl, P., Oh, B., Ravitharan, R., Stafford, M.: Using Wi-Fi technologies to count passengers in real-time around rail infrastructure. In: 2018 International Conference on Intelligent Rail Transportation (ICIRT), Singapore, pp. 1–5 (2018)

Rudnicka, J.: Polizeiliche Aufklärungsquote bei Wohnungseinbrüchen in Deutschland bis 2021. https://de.statista.com/statistik/daten/studie/152583/umfrage/entwicklung-der-polizeili chen-aufklaerungsquoten-bei-wohnungseinbruchdiebstahl-seit-1995/. Accessed 02 Feb 2023

Sapiezynski, P., Stopczynski, A., Gatej, R., Lehmann, S.: Tracking human mobility using Wi-Fi signals. PLoS ONE 10(7), e0130824 (2015)

Soundararaj, B., Cheshire, J., Longley, P.: Estimating real-time high-street footfall from Wi-Fi probe requests. Int. J. Geogr. Inf. Sci. 34(2), 325–343 (2020)

Spitz, M.: https://docs.google.com/spreadsheets/d/1PMjIkymwzYNGhENCi9BZst63H-UPagYg PO6DwHVdskU/edit?authkey=COCjw-kG&hl=en_GB&hl=en_GB&authkey=COCjw-kG# gid=0; https://www.zeit.de/datenschutz/malte-spitz-vorratsdaten; https://www.zeit.de/digital/ datenschutz/2011-02/vorratsdaten-malte-spitz. Accessed 31 Jan 2023

Unabhängiges Landeszentrum für Datenschutz Schleswig-Holstein, ULD: Tätigkeitsbericht (activity report) 2019. https://www.datenschutzzentrum.de/tb/tb37/uld-37-taetigkeitsbericht-2019.pdf. Accessed 02 Feb 2023

Vanhoef, M., Matte, C., Cunche, M., Cardoso, L.S., Piessens, F.: Why MAC address randomization is not enough: an analysis of Wi-Fi network discovery mechanisms. In: Proceedings of the 11th ACM SIGSAC Symposium on Information, Computer and Communications Security (AsiaCCS 2016), pp. 413 – 42 (2016)

Past and Present: A Case Study of Twitter's Responses to GDPR Data Requests

Daniela Pöhn[1]([⊠])(iD) and Nils Gruschka[2](iD)

[1] Universität der Bundeswehr München, Research Institute CODE, Munich,
Germany
daniela.poehn@unibw.de
[2] Department of Informatics, University of Oslo, Oslo, Norway
nilsgrus@ifi.uio.no

Abstract. The European General Data Protection Regulation (GDPR)
came into effect in May 2018. It requires organizations to give European
users access to their data. Although several requirements are contained in
the GDPR, such as machine-readable format and easily understandable
information, these kinds of regulations leave flexibility on how to achieve
them. In order to understand the past and the current practices emerging
from the GDPR, we evaluate data exports from 2018 and 2023 of one
reference account from the social media platform Twitter. We analyze
the service's compliance with the requirements of the GDPR, the changes
within the time span, and the differences between accounts. To compare
and verify the results, we incorporate the findings of data exports of four
verification accounts. The results show that the information presented
to the users is easier to understand with the present version. However,
the data is not provided in a machine-readable format and additional
files, such as more than 3,000 emoticons, are incorporated. In addition,
not all practices are according to GDPR. Based on the results, the study
suggests future research topics and practical improvements.

Keywords: GDPR · personal data · privacy · case study · Twitter

1 Introduction

The modern Internet is data-centric and dominated by a few big players that
provide multiple services. For example, Google offers a smartphone operating
system (OS), a search engine, YouTube, online office documents, and the service
of an identity provider ("Sign-in with Google"). In addition, advertising remains
one main source of income for many websites, apps, and online services [36]. With
ads and analytics services, websites personalize their products and services. To
target specific individuals, tracking services gather personal data with the help
of Hypertext Transfer Protocol (HTTP) cookies and other means.

In consequence, the collected data is often seen as an economic asset of an
organization [44]. The EU General Data Protection Regulation (GDPR), which

© The Author(s), under exclusive license to Springer Nature Switzerland AG 2024
K. Rannenberg et al. (Eds.): APF 2023, LNCS 13888, pp. 57–84, 2024.
https://doi.org/10.1007/978-3-031-61089-9_4

came into effect in May 2018, addresses this problem. The GDPR requires organizations to be transparent about how they collect, process, and store personal data. In addition, the GDPR gives individuals the right to request what personal data is being collected about them, why it is being collected, and how it is being used (GDPR Art. 15). This assists to empower individuals and give them greater control over their personal data. Since the GDPR became effective, organizations had time to optimize their processes and the data exports they provide.

However, there is still little research on data subject requests. Bowyer et al. [8] and Alizadeh et al. [4] conducted user studies where the participants requested their data. Urban et al. [41] evaluated the response of companies to access requests and portability with the purpose to learn more about the data collected by tracking services.

In this paper, we analyze how the implementation of data access rights has changed since the GDPR came into effect using the example of Twitter. Twitter as one of the largest social media platforms is also used by organizations and is known for its transparency and accountability, regularly publishing transparency reports, and complying with government requests for user data. We performed a case study examining Twitter's responses to Article 15 data access requests shortly after the GDPR came into effect and more than four years later, in order to assess the impact of the regulation on the company's practices and to identify any changes or improvements made in its handling of and presenting personal data. The results are compared with and verified by evaluating current data exports from various user accounts and Twitter's privacy statement.

The contribution of the paper is multi-fold: 1) analysis of the data request of one provider (Twitter) in detail; 2) comparison of the data exports from the beginning of the GDPR and present time; 3) evaluation of the data exports with regards to compliance with the GDPR and Twitter's privacy statement.

The remainder of the paper is as follows: In Sect. 2, we summarize related work in the area of GDPR. Based on that, we outline our methodology in Sect. 3. This is followed by the evaluation of the single data requests and their comparison in Sect. 4. The results are discussed in Sect. 5. Last but not least, we summarize the paper and outline future work in Sect. 6.

2   Related Work

In this section, we provide an overview of the GDPR respectively the articles concerning our paper (see Sect. 2.1) and give an outline of research approaches targeting the GDPR (see Sect. 2.2). Last but not least, we emphasize the need for this study in Sect. 2.3.

2.1   General Data Protection Regulation

The GDPR contains several articles that are relevant to the paper's topic.

Article 5: Principles for the processing of personal data, such as transparency, earmarking, data minimization, accuracy, integrity, and confidentiality.

Article 11: Implementation of appropriate measures to ensure that personal data is not kept for longer than necessary, related to Article 5.

Article 12: Providing clear, concise, and transparent information to data subjects (individuals) about the processing of their personal data in a manner that is easily accessible and understandable. The proper identification of the data subject is required, before answering the request in a timely manner.

Article 15: Right to obtain confirmation from the controller as to whether or not their personal data is being processed and, consequently, a copy of their personal data [7] and information about the processing of their data. Following, data subjects have the right to delete and amend the data.

Article 20: Right to data portability. In consequence, this requires personal data to be in a structured, commonly used, and machine-readable format.

2.2   Research Approaches Related to GDPR

In this section, we give a broad overview of research related to GDPR and then focus on approaches concerning data requests. Main research topics are, for example, tracking mechanisms, cookies, and consent under GDPR [5,19,21,27, 31], dark patterns related to these practices [18,28,34], and compliance [2,3,16, 22]. Shastri et al. [33] analyze bad habits related to GDPR generally, whereas Mehrnezhad et al. [25] compare GDPR practices with users' privacy protection habits, finding a disparity.

Other approaches regard more specific aspects. First, we outline publications on non-data subject requests. Based on two case studies, Gruschka et al. [13] show which types of information might become a privacy risk, the employed privacy-preserving techniques, and their influence on the research results. Mangini et al. [23] conducted an empirical study on the impact of the GDPR and the right to be forgotten, while Patil and Shyamasundar [29] analyze this right for Facebook. Additionally, Wong and Henderson [43] exercise the right to data portability. Zaeem and Barber [45] automatically evaluate the GDPR compliance focusing on privacy policies. Urban et al. [41] analyze how companies respond to subject access requests and portability to learn more about the data collected by tracking services. In a following publication, Urban et al. [42] measure the impact of the GDPR on data sharing in ad networks by focusing on the underlying information sharing networks between online advertising companies. Using graph analysis, the authors show that the number of ID syncing connections decreased by around 40% around the time the GDPR went into effect but slightly rebounded since then. Due to consolidations, fewer companies perform tracking on more sites. Last but not least, Raschke et al. [30] design a GDPR-compliant and usable privacy dashboard.

In contrast, fewer approaches address the data access requests. Bowyer et al. [8] present a study with ten participants, where each participant filed four to five data access requests. This practical part of the study was accompanied by interviews about the requests and the returned data. The authors conclude that the GDPR falls short due to non-compliance and low-quality responses. Similarly, Alizadeh et al. [4] conduct a study with 13 households, who request their personal data from their respective loyalty program providers. The authors conclude that the data exports should deliver detailed information and inform the users of the purpose of this data collection to prevent mistrust. In this regard, Tolsdorf et al. [37] examine ten privacy dashboards used by services. Following their study, the authors suggest steps to provide real value to the users. In contrast, Hansen and Jensen [14] suggest an implementation to create valid, complete, and legally compliant responses. Herrmann and Lindemann [15] analyze the responses to the data requests before the at that time upcoming GDPR. Around half of the providers answered with data exports, though several did not confirm the identity of the user. In addition, Bufalieri et al. [9] and Di Martino et al. [24] show that the requests for users' data can become a privacy threat due to inappropriate identification. Based on this issue, Lauradoux [20] analyzes if authoritarian governments could abuse this right. The author highlights the need for proper identification. However, identification can be a privacy risk in itself. In contrast, Boniface et al. [6] show that some providers require much stronger identification and authentication from the users for the right of access request than for normal usage of the service.

2.3   Summary

Although several approaches target GDPR, no approach – to the best of our knowledge – compares GDPR data exports from different years and users. Hence, we shed light on the changes from 2018 to 2023 by studying the case of Twitter.

3   Methodology

We describe the methodology of our case study, applied in the following section.

Preparation: The preparation concerns the reference account and further accounts for verification and comparison. The accounts belong to the authors and persons, which provided their account data for the study.

    Reference account: The reference account was created eight years ago and is actively used mostly in a web browser. Based on [46] (see definitions in Appendix A), the account can be characterized as profile averse, while the user is between identity-concerned to privacy fundamentalist. For the comparison, two main data exports from this account are evaluated: October 2018 (Past) and February 2023 (Present).

    Verification accounts: In addition, the present data are compared with the exported data from other user accounts.

        V1: This account is three years old and actively used mostly in a web browser. In contrast, this account is set up as identity-concerned.

        V2: This test account is four months old, fed with synthetic data, and actively used in Twitter's Android app. The account reflects the behavior of a non-concerned user.

V3: This account is 14 years old, but very rarely used. The account is configured in an Android Twitter app that is, however, opened only a few times per year and can be counted as profile averse.

V4: This account is seven years old. It is used mainly in a passive way (reading and following) by utilizing the Twitter app on an iPhone. The user is profile averse.

Data collection: After the data was ready, it was downloaded locally.

Data pre-processing: Then, the data was pre-processed if necessary.

Data analysis: The two data exports of the reference account were first analyzed separately and then compared to identify any changes in terms of the data that Twitter has collected, stored, and presented. In addition, the second data export was compared with the ones of the verification accounts.

Based on the data exports, compliance with GDPR (see Sect. 2.1) is evaluated and discussed by focusing on the following aspects.

Accuracy: The data must be accurate and up to date. Personal data must be erased or rectified if it is inaccurate or no longer necessary for the purpose for which it was collected (GDPR Article 5).

Format of personal data: Personal data should be in a format that is easily readable and accessible to the data subject (GDPR Article 12).

Timeliness: The data should be exchanged as soon as possible but latest after one month with the option for an extension (GDPR Article 12).

Data minimization: Personal data should only be stored for as long as necessary for the purpose for which it was collected. The duration of storage should be stated (GDPR Articles 5 and 15).

Structured format: Personal data should be structured in a way that makes it easy to locate and export specific data items. Where possible, the format of personal data should be standardized to ensure that data is easily comparable and interoperable between different systems and services. Hence, the data should be in a machine-readable format (GDPR Article 20).

In addition, we compare our findings with Twitter's privacy statement. The study respects the following to increase the quality of the results.

Validity and reliability: To increase the validity and reliability of the data and the study results, several accounts were included in the evaluation. The findings were then verified for validity.

Ethical considerations: The study was in compliance with the ethical boards of the involved universities. To protect the participants, personally identifiable information is neither shared in this paper nor as artifacts.

Limitations: The study focuses on Twitter with data exports from 2018 and 2023. No exports between these years and no further providers are incorporated. Hence, the results solely stand for this particular service on these specific dates. Although both authors verified the outcome by comparing several data exports, the results may still be the result of subjectivity.

4   Evaluation of Data Requests

The evaluation describes the analysis of both individual requests from 2018 (see Sect. 4.1) and 2023 (see Sect. 4.2) of the reference account, before comparing both data exports in Sect. 4.3. In each section, we outline the data exports and then compare the data with the requirements stated above. Where suited, we incorporate the results of the data exports from the verification accounts. Our results are then discussed in Sect. 5.

4.1   Past: First Request in 2018

The data was requested by going to the settings, then clicking on "My Twitter data", and finding the button to request the data. Within a short time frame of one day, the request was answered and the user was able to download their data.

Data Export. The data received by Twitter is compressed as a ZIP archive file and mainly contains 37 machine-readable, but not user-friendly JavaScript Object Notation (JSON) files, as shown in Table 1 in the Appendix B. In addition, the participants can find their uploaded media, such as pictures. As an example, Listing 1.1 shows the account timezone found in `account-timezone.json`.

Listing 1.1. Account-timezone.json

```
{
  "accountTimezone" : {
    "accountId" : "$id",
    "timeZone" : "Pacific Time (US & Canada)"
  }
}
```

Evaluation of the Data Export. In the following, we compare the past data export with the stated requirements related to the GDPR.

Accuracy: Most information is accurate besides the time zone. In addition, the age is stated as 13–54 and older than 65, which cannot be true at the same time. Ad information depends on the algorithms etc. and seems to be unfitting. Last but not least, the tweets are not contained as posted.

Format: Although the dashboard provides readable and accessible data, JSON cannot be used alone as a good format to comply with GDPR Article 5.

Timeliness: Due to presumably automated functions, the timeliness is given.

Data minimization: The current and previous email addresses can be found in the data, although the change took place several years ago. Ad engagement and interest groups are interesting for discussions due to over 800 results for an (at that time lightly active) account. IP audit shows the Internet Protocol (IP) addresses and login times of the past month. In addition, the IP address from the account creation can be found in the data export.

Structured format: JSON is a standard machine-readable format, while the file names summarize the content.

4.2   Present: Second Request in 2023

Similar to beforehand, the data is requested within the settings of the user. The exact location depends on browser or app usage and the version of the app and may differ from Twitter's description. After around 24 h, the user can download their data in a ZIP file. For verification, the user's password and a code sent to the corresponding email address or phone number are required.

Data Export. The archive consists of two folders (data, assets) and a Hypertext Markup Language (HTML) file, called `Your archive.html`.

Opening the HTML file, we obtain an overview of the core statistics related to tweets, likes, blocked and muted accounts, lists, and moments, as shown in Fig. 1. These can be displayed by clicking on the according links. We find information about the account, tweets, likes, direct messages, security, personalization, ads, lists, and moments in the user's settings. Further pages related to the account consist of information about the profile, linked application, contacts, sessions, and the course of the account accesses. The security category consists of muted and blocked accounts. The personalization category regards demography, interests, ad engagement, location, and saved searches. Ads list all advertisements, the user might have seen starting in August 2022.

The folder "assets" consists of the folders "fonts", "images", and "js". The 3,077 emoticons in two versions (see Fig. 2), JavaScript (JS) files, fonts, and further files are presumably applied to display the HTML page (understandable data according to Article 12) but are not necessary for machine-readable data (Article 20). This large number of emoticons blows up the size of the download file and users might be annoyed that most of the files (more than 98%) are not required to learn which data Twitter has stored.

Next, we investigate the "data" folder, which contains nine folders (which may contain media files most likely in JPEG format, see Fig. 3), 77 JS files, and a `README.txt`. The `README.txt` explains how to navigate through the archive and the content of each JS file. The favored variant is using the HTML file, which has the limitation that it does not render if the archive is bigger than 50 GB. According to the `README.txt`, the HTML archive does not include all data. In order to see all data, the user has to go through the files in the data folder. Some data is only kept for a certain time frame: location history for 60 days, `timeStampOfInteraction` in `user-link-clicks.js` for 30 days, data corresponding ads for 90 days. The JS files include the content for the HTML file in JSON format. Depending on the usage, some files might be empty. The file `protected-history.js`, for example, only contains one line (`window.YTD.protected_history.part0 = [ ]`), whereas Listing 1.2 shows the wrongly set timezone. The JSON input is similar to the corresponding JSON file of the past export in Sect. 4.1.

Fig. 1. Dashboard of the data export

Fig. 2. Emoticons in the data export

Listing 1.2. account-timezone.js

```
window.YTD.account_timezone.part0 = [
  {
    "accountTimezone" : {
      "accountId" : "$id$",
      "timeZone" : "Pacific Time (US & Canada)"
    }
  }
]
```

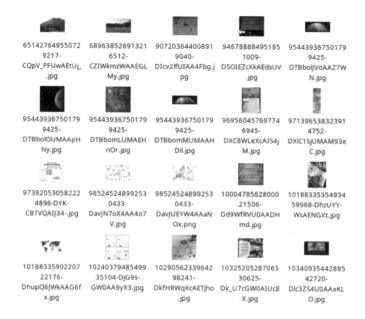

Fig. 3. Pictures in the data export

Evaluation of the Data Export. In the following, we compare the present data exports with the stated requirements related to the GDPR.

Accuracy: Although the usage of the account has not changed significantly and the wrong timezone is still set, we notice better fitting ad information. The timezone of V1 is also incorrect, in contrast to the other verification accounts. For unknown reasons, the likes cannot be shown in the HTML dashboard for some accounts, although included in the JS file. Data accuracy is further discussed in Sect. 5.1.

Format: The HTML file is comparably easy to access for standard users if the ZIP archive was previously unzipped. The file is basically a privacy dashboard with the typical Twitter menu, helping users to accustom to viewing their data. It might be difficult to find the setting after reviewing the initial dashboard. In addition, not all information is contained in the HTML representation. This is not transparent to the user if they do not find the README.txt in the data folder. If the user wants to see all their data, they have to go through the other files provided. Due to the incorporation of JSON into JS, this is unsuited for normal users.

Timeliness: Although the data export was requested during a time when several users still left Twitter [32], the request did not need much longer than 24 h to process. Hence we can conclude that automated functions collect and aggregate the data. The same behavior was observed with the verification accounts with exception of V1, where it took more than three days and the download was not possible within the Twitter app.

Data minimization: When comparing the statements about the duration of saving data with the information found in the archive, these time frames might not be correct all the time. The ad data contains, for example, information from at least four months. The email address was changed in 2017 and should, therefore, not be needed anymore. Similarly, the IP address during account creation is obsolete. This issue is further discussed in Sect. 5.2. In addition, ad behavior and different login behaviors are dependent on the platform respectively app, as outlined in Sect. 5.4.

Structured format: The structured format is embedded into JS, which requires an extra step to automatically process them. Thereby, we would conclude that the regulation is not completely met.

4.3   From Past to Present

In the following, we compare both data exports.

Data Export. Contrasting the first and the second export, we see an increase from 36 JSON files to 77 JS files for the data export itself. While the increase in JPG files is the result of the account activity, several files were added for the HTML dashboard: 1 EOT (Embedded OpenType), 3 GIF (Graphics Interchange Format), 1 HTML, 1 ICO (Icon), 115 JS (77 plus some for the functionality), 3081 PNG (Portable Network Graphics), 3079 SVG (Scalable Vector Graphics), 1 TTF (TrueType Font), and 1 WOFF (Web Open Font Format). This difference is highlighted in Fig. 4.

An overview of all files is given in Table 1 in Appendix B. Several file names are similar. As many JS files are mostly empty, we focus on those with content.

- device-token.js: A list of client application ID, token, creation time, last time seen, and the client application, for example, "Twitter Web App (Twitter. Inc)". The list goes back to September 2021.
- manifest.js: A manifest is according to W3C [11] a centralized place for the metadata associated with a web application. The file is typically JSON-based and includes, for example, a web application's name and links to icons. In

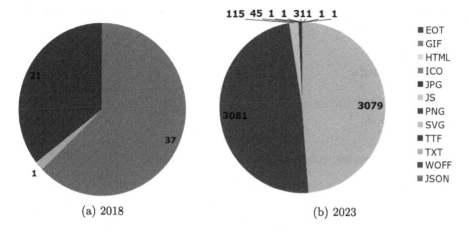

Fig. 4. Used data formats in the data exports

the manifest, we find information about the user, archives, README files, and data types, linking the different file names and folders with global names used in the HTML file.

- **phone-number:js** The actively added phone number(s).
- **tweets.js**: Tweets starting in 2020 (years after the account was created). Besides tweet text, name of mentioned accounts, their screen names, and IDs, the user ID, the tweet time, and source (such as web app), we notice likes, retweets, truncated (might be retweeted with own text), language, and a piece of possibly sensitive information.
- **tweet-headers.js**: Tweet ID, User ID, and creation time. The authors are unsure of the reason, why the headers are additionally stored, though being included in the tweets in **tweets.js**. It might enable a faster view of the overview, while the detailed data is loaded on request (clicking for details).
- **twitter-circle.js**: ID, user ID, and creation time.
- **verified.js**: Account ID and a Boolean value about the state of verification.

Comparison of the Data Exports. In the following, we compare the past and present data exports with the stated requirements related to the GDPR.

Accuracy: The age information and ad data are more accurate within the present data export. The timezone remains inaccurate.

Format: The format changed from JSON to HTML (easier to comprehend) with several underlying files and formats.

Timeliness: All exports were received in a timeliness manner due to presumably automated functions.

Data minimization: Concerning the data minimization, we find several data from previous years, such as an old email address and the IP address of registration. In the present export, the given duration of storage only partly holds true for the reference account.

Structured format: Due to the format change, the data export is not machine-readable anymore.

5   Discussion

In this section, we discuss our findings related to GDPR, privacy, and Twitter's privacy statement.

5.1   Completeness, Accuracy, and Transparency

Completeness in the Case Study. Completeness refers to the idea that personal data should be complete and not omit any (relevant) information. The GDPR does not explicitly mention this principle. However, the requirement to ensure that personal data is accurate and processed in a manner that ensures its accuracy (see Article 5) can be interpreted as requiring completeness. Additionally, the requirement to provide individuals with a complete copy of their personal data upon request (Article 15) implicitly necessitates completeness.

It is difficult to estimate the completeness as it is unknown which data Twitter has. What we find missing, is information about the authentication methods. One might assume that at least password changes are noted. We verified this with V2, which recently used a fallback method to set up a new password. Even if Twitter does not store changes, the authentication method is known.

Accuracy in the Case Study. The principle of accuracy necessitates organizations to ensure that the personal data they collect and the process are accurate and up-to-date. The GDPR mentions this principle in Articles 5 and 16 (data subjects have the right to rectify their personal data), among others.

In the HTML dashboard, Twitter explains some but not all data that is shown to the user. For example, it is unclear which information directly came from the user and which was inferred from Twitter. Regarding the past data export from 2018 (see Sect. 4.1), we have `ageinfo: 13-54, >65`, which changed to 13–54 in the present export (see Sect. 4.2) without any active alteration.

As noticed in Sect. 4.2, the timezone of the reference account is inaccurate. Verification of this feature with the others accounts revealed no consistent pattern: V1 has the wrong timezone, V3 has the correct timezone, and V2 and V4 have no timezone information at all. In addition, V1's languages (English, German, Indonesian) and gender (male) were not stated correctly. This is interesting, as no gender was given by the user and the account is mainly focused on geek topics. Here, the data is inferred by Twitter. Last but not least, the interests and hence the ads presumably are derived from information collected by Twitter (e.g., ads in Sect. 5.4). Consequently, it does not become clear, which data has which authorship respectively if it is declared or inferred data.

Transparency in the Case Study. Transparency is a principle that requires organizations to be transparent about the collection, processing, and use of personal data. This includes clear and concise information about how personal data will be used, who will have access to it, and for what purpose. The GDPR explicitly mentions the principle of transparency in, e.g., Articles 5 (transparent processing), 12 (requirements for transparent information), and 13 (directly informing users when personal data is collected).

It might be that not all information is displayed in the HTML file. The authors did not find any hint in the HTML dashboard but in the `README.txt`, which most standard users may not look at. Consequently, it could be the case that a user is not concerned with the information found in the dashboard, although more (serious) data were included.

5.2   Data Minimization

The principle of data minimization requires organizations to limit the collection and processing of personal data to the minimum, which is necessary for a specific purpose. The GDPR explicitly mentions the principle in several articles. Consequently, GDPR requires organizations to ensure and demonstrate that the data processing is performed in accordance with the law (Article 25).

What we notice in all data exports, are the IP address and email address used for creating the account. We assume that the IP address is not needed anymore after that long time period. A similar issue can be observed with changed email addresses, as noted in Sects. 4.1 and 4.2. According to Twitter's privacy statement [40], they keep profile information and content for the duration of the account but collect other personally identifiable data for a maximum of 18 months. The IP address used when creating the account is presumably neither profile information nor content and is for most of our accounts significantly older than 18 months. While Twitter states the duration of storage in `README.txt` for some data, it does not do that for all. In addition, we found exceptions from the stated storage duration. Hence, we conclude that data minimization is not always given.

In the present export, we found two JS files concerning deleted tweets, i. e., `deleted-tweets` and `deleted- tweet-headers`, and a corresponding media folder. Although it did not include any data in all accounts, it would be interesting to investigate the duration of storage. This is also the case with display names and other changes in the profile.

5.3   Understandable vs. Machine-Readable

GDPR Article 12 requires that the data export is "understandable" and "transparent" to the individual to whom the data relates. To achieve this, the information must be written in clear and plain language. In addition, GDPR Article 20 requires that personal data be processed in a "machine-readable" format. This means that personal data must be stored and processed in a format that can be easily processed by automated systems.

We notice that the first export is only machine-readable (JSON), while the present version focuses on understanding (HTML with underlying JS). The machine-readable information is incorporated in JavaScript files, which requires an additional step for the usage of algorithms and software. Regarding both requirements, there is an inherent tension. Machine-readable data is typically not understandable and thus required additional information, whereas this might contradict the machine-readability. A website can comply with Article 15 when using a commonly used electronic form. This means either of both is fine at least concerning Article 15. We want to explore how other providers solve this issue and if any tendencies towards understandable privacy dashboards can be observed. However, the data is not complete and further information, see ads, would be necessary for transparent usage.

5.4   Advertisement and Tracking

According to Twitter's privacy page, it collects data, which is released by the user, during the usage of Twitter, and by third parties (discussed in Sect. 5.5). Furthermore, Twitter states to apply fingerprinting and cookies for profiling users. Another source of information is browsing behavior: "Tailored audiences are often built from email lists or browsing behaviors. They help advertisers reach prospective customers or people who have already expressed interest in their business." [40]

Traces of Advertisement in the Data. When regarding the past data export, we find a target group of 16 members, which fits for two third of them. In addition, a look-alike (see Appendix A for the definition) list can be found, where of a long list of accounts, only two match the actual user. Interests, which are partly linked to these, consist of another long list, which does not seem to fit either. Ad engagement with over 800 lines of code is of similar quality.

The present advertiser lists consist of the following advertisers, which have added the user to their audiences. These are, again, only partly interesting for the participant.

- @AlgoFoundation
- @DellTechDE
- @DellTechNL
- @DisneyPlusDE
- @FrontierCorp
- @HCLSoftware
- @HPE
- @HPE_Storage
- @HPUK
- @HuaweiMobileDe
- @IBM
- @MS_ITProCA
- @MySocialData
- @NEOM
- @RevolutBusiness
- @SocialDatabase_
- @SquareUK
- @Swisscom_B2B
- @TwitterBlue
- @WSJ
- @canva
- @mondaydotcom
- @pim_id_app
- @pr_canadel
- @sega_pso2
- @smart_worldwide

Possible Reasons for These Advertisements. It is unknown how the user actually became a member of the advertiser lists. Interestingly, the ads lately shown to the user did not come from these advertisers. For example, the reasons for displaying an Apple TV ad were listed as age 18 and up, interests in comedy, language German, location Germany, and platforms Android (though the account is mainly used in a web browser). Another reason for displaying an ad is follower look-alike. The follower look-alike list can be found in `personalization.js`. In the file `ad-impressions.js`, we see the actual location of the ads. For Apple TV, this was on "TimelineHome". In addition, the OS type (e.g., Desktop, Android, etc.) is displayed.

Advertisement Behavior Based on Tracking. The ad behavior was evaluated and verified with V2. The user had to add interests and follow at least a few other users to start using Twitter. Here, the ads started after 17 days. Some ads were selected to due age and location, meaning the city. Hence, Twitter uses IP geolocation [10] or other location tracking methods such as utilizing smartphone sensors [26], since the city was otherwise not specified by the user. According to Diel et al. [12], tracking mechanisms used by web pages and apps are from the user's perspective not always transparent. This might be true even if evaluating the data export. Looking in "Location", we cannot find any place Twitter has associated V2 with based on the activity. In addition, some ads targeted the user due to the language (German), which is not the selected language (English).

Furthermore, the age is further delimited in contrast to the age set in the "ageinfo". While it states "13–54", few ads focus on the age of "21 to 49" or "18 and up" respectively similar, as shown in Fig. 5. This is the case, even though no age was set. This behavior was also observed with the reference account, where the age partly appears even more restricted and the location of a trip appears as the reason for displaying the ad, see Fig. 6. At that time, Twitter was only used in the web browser. The collection of this data is in accordance with Twitter's privacy statement but is not included in the data exports. Another example of V2 is shown in Fig. 7. Here, the ad was displayed to the user due to the device ID and Android OS version. Thereby, we can conclude that Twitter (temporarily) collects more information than stated in the data export. Not always, an explanation for showing the ad is given, as displayed in Fig. 8.

App Behavior. The number of sessions and IP connections varies between the accounts. While the reference account and V1 have a comparably low amount, V2 – V4 have a (significantly) higher amount. This might be due to the OS. The reference account and V1 are mainly opened in a web browser, in addition to Twitter's app on GrapheneOS for V1 since December 2022. Here, no difference between usage with and without the app can be noted. This is verified as ads for V1 are targeted due to the desktop platform. The Android app of V2 has around two connections per day (with the exception of the smartphone running out of battery), the Android app of V3 typically has one connection, and the

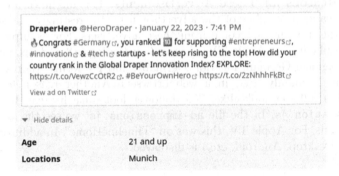

Fig. 5. Specific ad displayed to a user due to age and location

Fig. 6. Specific ad displayed to a user due to keyword and temporary location

Fig. 7. Specific ad displayed to a user due to platform Android and a specific OS version, among other things

Fig. 8. No information is given for showing a specific ad to a user

iOS app of V4 has several connections per day. The authors are unsure of the implications between IP connections and tracking.

Future Work Related to Advertisement and Tracking. Even though the advertisement data better fit the participant in the present version, it still seems that data is arbitrary. The source of the data is not contained, which would be interesting for inferred data and information gained by fingerprinting and other tracking mechanisms. To better understand the data export, further explanations would be needed. The development and all the data stored related to advertisements is alarming – even for a normal user. The authors would be interested in seeing these data for power users.

5.5 Comparison with Twitter's Privacy Statement

Twitter's privacy statement [40] informs the user about three types of information they collect: (1) information the user provides, (2) information Twitter collects during the usage, and (3) information Twitter receives from third parties. As we noticed indicators of tracking, we compare the data we received with the privacy statement and investigate if Twitter might have further data.

Information by the User. When registering a Twitter account, the user provides several pieces of information, which might be updated and extended during the usage of the service. Twitter explicitly notes personal accounts, professional accounts, payment information, and preferences.

Personal account includes a display name, a username, a password, an email address or phone number, a date of birth, a display language, and third-party single sign-in information if chosen. In addition, location, tweets, and an uploaded address book (in `contact.js`) might be possible. Comparing the received data with this statement, we again cannot find any information about authentication methods. In contrast, changed data such as display names and email addresses are not explicitly included in the privacy statement.

Payment information consists of credit or debit card numbers, card expiration dates, CVV codes, and billing addresses. As none of our accounts uses this functionality, we cannot measure the data in the export.

Preferences are explained as the items the user expresses in the setting. Here, it is interesting to notice that the personalization based on the places the user has been to is disabled but, as advertisements were shown based on the location, we assume that this setting is not always complied with. Last but not least, although some Periscope (application for real-time video) data is included, the user's setting forwards the user to Periscope. This information is though not given in the data export.

Information by Usage. Twitter states several ways to collect information about the user during usage: (1) usage information, (2) purchase and payments, (3) device information, (4) location information, (5) inferred identity, (6) log information, (7) advertisements, (8) cookies and similar technologies, and (9) interactions with Twitter content on third-party sites.

Usage Information includes tweets and other posted resp. followed content, the interaction with other users' content (retweets, likes, shares, replies, tagging, etc.) and other users (followers, following, direct messages with metadata), communication with Twitter via email, and the interaction with links. To the best of our knowledge, this information is (mostly) included in our data exports.

Purchase and payments concerns the payments and money sent using Twitter features or services, including intermediaries. The collected data contains information about the transactions, subscriptions, and amounts paid or received. This aspect could not be verified due to not using this feature but at least some corresponding JS files were found in the data export.

Device Information relates to the information collected from and about the devices used to access Twitter. According to Twitter, this includes information about the connection (e.g., IP address and browser type), information about the device and its settings (e.g., device and advertising ID, OS, carrier, language, memory, apps installed, and battery level), and the device address book if shared. Information about the connection was found in the HTML file respectively in `ip-audit.js`, `device-token.js`, and maybe in `tweets.js` at least, though the browser type was not explicitly marked as data. With the information about the device and its settings, the authors assume that Twitter uses fingerprinting techniques. Based on personal experiences, the authors further conclude that Twitter applies risk-based authentication, which might be based on these fingerprinting techniques. Spooring et al. [35] showed in 2015 that device fingerprinting is not suited for risk-based authentication but devices matured since then. In contrast, Adamsky et al. [1] reason that device fingerprinting is a comparably simple technique. In consequence, the usage of risk-based authentication, the applied fingerprinting techniques, and their combination require further research. In addition, this information was only partially found in the data export (see advertisement based on an Android app running on a specific version of the Android OS in Sect. 5.4). Hence, the authors conclude that the data export is not complete in this respect.

Location Information collected by Twitter concern the approximate location "to provide the service you expect, including showing you relevant ads" [40]. The user can choose to share the current precise location or places where they previously used Twitter by enabling these settings in their account. We can verify both, advertisements based on the location and the possibility to activate the precise location. The authors though are unsure if the approximate location is stored or only used for a short time. Due to the fingerprinting and risk-based authentication behavior, the authors assume that at least a short time usage is the case but this topic requires further investigation by comparing the data of accounts with different privacy settings in a long-term study.

Inferred Identity relates to collected or received information corresponding to the information provided by the user. This includes the association of browsers and/or devices with the account, closely related information to those provided (e.g., email address and phone number), and usage behavior when not signed in. This option was deactivated at the chosen accounts and, therefore, no information was contained in the data export. Nevertheless, the number of accounts associated with an email address or phone number is limited by Twitter. Hence, the authors conclude that Twitter uses this information for security reasons and profile formation among others. Tests concerning the creation of several accounts with the same browser or device could be future work. The latter (usage behavior when not signed in) is probably related to profile formation. In [17], the authors describe the creation of shadow profiles due to tweets. It would be interesting to analyze the creation of shadow profiles caused by the usage of Twitter. Concluding, the authors assume that the data exports were not complete concerning inferred identity but this topic also opens several research questions.

As Article 20 (1) focuses on the data provided by the user to the controller, it is unclear how to handle inferred data. The data relates to the user but is not included in the article concerning portability on GDPR. In addition, users cannot estimate if the data provided to them is complete or not. We tried to evaluate the completeness based on the information we provided to Twitter, the differences between several data exports, and a comparison with Twitter's privacy statement. This workflow though requires knowledge, time, and the willingness to carry it out – and cannot be expected from normal users.

Log Information may include IP address, browser type and language, operating system, the referring web page, access time, pages visited, location, mobile carrier, device information, search terms and IDs, ads shown, Twitter-generated identifiers, and identifiers associated with cookies. This data is received when interacting with Twitter and corresponding resp. intermediate services independently if logged in or not. Although no further information is given in the privacy statement in PDF format [38] (e.g., about the duration of storage), the amount of log information seems more than required. In addition to shadow profiles, the data might be applied for risk-based authentication and restricting the number of accounts per user and hence needs further investigation.

Advertisements are shown on Twitter. Data about these views and interactions, such as watching videos, clicking on advertisements, interacting with retweets, or replying to advertisements, may be collected. Due to the participants, only information about the shown advertisements can be found. Nonetheless, the behavior around advertisements is arbitrary for the authors.

Cookies and similar technologies are applied by Twitter to collect additional website usage data and to operate Twitter. The information concerning the usage of cookies is described in a separate page [39]. Here, Twitter states that they use cookies to keep the user logged in to Twitter, to deliver features and functionalities of Twitter services, apply the user's preferences, personalize the content, protect against spam and abuse, show more relevant ads, provide subscriptions features and certain content, understand the interaction of the user with Twitter for further improvements, measure the effectiveness of advertisements and marketing, rate the performance of Twitter, and gather data used to operate Twitter. The life span of cookies may be 13 months according to Twitter. Based on the list provided by Twitter containing 165 cookies on the day of access, we notice that Twitter applies Google Analytics, which is not specified elsewhere. As YouTube videos, Giphy animations, and MoPub (web ad platform) authentication services can be embedded in, for example, tweets, the corresponding cookies are applied for integration and analytics. Further tracking services include Google Ads Targeting, Google DoubleClick, Adobe, and Branch Metrics. A specific cookie, `guest_id_marketing`, is used for advertising when logged out. Practically using Twitter, we see data in local storage, session storage (including "currentlocationIndex"), cookies, IndexedDB, and cache storage. In the data exports, only a little to no information concerning cookies and similar technologies is given. Though the `README.txt` mentions cookies, there were not contained in any files.

Interactions with content on third-party sites are collected if the user views content on third-party websites that integrate Twitter content, such as Tweet buttons. In the data exports, the authors could not find any hints about information from third parties, e.g., web pages. This though does not imply that no data is actually collected. Hence, future work is required.

Information by Third Parties. Last but not least, Twitter informs about the data received from third parties. This includes (1) ad partners, developers, and publishers and (2) other third parties, account connections, and integrations.

Twitter's partners share information, such as cookie IDs, Twitter-generated identifiers, mobile device IDs, hashed user information (e.g., email addresses, demographics, and interest data), and content viewed respectively actions taken on a website or app. Twitter states that it may combine this information with otherwise collected information. This shows that Twitter generates comprehensive profiles, which are not directly reflected by the data exports though this might be the reason for the better-fitting advertisements.

Third parties such as other Twitter users, developers, partners, and services, which are linked to the user's Twitter account, may collect additional data. For example, the account of V2 was linked with Google, displayed in `sso.js` by the corresponding "ssoEmail". Although the past export had a JSON file for Facebook connection, this functionality was not used and, therefore, cannot be traced in the present export.

6   Conclusion and Outlook

In the data-centric Internet, the GDPR provides users with several rights related to their data. By applying GDPR Article 15, users can request a copy of their data. Organizations such as Twitter had five years' time to optimize their functions since the GDPR was implemented. Based on related work in Sect. 2 and our methodology in Sect. 3, we described, evaluated, and compared two data exports, one from 2018 and the second from 2023, requested from one Twitter reference account (see Sect. 4). In addition, we verified and contrasted the results with the data exports from four verification accounts. The results were then discussed based on our observations, the GDPR, and Twitter's data privacy statement in Sect. 5. What is noticeable is the change from machine-readable data to easily understandable information. In the data exports, we find hints on fingerprinting, risk-based authentication, and further information Twitter may have. This observation is backed up by their privacy statement.

In future work, we plan to investigate tracking, fingerprinting, and risk-based authentication applied by Twitter. Although the data related to interests and advertisements seem to gain accuracy, this topic will be further focused in regard to future developments and the user perspective. Furthermore, we want to explore the duration Twitter keeps data. In order to observe future progress, we want to regularly export and analyze data from users. By exporting and evaluating the data from other organizations, we may be able to see the differences and gain a better understanding of the usage of data.

A   Definitions

Not concerned: Individuals who do not value the handling of their data.

Identity-concerned: Individuals who transfer information to services for personalization, but try to pass not any information that points to a real, identifiable person.

Profile averse: Individuals acting under their real name, but not releasing profile-related data.

Privacy fundamentalist: Individuals who want to disclose as little information about themselves as possible and, as a precaution, do not use specific services.

Look-alike: Follower look-alike targeting focuses on people with similar interests to an account's followers.

Shadow profile: These profiles describe the situation when users' or non-users' information is collected without their consent. See [17] for more information.

Declared data: Data that has been explicitly shared by the user, for example, by interactions.

Inferred data: Data developed around the user without their input, such as behavioral and transactional data.

B   Comparison of Past and Current Files

Table 1. Comparison of files within the data exports

Past (JSON)	Present (JS)
account	account
account-creation-ip	account-creation-ip
	account-label
account-suspension	account-suspension
account-timezone	account-timezone
ad-engagement	ad-engagement
	ad-free-article-visits
ad-impressions	ad-impressions
ad-mobile-conversions-attributed	ad-mobile-conversions-attributed
ad-mobile-conversions-unattributed	ad-mobile-conversions-unattributed
ad-online-conversions-attributed	ad-online-conversions-attributed
ad-online-conversions-unattributed	ad-online-conversions-unattributed
ageinfo	ageinfo
	app
block	block
	branch-links
	catalog-items
	commerce-catalog
	community-note
	community-note-rating
	community-note-tombstone
	community-tweet
connected-applications	connected-applications
contacts	contacts
	deleted-tweet-headers
	deleted-tweets
	device-tokens

continued

Table 1. continued

Past (JSON)	Present (JS)
direct-message	direct-messages
	direct-message-group-headers
direct-message-headers	direct-message-headers
direct-message_media	
	direct-message-mute
	direct-messages-group
email-address-change	email-address-change
facebook-connection	
follower	follower
following	following
ip-audit	ip-audit
like	like
lists-created	lists-created
lists-member	lists-member
lists-subscribed	lists-subscribed
	manifest
moment	moment
mute	mute
ni-devices	ni-devices
periscope-account-information	periscope-account-information
	periscope-ban-information
periscope-broadcast-metadata	periscope-broadcast-metadata
periscope-comments-made-by-user	periscope-comments-made-by-user
periscope-expired-broadcasts	periscope-expired-broadcasts
periscope-followers	periscope-followers
	periscope-profile-description
personalization	personalization
	phone-number
	product-drop
	product-set
	professional-data

continued

Table 1. continued

Past (JSON)	Present (JS)
`profile`	`profile`
`profile_media`	
	`protected-history`
	`rely-prompt`
	`saved-search`
	`screen-name-change`
	`shopify-account`
	`shop-module`
	`smartblock.js`
	`spaces-metadata`
	`sso`
	`tweetdeck`
	`tweet-headers`
	`tweets`
	`twitter-article`
	`twitter-article-metadata`
	`twitter-circle`
	`twitter-circle-member`
	`twitter-circle-tweet`
	`twitter-shop`
	`user-link-clicks`
	`verified`

References

1. Adamsky, F., Schiffner, S., Engel, T.: Tracking without traces - fingerprinting in an era of individualism and complexity. In: Antunes, L., Naldi, M., Italiano, G.F., Rannenberg, K., Drogkaris, P. (eds.) APF 2020. LNCS, vol. 12121, pp. 201–212. Springer, Cham (2020). https://doi.org/10.1007/978-3-030-55196-4_12
2. Agarwal, S., Steyskal, S., Antunovic, F., Kirrane, S.: Legislative compliance assessment: framework, model and GDPR instantiation. In: Medina, M., Mitrakas, A., Rannenberg, K., Schweighofer, E., Tsouroulas, N. (eds.) APF 2018. LNCS, vol. 11079, pp. 131–149. Springer, Cham (2018). https://doi.org/10.1007/978-3-030-02547-2_8
3. Alamri, B., Javed, I.T., Margaria, T.: A GDPR-compliant framework for IoT-based personal health records using blockchain. In: Proceedings of the 11th IEEE/IFIP International Conference on New Technologies, Mobility and Security (NTMS), Paris, France, 19–21 April 2021, New York, NY, USA, pp. 1–5 (2021). https://doi.org/10.1109/NTMS49979.2021.9432661

4. Alizadeh, F., Jakobi, T., Boden, A., Stevens, G., Boldt, J.: GDPR reality check - claiming and investigating personally identifiable data from companies. In: Proceedings of the IEEE European Symposium on Security and Privacy Workshops (EuroS&PW), Genoa, Italy, 7–11 September 2020, New York, NY, USA, pp. 120–129 (2020). https://doi.org/10.1109/EuroSPW51379.2020.00025

5. Bollinger, D., Kubicek, K., Cotrini, C., Basin, D.: Automating cookie consent and GDPR violation detection. In: Proceedings of the 31st USENIX Security Symposium (USENIX Security 22), Boston, MA, USA, 10–12 August 2022, Boston, MA, pp. 2893–2910 (2022). https://www.usenix.org/conference/usenixsecurity22/presentation/bollinger

6. Boniface, C., Fouad, I., Bielova, N., Lauradoux, C., Santos, C.: Security analysis of subject access request procedures: how to authenticate data subjects safely when they request for their data. In: Naldi, M., Italiano, G., Rannenberg, K., Medina, M., Bourka, A. (eds.) APF 2019. LNCS, vol. 11498, pp. 182–209. Springer, Cham (2019). https://doi.org/10.1007/978-3-030-21752-5_12

7. Bottis, M., Panagopoulou-Koutnatzi, F., Michailaki, A., Nikita, M.: The right to access information under the GDPR. Int. J. Technol. Policy Law 3(2), 131–142 (2019). https://doi.org/10.1504/IJTPL.2019.104950. https://www.inderscienceonline.com/doi/abs/10.1504/IJTPL.2019.104950

8. Bowyer, A., Holt, J., Go Jefferies, J., Wilson, R., Kirk, D., David Smeddinck, J.: Human-GDPR interaction: practical experiences of accessing personal data. In: Proceedings of the ACM Conference on Human Factors in Computing Systems (CHI), New Orleans, LA, USA, 29 April–5 May 2022, New York, NY, USA (2022). https://doi.org/10.1145/3491102.3501947

9. Bufalieri, L., Morgia, M.L., Mei, A., Stefa, J.: GDPR: when the right to access personal data becomes a threat. In: Proceedings of the IEEE International Conference on Web Services (ICWS), Beijing, China, 19–23 October 2020, New York, NY, USA, pp. 75–83 (2020). https://doi.org/10.1109/ICWS49710.2020.00017

10. Cozar, M., Rodriguez, D., Del Alamo, J.M., Guaman, D.: Reliability of IP geolocation services for assessing the compliance of international data transfers. In: Proceedings of the IEEE European Symposium on Security and Privacy Workshops (EuroS&PW), Genoa, Italy, 6–10 June 2022, New York, NY, USA, pp. 181–185 (2022). https://doi.org/10.1109/EuroSPW55150.2022.00024

11. Cáceres, M., et al.: Web Application Manifest. Working draft, W3C (2023). https://www.w3.org/TR/appmanifest/

12. Diel, S., Heereman, W., Spychalski, D.: The use of web tracking technologies and its compliance with the consent-requirement. In: INFORMATIK 2021, virtual, 27 September–01 October 2021, pp. 789–794. Gesellschaft für Informatik, Bonn, Germany (2021). https://doi.org/10.18420/informatik2021-067

13. Gruschka, N., Mavroeidis, V., Vishi, K., Jensen, M.: Privacy issues and data protection in big data: a case study analysis under GDPR. In: Proceedings of the IEEE International Conference on Big Data (Big Data), Seattle, WA, USA, 10–13 December 2018, New York, NY, USA, pp. 5027–5033 (2018). https://doi.org/10.1109/BigData.2018.8622621

14. Hansen, M., Jensen, M.: A generic data model for implementing right of access requests. In: Gryszczyńska, A., Polański, P., Gruschka, N., Rannenberg, K., Adamczyk, M. (eds.) APF 2022. LNCS, vol. 13279, pp. 3–22. Springer, Cham (2022). https://doi.org/10.1007/978-3-031-07315-1_1

15. Herrmann, D., Lindemann, J.: Obtaining personal data and asking for erasure: do app vendors and website owners honour your privacy rights? In: Meier, M., Reinhardt, D., Wendzel, S. (eds.) Sicherheit 2016 - Sicherheit, Schutz und Zuverlässigkeit, pp. 149–160. Gesellschaft für Informatik e.V, Bonn, Germany (2016)

16. Horák, M., Stupka, V., Husák, M.: GDPR compliance in cybersecurity software: a case study of DPIA in information sharing platform. In: Proceedings of the 14th ACM International Conference on Availability, Reliability and Security (ARES), Canterbury, United Kingdom, 26–29 August 2019, New York, NY, USA (2019). https://doi.org/10.1145/3339252.3340516

17. Keküllüoglu, D., Magdy, W., Vaniea, K.: Analysing privacy leakage of life events on Twitter. In: Proceedings of the 12th ACM Conference on Web Science (WebSci), WebSci 2020, Southampton, United Kingdom, 6–10 July 2020, New York, NY, USA, pp. 287–294 (2020). https://doi.org/10.1145/3394231.3397919

18. Keleher, M., Westin, F., Nagabandi, P., Chiasson, S.: How well do experts understand end-users' perceptions of manipulative patterns? In: Proceedings of the ACM Nordic Human-Computer Interaction Conference (NordiCHI), Aarhus, Denmark, 8–12 October 2022, New York, NY, USA (2022). https://doi.org/10.1145/3546155.3546656

19. Kretschmer, M., Pennekamp, J., Wehrle, K.: Cookie banners and privacy policies: measuring the impact of the GDPR on the web. ACM Trans. Web **15**(4) (2021). https://doi.org/10.1145/3466722

20. Lauradoux, C.: Can authoritative governments abuse the right to access? In: Gryszczyńska, A., Polański, P., Gruschka, N., Rannenberg, K., Adamczyk, M. (eds.) APF 2022. LNCS, vol. 13279, pp. 23–33. Springer, Cham (2022). https://doi.org/10.1007/978-3-031-07315-1_2

21. Lisičar, H., Katulić, T., Jurić, M.: Implementation of GDPR transparency principle in personal data processing by croatian online news sites. In: Proceedings of the 45th IEEE Jubilee International Convention on Information, Communication and Electronic Technology (MIPRO), Opatija, Croatia, 23–27 May 2022, New York, NY, USA, pp. 1264–1269 (2022). https://doi.org/10.23919/MIPRO55190.2022.9803637

22. Liu, S., Zhao, B., Guo, R., Meng, G., Zhang, F., Zhang, M.: Have you been properly notified? Automatic compliance analysis of privacy policy text with GDPR article 13. In: Proceedings of the ACM Web Conference (WWW), Ljubljana, Slovenia, 19–23 April 2021, New York, NY, USA, pp. 2154–2164 (2021). https://doi.org/10.1145/3442381.3450022

23. Mangini, V., Tal, I., Moldovan, A.N.: An empirical study on the impact of GDPR and right to be forgotten - organisations and users perspective. In: Proceedings of the 15th International ACM Conference on Availability, Reliability and Security (ARES), Virtual Event, Ireland, 25–28 August 2020, New York, NY, USA (2020). https://doi.org/10.1145/3407023.3407080

24. Martino, M.D., Robyns, P., Weyts, W., Quax, P., Lamotte, W., Andries, K.: Personal information leakage by abusing the GDPR 'right of access'. In: Fifteenth Symposium on Usable Privacy and Security (SOUPS 2019), Santa Clara, CA, USA, 11–13 August 2019, pp. 371–385. USENIX Association, Santa Clara, CA (2019). https://www.usenix.org/conference/soups2019/presentation/dimartino

25. Mehrnezhad, M., Coopamootoo, K., Toreini, E.: How can and would people protect from online tracking? In: Proceedings on Privacy Enhancing Technologies (PETS), Sydney, Australia, 11–15 July 2022, vol. 1, pp. 105–125 (2022). https://doi.org/10.2478/popets-2022-0006. http://dro.dur.ac.uk/34795/

26. Nguyen, K.A., Akram, R.N., Markantonakis, K., Luo, Z., Watkins, C.: Location tracking using smartphone accelerometer and magnetometer traces. In: Proceedings of the 14th ACM International Conference on Availability, Reliability and Security (ARES), Canterbury, United Kingdom, 26–29 August 2019, New York, NY, USA (2019). https://doi.org/10.1145/3339252.3340518

27. Nguyen, T.T., Backes, M., Marnau, N., Stock, B.: Share first, ask later (or never?) studying violations of GDPR's explicit consent in android apps. In: Proceedings of the 30th USENIX Security Symposium (USENIX Security 2021), online, 11–13 August 2021, pp. 3667–3684 (2021). https://www.usenix.org/conference/usenixsecurity21/presentation/nguyen

28. Nouwens, M., Liccardi, I., Veale, M., Karger, D., Kagal, L.: Dark patterns after the GDPR: scraping consent pop-ups and demonstrating their influence. In: Proceedings of the ACM Conference on Human Factors in Computing Systems (CHI), Honolulu, HI, USA, 25–30 April 2020, New York, NY, USA, pp. 1–13 (2020). https://doi.org/10.1145/3313831.3376321

29. Patil, V.T., Shyamasundar, R.K.: Efficacy of GDPR's right-to-be-forgotten on Facebook. In: Ganapathy, V., Jaeger, T., Shyamasundar, R. (eds.) ICISS 2018. LNCS, vol. 11281, pp. 364–385. Springer, Cham (2018). https://doi.org/10.1007/978-3-030-05171-6_19

30. Raschke, P., Küpper, A., Drozd, O., Kirrane, S.: Designing a GDPR-compliant and usable privacy dashboard. In: Hansen, M., Kosta, E., Nai-Fovino, I., Fischer-Hübner, S. (eds.) Privacy and Identity Management, pp. 221–236. Springer, Cham (2018). https://doi.org/10.1007/978-3-319-92925-5_14

31. Sakamoto, T., Matsunaga, M.: After GDPR, still tracking or not? Understanding OPT-out states for online behavioral advertising. In: Proceedings of the IEEE Security and Privacy Workshops (SPW), San Francisco, CA, USA, 19–23 May 2019, New York, NY, USA, pp. 92–99 (2019). https://doi.org/10.1109/SPW.2019.00027

32. Schulman, R., Callas, J.: Leaving Twitter's Walled Garden (2022). https://www.eff.org/deeplinks/2022/11/leaving-twitters-walled-garden. Accessed 15 May 2024

33. Shastri, S., Wasserman, M., Chidambaram, V.: The seven sins of personal-data processing systems under GDPR. In: Proceedings of the 11th USENIX Workshop on Hot Topics in Cloud Computing (HotCloud 2019), Renton, WA, USA, 8 July 2019, Renton, WA (2019). https://www.usenix.org/conference/hotcloud19/presentation/shastri

34. Shastri, S., Wasserman, M., Chidambaram, V.: GDPR anti-patterns. Commun. ACM **64**(2), 59–65 (2021). https://doi.org/10.1145/3378061

35. Spooren, J., Preuveneers, D., Joosen, W.: Mobile device fingerprinting considered harmful for risk-based authentication. In: Proceedings of the 8th ACM European Workshop on System Security (EuroSec), Bordeaux, France, 21 April 2015, New York, NY, USA (2015). https://doi.org/10.1145/2751323.2751329

36. Starov, O., Nikiforakis, N.: Extended tracking powers: measuring the privacy diffusion enabled by browser extensions. In: Proceedings of the 26th International Conference on World Wide Web (WWW), Perth, Australia, 3–7 April 2017, pp. 1481–1490. International World Wide Web Conferences Steering Committee, Republic and Canton of Geneva, CHE (2017). https://doi.org/10.1145/3038912.3052596

37. Tolsdorf, J., Fischer, M., Lo Iacono, L.: A case study on the implementation of the right of access in privacy dashboards. In: Gruschka, N., Antunes, L.F.C., Rannenberg, K., Drogkaris, P. (eds.) APF 2021. LNCS, vol. 12703, pp. 23–46. Springer, Cham (2021). https://doi.org/10.1007/978-3-030-76663-4_2

38. Twitter: Twitter Privacy Policy. Privacy statement, Twitter (2022)
39. Twitter: How cookies are used on Twitter (2023). https://twitter.com/en/rules-and-policies/twitter-cookies. Accessed 15 May 2024
40. Twitter: Twitter Privacy Policy (2023). https://twitter.com/en/privacy. Accessed 15 May 2024
41. Urban, T., Tatang, D., Degeling, M., Holz, T., Pohlmann, N.: A study on subject data access in online advertising after the GDPR. In: Pérez-Solà, C., Navarro-Arribas, G., Biryukov, A., Garcia-Alfaro, J. (eds.) DPM CBT 2019. LNCS, vol. 11737, pp. 61–79. Springer, Cham (2019). https://doi.org/10.1007/978-3-030-31500-9_5
42. Urban, T., Tatang, D., Degeling, M., Holz, T., Pohlmann, N.: Measuring the impact of the GDPR on data sharing in ad networks. In: Proceedings of the 15th ACM Asia Conference on Computer and Communications Security (ASIA CCS), Taipei, Taiwan, 5–9 October 2020, New York, NY, USA, pp. 222–235 (2020). https://doi.org/10.1145/3320269.3372194
43. Wong, J., Henderson, T.: How portable is portable? Exercising the GDPR's right to data portability. In: Proceedings of the 2018 ACM International Joint Conference and 2018 International Symposium on Pervasive and Ubiquitous Computing and Wearable Computers (UbiComp), Singapore, Singapore, 8–12 October 2018, New York, NY, USA, pp. 911–920 (2018). https://doi.org/10.1145/3267305.3274152
44. World Economic Forum: Personal Data: The Emergence of a New Asset Class. Report, World Economic Forum (2011)
45. Zaeem, R.N., Barber, K.S.: The effect of the GDPR on privacy policies: recent progress and future promise. ACM Trans. Manage. Inf. Syst. **12**(1) (2020). https://doi.org/10.1145/3389685
46. Zhang, N., Wang, S., Zhao, W.: A new scheme on privacy-preserving data classification. In: Proceedings of the 11th ACM SIGKDD International Conference on Knowledge Discovery in Data Mining (KDD), Chicago, Illinois, USA, 21–24 August 2005, New York, NY, USA, pp. 374–383 (2005). https://doi.org/10.1145/1081870.1081913

Modelling Data Protection and Privacy

No Children in the Metaverse? The Privacy and Safety Risks of Virtual Worlds (and How to Deal with Them)

Diletta De Cicco[1], James Downes[2], and Charles Helleputte[1(✉)]

[1] Brussels, Belgium
charles.helleputte@squirepb.com
[2] London, UK

Abstract. This paper examines how the Metaverse could impact on both the privacy and safety of children. It assesses the challenges both of designing virtual reality devices for the Metaverse and of designing the virtual reality spaces in the Metaverse and posits solutions which ensure that child safety remains paramount. It also examines the relevant child data privacy laws vis-à-vis the Metaverse and how potential regulatory difficulties could be overcome. Lastly, it analyses the threats that children may experience when using the Metaverse and how these could be mitigated.

Keywords: Metaverse · Data Privacy · Child Safety · Child Protection · PETs · Privacy By Design

1 Introduction

The aim of this paper is to consider the privacy challenges the Metaverse could create in relation to the protection of children and explore options to best tackle those challenges. Firstly, it defines the Metaverse. It will then describe the Metaverse's increasing relevance and identify the risks to children. Next, it will introduce the overarching international and EU laws which enshrine the protection of children as well as the EU laws which protect children in the context of data protection. It will then look at the safety challenges of designing the hardware of virtual reality devices for children, as well as some potential solutions. In terms of the design of the virtual spaces in the Metaverse, it will examine how new technologies and accountability tools could mitigate the risks to children and how consumer laws in lockstep with data protection laws could provide an effective combination to ensure children are kept safe. It will then look at how the Metaverse could present challenges to existing data protection laws, in particular the legal bases for the GDPR. Lastly, it will look at the threats the Metaverse could present to children in terms of sexual exploitation and gambling and ways to combat these threats. For clarity, and unless specified otherwise, reference to "child" or "children" means any person under the age of 18 years old, as defined in the UN Convention on the Rights of the Child [1].

K. Rannenberg et al. (Eds.): APF 2023, LNCS 13888, pp. 87–108, 2024.
https://doi.org/10.1007/978-3-031-61089-9_5

2   What is the "Metaverse"?

There is currently no universally accepted definition of the "Metaverse." The term was likely first mentioned in the science fiction novel *Snow Crash*, written by Neal Stephenson in which the characters of the novel were able to access a vast virtual world using electronic goggles [50].

The Metaverse could encompass all technologies which can be described as extended reality ("ER") [34]. ER is an umbrella term which covers augmented reality ("AR"), virtual reality ("VR"), and mixed realities ("MR") [34]. In essence, AR technologies incorporate the real-world environment, while VR technologies replace it with a virtual one [34]. Mixed reality technologies sit somewhere between the two, by imposing virtual elements into a real world setting with a persistence similar to a material object [34]. What unifies ER technologies is the ability for the user to look and move around an environment which is either enhanced or virtual [34]. The current definition of the Metaverse is not exclusive to those digital spaces which are accessed without ER [60]. For example, video games such as *Second Life* could qualify within the definition of a Metaverse. However, for the purposes of this paper, references to the "Metaverse" will mean digital spaces which are accessed by one of the forms of ER (unless stated otherwise). VR appears to be the direction intended by Meta (formerly Facebook) which is investing heavily in the creation of a Metaverse [57]. To be clear, the Metaverse is not intended to be owned by Meta or any one company [59]. The Metaverse (if such thing was to exist) will act as a platform which would facilitate the virtual worlds created by different companies or organizations to inter-operate and interconnect [59]. For example, an item bought in Amazon's virtual world could be "taken" to another virtual world created by Microsoft [59]. The Metaverse should therefore be seen as a collective space allowing different virtual worlds to connect with one another.

3   Relevance and Risks to Children

Gartner has predicted that by 2026, around one quarter of people will spend at least one hour per day on the Metaverse either for work, shopping, or entertainment [47, 65]. If this trend proves even slightly correct, then children will inevitably become significant users of the Metaverse as well. As it stands, children are already at risk from other Internet users in the form of bullying, sexual abuse, and radicalization [44]. In addition, children are at risk from exposure to sites which promote self-harm, eating disorders, or pornography [44]. The European Commission (the "Commission") has set out a political strategy to better protect children online called the new European strategy for a better internet for kids ("BIK+") [44]. One of the key pillars of BIK+ is to ensure that children have safer digital experiences [44]. It aims to protect children from harmful and illegal online content and aims to improve their wellbeing by creating an age-appropriate digital environment [44].

4 Overarching Child Privacy and Safeguarding Legal Framework

The concept that children are vulnerable to exploitation and require special protection is an accepted legal principle. At an international level, the rights of children are enshrined in the UN Convention on the Rights of the Child ("Convention"). All UN Member States have ratified the treaty except the United States [62]. Under Article 3(1), the Convention states that:

> "In all actions concerning children, whether undertaken by public or private social welfare institutions, courts of law, administrative authorities or legislative bodies, the best interests of the child shall be a primary consideration [1]."

This places an extensive obligation on UN Member States to ensure that the best interests of children are upheld in their national affairs. At a European level, the Charter of Fundamental Rights of the European Union ("Charter") also contains a similar obligation under Article 24(2) [2]. This obliges public authorities and private institutions to put the best interests of a child as their primary consideration [2]. This obligation applies both to the institutions of the EU, as well as to EU Member States (when implementing EU law) [3]. Under Article 8, the Charter also enshrines the right to the protection of personal data [2]. These overarching obligations underpin the General Data Protection Regulation ('GDPR') which is the EU's primary piece of legislation for the protection of personal data [7]. Recital 38 of the GDPR emphasizes the need for children [66] to have specific protection, stating:

> "Children merit specific protection with regard to their personal data, as they may be less aware of the risks, consequences and safeguards concerned and their rights in relation to the processing of personal data. Such specific protection should, in particular, apply to the use of personal data of children for the purposes of marketing or creating personality or user profiles and the collection of personal data with regard to children when using services offered directly to a child. The consent of the holder of parental responsibility should not be necessary in the context of preventive or counselling services offered directly to a child [8]."

The Information Commissioner's Office ("ICO") has created guidance called 'Age Appropriate Design: A Code of Practice for Online Services' (the "ICO Code") [51]. The ICO Code is the first of its kind and seeks to set out how the (UK) GDPR applies to online services which are provided to children. The code is based on 15 risk-based standards which are categorized as follows (Table 1):

Table 1. 15 Risks-based Standards (ICO Code)

1	Best interest of the child	9	Data Sharing
2	Data protection impacts assessments	10	Geolocation
3	Age-appropriate application	11	Parental Controls
4	Transparency	12	Profiling
5	Detrimental use of data	13	Nudge techniques
6	Policies and community standards	14	Connected toys and devices
7	Default settings	15	Online Tools [51]
8	Data minimization		

Where relevant, this paper will expand in more detail as to what these standards mean. In a nutshell though, the standards strive to strike a balance between ensuring that children have the best possible access to online services whilst also ensuring that the collection and use of their personal data is minimized by default [51].

5   Design of Virtual Reality Devices

This section will focus on what can be done to protect children at the design phase of the Metaverse. It will cover the obligations on manufacturers which create the VR devices for children.

As children have become increasingly connected to the Internet, it perhaps comes as no surprise that their toys have as well. Toys which are linked to the Internet are known as "connected toys" and they are becoming increasingly popular [35]. Connected toys can contain an array of sensors, microphones, or cameras which collect information which is then stored by the manufacturer or a cloud service provider [49]. This information can include voice recordings, web application passwords, Wi-Fi information, or home addresses [49]. This puts children at considerable risk of their personal data being abused and has caused increasing concern. The Commission has responded to this and adopted new legislation which seeks to address the risks posed by connected toys.

Under the Radio Equipment Directive ("RED"), manufacturers of radio equipment (which includes connected devices) are required to incorporate safeguards in their products which ensure that the personal data and privacy of the user and of the subscriber are protected [4]. The obligation to do this has now been specifically extended to radio devices designed or intended exclusively for childcare as well as to devices which are worn, strapped, or hung from any part of the human body (or clothing worn by human beings) [6]. When children use devices which connect to the Metaverse (i.e., goggles or virtual reality suits), these have the potential to be captured by this obligation as a form of "connected toy." The obligation on these devices to protect a child user's privacy is particularly important given the increased scope of the personal data they could process. For example, it is anticipated that the devices could allow companies in the Metaverse to track body movements and physiological responses; in the future the technology could even develop to track electrical signals generated in the brain [58]. The sheer scale of personal data which could be processed and stored about children therefore provides an enormous opportunity for hackers to exploit this data for criminal or malicious purposes.

From a manufacturer's perspective, an important aspect of the design of virtual reality goggles and suits is to prevent someone from being able to externally access them. For example, some connected toys have been found to have flaws with their Bluetooth capabilities which would have allowed hackers access to the toys and, in some instances, to communicate with children [64]. Manufacturers would need to ensure that similar flaws are not replicated with virtual reality hardware so that hackers are unable to steal personal data or inappropriately communicate with children whilst they use the Metaverse.

To encourage the development of devices which meet an adequate standard for the protection of child privacy, the EU could also propose new standards or certifications. Currently, RED requires an EU declaration of conformity and the affixing of CE marking to radio equipment before it goes onto the market [5]. These requirements could be extended so that devices, for example VR goggles, have a separate declaration of conformity which confirms the device is designed specifically to address risks to child privacy. Alternatively, the Commission could create a completely new certification scheme for radio equipment marketed to children which would require VR devices to be manufactured to a particular standard which protects child privacy. Privacy by design requirements under GDPR might also offer some frameworks mandating to embed privacy from start to finish, as the next section explains.

6 Design of the Virtual Spaces in the Metaverse

In this section, we will analyze the obligations on companies to design their virtual spaces in the Metaverse in a way which best protects child privacy. The GDPR requires data controllers to implement "data protection by design and default [16]." This means that when companies design their virtual worlds (and hardware to enter it), they need to ensure that there are technical measures in place which limit the processing of data to what is necessary for each purpose of processing [16]. In addition, they must ensure that personal data is not available to an indefinite number of persons [16]. There are two ways to help achieve this. Firstly, a company could employ Privacy Enhancing Technologies ("PETs") which are designed specifically to address the risks that the Metaverse could present to children. Secondly, given the Metaverse's technological novelty, specific safeguards would have to be put in place by anyone willing to process data within a Metaverse as a controller. Data Protection Impact Assessment ("DPIA") is one of them, helping to identify additional privacy safeguards for children *ex ante*.

6.1 PETs (and Other 'Privacy by Law' Initiatives)

The European Union Agency for Cybersecurity ('ENISA') describes PETs as:

> *"software and hardware solutions, i.e. systems encompassing technical processes, methods or knowledge to achieve specific privacy or data protection functionality or to protect against risks of privacy of an individual or a group of natural persons* [67]."

Put simply, they are technological solutions which can assist companies in showing that they are following a "data protection by design and default approach [52]." They achieve this by assisting with compliance of the data minimization principle, providing appropriate security measures, implementing strong anonymization or pseudonymization solutions, or by minimizing the risk of personal data beaches [52]. Given the scale of personal data which companies could collect in the Metaverse, PETs could be a useful way of minimizing risks to children. In terms of risks, the ICO Code lists as follows (Table 2):

Table 2. List of Risks to Children (ICO Code)

1	Physical harm	8	Loss of autonomy or rights (including control over data)
2	Online grooming or other sexual exploitation	9	Compulsive use or attention deficit disorders
3	Social anxiety, self-esteem issues, bullying or peer pressure	10	Excessive screen time
4	Access to harmful or inappropriate content	11	Interrupted or inadequate sleep patterns
5	Misinformation or undue restriction on information	12	Economic exploitation or unfair commercial pressure
6	Encouraging excessive risk-taking or unhealthy behavior	13	Any other significant economic, social, or developmental disadvantage [51]
7	Undermining parental authority or responsibility		

What can be done to mitigate the risk of children having "access to harmful or inappropriate content"? We explore two options: (1) prospective uses of digital identities and (2) Zero Knowledge Proof ("ZKP") and come up unexpectedly with a third one that we named "privacy by law". For example, a "virtual brothel", will need to mitigate against the risk of this content being available to children. The Commission is currently in the process of developing personal digital wallets which would make it easier for users to access services which require identification in other member states [36]. Crucially, it will also provide a new qualified trust service which will enable the attestation of attributes such as age [36]. This could prove a useful way for Metaverse companies to efficiently and securely ensure that users are the correct age.

To assist companies in complying with the data minimization principle, a ZKP could provide a useful solution whereby the age of a user is verified without the need to reveal their actual age [52]. The way it works is that a user proves to a company that they know a value X (i.e., proof they over the age of 18 or 21) [52]. This is conveyed to the company without revealing any information other than the fact the statement is true (i.e., they over 18 or 21 years old) [52]. The company then challenges the user in such a way that the response from the user will convince the company that X is true (i.e., that they are over the age of 18) [52]. A ZKP is not an anonymization technique, because the information processed (i.e., proof the user is over a certain age) is still information which can relate to an individual and constitutes personal data under the GDPR [52]. However, a company not querying the exact age of each user helps to comply with the data minimization principle by limiting the amount of personal data processed and it helps to comply with the security principle as confidential data about someone's age does not have to be shared with third parties [52]. Most importantly, it is also a neat way of designing a virtual space which ensures that children do not have access to harmful content.

Other regulatory initiatives could play an (unexpected) key role as well. For example, the new Digital Services Act ("DSA") will require online providers, when assessing the age of a minor, to minimize the personal data which is collected [19]. It states that the protection of children should not automatically act as an incentive to collect a child's age [19]. BIK+ also states that the Commission will support methods that prove age in a way that preserves privacy and security [44].

Alternatively, a broader strategy to overcome this challenge would be a Metaverse aimed specifically at children. This would not dispense with the complications of verifying ages as children navigate across the virtual world. However, the problem with this model is that differing jurisdictions have differing standards of what is appropriate for children. For example, one country might want to ensure a space for children which is LGBTQIA+ friendly, but another country may not want any promotion of this at all. Age verification also needs to be put in place to mitigate the risks of adults navigating the Metaverse for children. There is also the option to ban children on the Metaverse, but this would cut-off their ability to interact, play, and learn in a digital friendly manner which is not promoted by the BIK+ strategy [44].

As previously highlighted, companies which operate in the Metaverse could potentially process vast amounts of personal data from children which heightens the risk of loss of autonomy or rights. There are currently three computing states for data: (1) data 'in use' which is the term to describe data which is being processed, (2) data 'in transit' which is when data is traversing a network, and (3) data 'at rest' which is when data is stored [37]. Traditionally, data 'in use' has been a weak point from a security perspective [37]. This presents a serious security challenge for companies in the Metaverse, particularly given the volume of child data which could be processed whilst children use the platform. To reduce the security risk to data 'in use,' a PET which is increasingly being deployed is a Trusted Execution Environment ("TEE"). The Confidential Computing Consortium ("CCC") defines a TEE as:

> "[...] an environment that provides a level of assurance of data integrity, data confidentiality, and code integrity [37]."

Data integrity means the prevention of unauthorized entities from altering data whilst data is being processed [37]. Data confidentiality means preventing unauthorized entities from accessing the data in a TEE [37]. Code integrity means preventing an unauthorized entity from replacing or modifying the code in a TEE [37]. These three differing attributes help to ensure that the personal data processed in a TEE is kept confidential and that the computations being performed are the correct ones [37]. Of most utility to companies operating in the Metaverse is the fact they can be applied in the context of biometric identification (see Sect. 8.2 below) and cloud computing [52]. For example, if an education provider wanted to use an iris scan performed by a set of virtual reality goggles to identify a student, it could use a TEE to run the matching and processing of the student [52]. The TEE would protect the student's biometric data by processing it separately and acting as a buffer against any non-secure applications in the other parts of the operating system [52]. It is also expected that the main use case for TEEs will be in the context of cloud computing [48]. This is because they have the potential to offer the same level of security which organizations are already familiar with from onsite premises [48]. TEEs are not a silver bullet though; they are still vulnerable to hacking such as "side-channel attacks" which attack a system based on the information that a TEE communicates with the other parts of an operating system [52]. Nevertheless, the adoption of TEEs could be an effective way for companies operating in the Metaverse to securely process sensitive or biometric data of children. Depending on the industry and the type of personal data, a company could even decide to process all forms of child personal data which require parental consent in a TEE. This might be easier from a cost perspective, as it would mean there would be no need to segment which child personal data should be processed in a TEE and which should not. Using a TEE would also assist companies in showing that whilst children are using their services, they are complying with the ICO Code and the security principle of the GDPR [11].

6.2 DPIA

A DPIA is a process which describes the processing of personal data, assesses its necessity and proportionality, and then manages the risks to the rights and freedoms of natural persons as a result of that processing by assessing and determining measures to address those risks [33]. It is a key requirement of the GDPR to conduct a DPIA where a processing activity is considered to *"[...] result in a high risk to the rights and freedoms of natural persons* [17]." The WP29 (the predecessor to EDPB) produced a set of guidelines which lists the activities which it considers to be "high risk" [33]. It considered that data concerning vulnerable data subjects, such as children, presented an inherently high risk because children cannot be considered to knowingly and thoughtfully oppose or consent to the processing of their personal data [33]. This is a position which is supported by the ICO Code which recommends in Standard 2 that a DPIA is conducted when the personal data of children is used for marketing purposes, profiling or other automated decision-making, or to offer direct online services [51]. It is likely that one or more of these activities will occur when children use a company's virtual space in the Metaverse.

Companies operating in the Metaverse would need to conduct DPIAs for any processing activities which fall within the scope of "high risk". The crux is to identify risks to children and how to mitigate them. For example, the risks listed in the ICO Code include social anxiety, self-esteem issues, and bullying. These are already common issues amongst young people who use existing social media. In a virtual space, there might be even less escape from this behavior as school colleagues could continue to bully through 'avatars' thereby inflicting the same misery already inflicted within school gates. A mitigation measure a DPIA could consider is a blocking feature or a "ghost" feature where users could become invisible in the event that they are subjected to harassment [58]. There could also be a reporting feature so that those who harass online face sanctions to ensure that this behavior is not repeated. There will no doubt be further risks in addition to those listed in the ICO Code and it might be that the Metaverse presents such an overwhelming risk to children that a completely new approach will need to be taken. This would most sensibly involve supervisory authorities, which under the existing GDPR arrangements, are already required to consult on high-risk activities which cannot be sufficiently addressed by companies acting as data controllers [18].

7 Could Consumer Laws Be the/an Answer?

DPIAs, PETs, and designing virtual reality hardware with in-built security features are all ways which could protect children from a privacy law perspective. However, at the design phase, it is possible that consumer laws are also an effective solution. At an international level, the UN has produced a set of guidelines relating to consumer protection [63]. One of the key general principles is that Member States should develop consumer protection policies which protect vulnerable and disadvantaged consumers [63]. This group is not defined in the guidelines, but it will include children. Extended to an EU level, one of the key consumer laws is the Unfair Commercial Practices Directive 2005 ("UNPD") [24]. Article 5(3) of the UNPD states:

> "Commercial practices which are likely to materially distort the economic behavior only of a clearly identifiable group of consumers who are particularly vulnerable to the practice or the underlying product because of their mental or physical infirmity, age or credulity in a way which the trader could reasonably be expected to foresee, shall be assessed from the perspective of the average member of that group. This is without prejudice to the common and legitimate advertising practice of making exaggerated statements or statements which are not meant to be taken literally."

What this means is that the impact of an unfair commercial practice will be judged against the average member of a child of a particular age group. The UNPD has a list of commercial practices which it considers to be unfair in all circumstances [25]. In this list, it states that it is an unfair commercial practice for an advertisement to be a direct exhortation for children to buy advertised products, or for the advertisement to persuade parents or other adults to buy an advertised product for children [26]. Therefore, companies creating virtual reality hardware will need to ensure that the devices are not sold in a manner which directly encourages children or their parents to buy them. Advertising which tempers the way it targets children means that parents have more control over the decision to buy a product and are under less pressure from children to buy products. This provides an initial safeguard against children being induced to buy the virtual reality devices at the expense of the potential privacy risks.

In an online context, the DSA has introduced several provisions to improve the safeguarding of children. Intermediary services, such as social media, will be required to design their systems in a way which ensures that children can understand the terms and conditions of the services offered [20, 38]. Providers of online platforms will be required to adopt appropriate and proportionate measures which ensure the privacy, safety, and security of children on their services [21]. They will also be prohibited from presenting adverts to children based on the profiling of their personal data [22]. Lastly, very large online platforms and search engines will be required to carry out risk assessments which consider any actual or foreseeable negative effects on children [23]. In the context of the Metaverse, these are very broad obligations for companies to put in place, but not impossible. With the assistance of Artificial Intelligence, companies could create safety avatars which would accompany children and ensure they comply with the requirements of the DSA. For example, a child who shouts abuse at another child could be chided by the safety avatar and warned of expulsion from the virtual space.

EU-wide consumer laws aimed specifically at the risks of obtaining VR hardware could also go some way to safeguarding the privacy interests of children. For example, laws could create criteria on the design of the packaging for VR devices. Such criteria could require that children and parents be specifically warned of the quantity and type of personal data which is processed by the device and the risks in the event it is hacked. For children, logos or labels on VR hardware packaging (depending on their age) could provide similar warnings. At the more extreme end, there could even be consumer laws which ban the sale or supply of virtual reality hardware for children under a certain age. This would be a powerful initial safeguard if it were decided that the risks to child privacy of a particular age group outweighed any benefits.

At the design phase of both virtual reality hardware and virtual spaces, it is difficult to judge whether privacy laws or consumer laws are better suited to safeguarding children. However, it is likely that consumer laws which work in lockstep with privacy laws will be the most effective combination to safeguard child privacy.

8 Data Protection Challenges in the Metaverse

This section will look at some of the data protection specific issues which could arise from the Metaverse. Firstly, it will analyze the jurisdictional issues which could arise in terms of the application of the various data protection laws which exist globally. Secondly, it will look at the complexities which could arise in terms of the legal bases for processing child personal data. Lastly, it will discuss the complications which could arise in terms of the requirement for children to be properly informed of the processing of their personal data.

8.1 Territorial Scope

Given that the Metaverse is expected to be a global virtual world, one of the main issues which will arise is the jurisdictional application of the differing data protection laws which exist globally. For example, a child using Twitter in California will be subject to the California Privacy Rights Act. However, that same child might then decide to attend a virtual concert in Japan and then have a virtual class with a language school based in France. As the child user moves between these differing jurisdictions globally, it might be difficult to ascertain which data protection laws will apply (or how to enforce them). One solution is to ensure that the laws have extra-territorial effect. For example, GDPR currently applies to any company which has an establishment in the EEA (regardless of whether the processing occurs in the EEA or not) as well as to companies based outside the EEA, but which are still "targeting" and/or "monitoring" data subjects based in the EU [9].

8.2 Consent

The GDPR defines consent as:

> *"[...] any freely given, specific, informed and unambiguous indication of the data subject's wishes by which he or she, by a statement or by a clear affirmative action, signifies agreement to the processing of personal data relating to him or her;* [10] *"*

'Freely given' implies that there is a genuine free choice for the data subject. In particular, the choice must not be conditional on access to a service offered by a data controller and that there must be no detriment to the data subject by choosing not to consent [40]. In the context of children, it is more difficult to achieve valid consent because the data controller needs to consider the competence of the child (i.e., whether they have the capacity to understand the implication of the processing of their data) [54]. If the child does not have capacity, then they will not be considered informed within the meaning of the GDPR so the consent will not be valid [54]. If consent is still required, then the data controller will need to seek the consent of a parental authority [54]. In addition to this, the GDPR places a specific obligation on "information society services." These are services offered online, even if renumeration or funding is not directly obtained from the end user [53]. This definition will most likely cover companies which offer services on the virtual spaces created in the Metaverse. Under Article 8(1), companies which offer information society services directly to children, and rely on consent as the legal basis for processing child personal data, must ensure that those services are only offered to children above the age of 16 years old. If not, then the processing will only be lawful if consent is given by the authorized holder of parental responsibility [14]. Member States have discretion to reduce this threshold to 13 years old [14].

This requirement for valid consent is made more complex by the Metaverse as it is likely that companies will also process 'special category data.' Under the GDPR, there are several different types of special category data, but the one most relevant to ER is likely to be biometric data [15]. Biometric data is defined in Article 4(14) as:

> *"[...] personal data resulting from specific technical processing relating to the physical, physiological or behavioral characteristics of a natural person, which allow or confirm the unique identification of that natural person, such as facial images or dactyloscopic data;"*

Given that VR goggles are likely to record eye movements and that VR suits will be able to record specific body movements (or even the electronic signals in the brain), it is very likely that the personal data which companies record on the Metaverse will constitute biometric data. As this constitutes special category data, the GDPR has a set of additional legal bases which need to be complied with for the processing to be lawful [15]. The most applicable for the type of online services which companies on the Metaverse will be offering is 'explicit consent' [15]. The term 'explicit' refers to the way that consent is expressed from a data subject [40]. In essence, it means that the data subject must give an express statement of consent to the processing of their special category data [15]. A common way that online services fulfil this requirement is by offering Yes/No checkboxes. For this method to be valid, the options available for each checkbox need to be clear and the data subject needs to actively click the checkbox [15, 31]. There are also other methods, but each is predicated on the data subject making a positive action to confirm their consent.

This creates difficulties for companies which operate in the Metaverse. The main overarching issue is the requirement to verify the age of users using the virtual space and then obtaining the required parental consent for users under the age of 16 (or under 13 depending on the jurisdiction). Firstly, the company will need to adapt their systems to apply the right verification depending on the requirements of each Member State. The need to seek parental consent could also cause a variety of issues. If a child is too young to consent to a processing activity, then how is the processing activity stopped in the event the child ignores a notice and continues to use the virtual space? It might also be difficult to verify that the person who consents to a child's use of the virtual space is the correct person. Another issue might be the requirement to allow a user to withdraw consent. Once a child reaches the digital age of consent, then they will have the right to withdraw the consent which was taken on their behalf by their parent [40]. Companies have a duty to inform the child about this possibility in accordance with the principle of fairness and accountability [40]. This could create an especially difficult problem for companies in terms of respecting the data minimization principle because they will need to retain sufficient information about each child data subject so that they can notify them of this possibility at the right time in the future.

As explained in Sect. 6, a way these issues might be solved, is to use ZKPs so that companies can verify the age of consent of child users as well as verify the identity of parents without the need to collect unnecessary amounts of personal information. The ZKPs could be set to ask the same child annually their age so that when they reach the digital age of consent, they can choose whether to withdraw the consent made on their behalf previously. In terms of privacy consent notices, UX designers could be employed so that consent is an interactive experience. For example, the necessary information on the notice could be presented as a game so that children must read all the information on the notice before they "win" and consent to it.

8.3 Necessity for the Performance of a Contract and Legitimate Interest

Necessity for the performance of a contract is one of the legal bases that a company in the Metaverse might want to rely on for processing child personal data [12]. It might prove uneasy. Firstly, there is the complexity that different jurisdictions have different ages at which children are deemed to be able to enter contracts. For example, in the United Kingdom alone, the legal age of capacity to enter a contract is 16 in Scotland, whereas in England & Wales it can be as young as 7 (with the caveat that the contracts are voidable minus some limited exceptions) [54]. Secondly, the Irish Data Protection Commission (pressed by the EDPB) recently published a decision in relation to Meta which confirms that companies cannot rely on the performance of a contract as the legal basis for behavioral advertising when this does not form the core of the contract performed with data subjects [39]. It is not meant to act, therefore, as a circumvention of consent if that is the more appropriate legal basis [32].

Where possible, the most likely legal basis that companies will rely on for processing the personal data of children is legitimate interest [13]. Before relying on this legal basis, a legitimate interest impact assessment ("LIA") needs to be carried out which identifies the legitimate interest, shows that the processing is necessary to achieve it, and balances this against the interest, rights, and freedoms of the child [54]. When relying on 'legitimate interest', the onus is on the data controller to protect children from risks which the children themselves might not fully appreciate or anticipate [54]. It is also up to the controller to identify issues and to come up with appropriate safeguards for children [54]. The benefit of relying on legitimate interest is that it is less onerous than consent. However, the requirement to design processing at the outset so that children are protected is itself an onerous obligation. In addition, if companies are processing any biometric data, then they will not be able to rely on legitimate interest and will likely need to still rely on explicit consent.

8.4 Augmented Privacy Notice

One of the key principles of the GDPR is transparency and this is reiterated in Standard 4 of the ICO Code. Articles 13 and 14 of the GDPR require users to be informed about the nature of the processing of their personal data, their rights as data subjects, and the identity of the controller of their personal data (amongst other obligations).

This information is usually presented through privacy notices, served to users at various points in time. The notices need to be clear, concise, and in language suitable for a child. It is recommended that information is presented in a "bite-sized" manner at the point that use is activated [51]. Currently, most websites put a link at the bottom of their webpage to access the wording of their privacy policy. Like the consent notices discussed above, a solution to this could be to present the information as a game so that information is provided interactively an in a manner which is modulated and concise. Alternatively, a privacy avatar which accompanies the child could inform them (depending on their age) as to what personal information is being processed as they traverse the Metaverse. This could ensure that information is kept "bite-sized" and kept strictly to the point of use. Children might also be more reactive to a figure they see as a guardian or friend.

9 Safety of Children in the Metaverse

In this section, we look at the some of the safety threats which come to the fore when children interact and play in the Metaverse.

9.1 Child Exploitation

When children are using the Metaverse, one of the key dangers which is likely to emerge is the risk of sexual exploitation. Currently, at an EU level, the Directive on combating the sexual abuse and exploitation of children obliges Member States to provide law enforcement authorities with the tools to combat child sexual abuse [27]. For example, it requires Member States to have minimum penalties for the acquisition and transmission of child pornography as well as for the solicitation of children for sexual purposes [28]. However, the continued proliferation of online child sexual material has meant the EU is now proposing to place obligations on online service providers as well [29]. In short, the regulation proposes placing obligations on internet companies to have procedures in place that limit and prevent the dissemination of child abuse material as well as to report material when it is detected [30]. It also empowers national authorities to coordinate and issue orders to detect abuse material and remove it [30]. The law will encompass end-to-end encrypted chat platforms such as WhatsApp and Telegram which has proved controversial with some Member States from a surveillance perspective [55]. The Metaverse could enormously increase the scope upon which child abuse activities could occur, particularly solicitation and grooming. This is likely to be an extremely complex issue which will require a high degree of international coordination if children are able to virtually cross borders globally.

An effective way to combat these threats is to ensure that children have specific training which means they avoid unwanted or dangerous contact from strangers. The police could also set up 'virtual police stations' so that parents can contact and report predatory behavior to the police in a manner which mirrors what would be done in the real world. As discussed previously, another option would be to create a Metaverse which is specific to children or, as also mentioned, to ensure there is a "ghost" function so that children can disappear if they sense they are in danger or want to avoid the unwanted attention of an adult [58].

There are also certain functionalities at the design stage of the hardware which could help to mitigate these risks. For example, virtual reality hardware could be configured with parental control features which mean that children can only access the Metaverse when a parent is present with a child in the Metaverse or after permission has been specifically granted by a parent. This would be particularly applicable to young children. The hardware could also be designed so that software can be configured to allow parents to monitor their children whilst they are on the Metaverse. The strength of such controls could be loosened as the children grow older, bearing in mind that as a child reaches adulthood, they also have an increasing right to personal autonomy. Whilst these types of controls have limits (i.e., a child working out a way to bypass the controls), they would provide a first step towards safeguarding children's privacy before entering the Metaverse and they would help companies to comply with their obligation to manufacture devices in a way that protects the privacy of children.

9.2   Gambling

In addition to sexual exploitation, there are also other problematic uses for children such as gambling. Studies have shown that children are less able to disentangle costs and are most at risk of developing gambling problems by comparison to adults when using virtual currencies [69, 72]. In addition, children have been found to have more problems in taking probabilities into account and are more vulnerable to develop hyperactivity and symptoms of inattention because of reward stimuli [68, 70, 71]. This makes children particularly vulnerable to online gambling. An example which presents the complexity of this problem in the online environment are 'loot boxes.' A European Parliament report defines loot boxes as:

> *"features in video games which are usually accessed through gameplay, or which may optionally be paid for with real-world money. They are 'mystery boxes' which contain randomised items, so players do not know what they will get before opening* [46].*"*

For loot boxes to be considered gambling, most EU Member States require that (1) there is an initial consideration to play the loot box, (2) the outcome of the box is determined wholly or partly by chance, and (3) the participant can win a prize of money or an item of monetary value [46]. However, some Member States such as Belgium still regard this activity as gambling even when the prize is not of monetary value – it is simply sufficient if the prize has some value to the player [46]. Loot boxes are therefore banned for video games sold in Belgium [46].

As the Metaverse develops, these types of applications will increase in sophistication and the scope with which children could be exposed to activities which constitute gambling. Given the international nature of the Metaverse, there will need to be agreed EU or global rules on what constitutes gambling and how best to ensure that the Metaverse does not become a gateway to children developing gambling addictions. Without agreed international standards, it could be easy for companies in the Metaverse to develop activities which encourage child gambling by the backdoor.

10   Broader Policy Options

The complexities of existing data protection laws and the legal challenges raised by the Metaverse present a wider policy question for the EU: whether the Metaverse requires its own regulation or whether the existing and upcoming body of laws are sufficient.

The Commission's Work Programme for 2023 states as one of its aims to develop *"[...] open human-centric virtual worlds, such as metaverses* [41].*"* There is not much further elaboration on what this might look like, but there have been some hints from Thierry Breton, the European Commissioner for the Internal Market [43]. In a statement in September 2022, he stated that *"private metaverses"* should be developed on interoperable standards and that *"no single private player should hold the key to the public square* [43].*"* This is clearly a veiled warning to Meta and shows the Commission's intention to avoid a monopoly emerging in the Metaverse. He also expressed a desire for a *"creative and interdisciplinary movement"*, similar to the European Bauhaus, which aims to develop standards and maximize the help of IT and regulatory experts [43]. This seems to point towards an intention by the Commission to include a more diverse mix of expertise in the development of the Metaverse and avoid it being developed by any one group [56].

In the same statement, Mr. Breton also launched the Virtual and Augmented Reality Industrial Coalition ("Coalition") [43]. The aim of the Coalition is to improve the performance of the VR/AR industry in Europe by creating a platform for dialogue between the European VR/AR ecosystem and policymakers [42]. So far, the Coalition has held workshops with stakeholders, produced a strategic paper with a market assessment of the

European VR/AR system and organized an event in April 2022 where the results of the assessment were discussed with key industry actors [42]. These activities are designed to inform policymakers as to the next steps for better integrating VR/AR technologies in Europe [42]. From a policymaking perspective though, there already appears to be some divergence as how best to tackle the challenges of the Metaverse.

Margrethe Vestager, the European Commissioner for Competition has argued that the EU should start considering regulation for the Metaverse [61]. She is due to present a specific initiative on virtual worlds which has now been pushed to 31 May 2023 [45]. One of her ambitions is to ensure that the virtual worlds in the Metaverse are interoperable so that users do not become locked in one virtual world and prevented from using services in other worlds [61]. However, Mr. Breton appears to argue that existing laws, such as the DSA, should be sufficient for now [43]. The problem with Vestager's proposal is that it is probably still too early to say how the issues with the Metaverse are going to play out given the nascent nature of the concept. More pragmatically, a proposal now (or in the immediate future) has very little chances to become law during this legislative tenure. More effective regulation may come from seeing where the gaps appear in the existing laws as the Metaverse progresses by spotting deficiencies in existing and upcoming (such as the regulation on artificial intelligence) body of laws. This would make it more targeted and would help to focus on where there is a lack of harmonization for current and upcoming laws applicable to the Metaverse.

11 Conclusion

Whilst the Metaverse presents numerous data protection issues in relation to the protection of children, there are options available to companies and policymakers which means they are not insurmountable (and that children would be protected in the Metaverses).

- Manufacturers should design ER devices which are secure from external interference and the EU could create an accompanying certification scheme which means that parents have confidence in the protections put in place.
- To ensure that virtual spaces are designed safely, companies could employ the use of PETs which verify ages in a manner that minimizes the use of personal data and segments it safely in a trusted environment. DPIAs could also ensure that risks to children are properly identified and mitigated against.
- In terms of the legal bases for processing child personal data, territorial issues are probably best solved with extraterritorial regulation and the difficulties seeking consent best solved with effective use of ZKPs and notices which are presented in a child-friendly manner. Alternatively, companies could rely on necessity for the performance of a contract or legitimate interest, but the former is probably an uneasy option owing to the recent Meta decision as well as the difficulties of forming contracts with children.
- The threat of sexual exploitation whilst children use the Metaverse could be mitigated against through education, virtual police stations, "ghost features", and ER devices which only allow children to be accompanied by an adult in the Metaverse.
- More broadly, the EU could also consider whether children should be allowed to use the Metaverse at all, but this will need to be balanced against the risk of leaving children digitally excluded.

All technological advances come with new threats, but by employing the use of privacy centered technology and nimble legislation, there is scope for ensuring that children can safely benefit from the Metaverse.

References

Primary: Charters and Conventions

1. UN Convention on the Rights of the Child, Article 1, Article 3(1). https://www.ohchr.org/en/instruments-mechanisms/instruments/convention-rights-child. Accessed 7 Feb 2023
2. EU Charter of Fundamental Rights of the European Union, (2012/C 326/02). https://eur-lex.europa.eu/legal-content/EN/TXT/PDF/?uri=CELEX:12012P/TXT&from=EN. Accessed 7 Feb 2023
3. EU The Charter of Fundamental Rights of the European Union, Article 51, (2012/C 326/02). https://eur-lex.europa.eu/legal-content/EN/TXT/PDF/?uri=CELEX:12012P/TXT&from=EN. Accessed 7 Feb 2023

RED and Delegated Regulation

4. Article 3(3)(e) of Directive 2014/53/EU of the European Parliament and of the Council of 16 April 2014 on the harmonisation of the laws of the Member States relating to the making available on the market of radio equipment and repealing Directive 1999/5/EC (Text with EEA relevance)
5. Articles 18–20 of Directive 2014/53/EU of the European Parliament and of the Council of 16 April 2014 on the harmonisation of the laws of the Member States relating to the making available on the market of radio equipment and repealing Directive 1999/5/EC (Text with EEA relevance)
6. Articles 2(b) and 2(d) of Commission Delegated Regulation (EU) 2022/30 of 29 October 2021 supplementing Directive 2014/53/EU of the European Parliament and of the Council with regard to the application of the essential requirements referred to in Article 3(3), points (d), (e) and (f), of that Directive (Text with EEA relevance)

GDPR

7. Recital 4 of the Regulation (EU) 2016/679 of the European Parliament and of The Council of 27 April 2016 on the protection of natural persons with regard to the processing of personal data and on the free movement of such data, and repealing Directive 95/46/EC (General Data Protection Regulation) (Text with EEA relevance)
8. Recital 38 of the Regulation (EU) 2016/679 of the European Parliament and of The Council of 27 April 2016 on the protection of natural persons with regard to the processing of personal data and on the free movement of such data, and repealing Directive 95/46/EC (General Data Protection Regulation) (Text with EEA relevance)
9. Article 3 of the Regulation (EU) 2016/679 of the European Parliament and of The Council of 27 April 2016 on the protection of natural persons with regard to the processing of personal data and on the free movement of such data, and repealing Directive 95/46/EC (General Data Protection Regulation) (Text with EEA relevance)

10. Article 4(11) of the Regulation (EU) 2016/679 of the European Parliament and of The Council of 27 April 2016 on the protection of natural persons with regard to the processing of personal data and on the free movement of such data, and repealing Directive 95/46/EC (General Data Protection Regulation) (Text with EEA relevance)

11. Article 5(1)(f) of the Regulation (EU) 2016/679 of the European Parliament and of The Council of 27 April 2016 on the protection of natural persons with regard to the processing of personal data and on the free movement of such data, and repealing Directive 95/46/EC (General Data Protection Regulation) (Text with EEA relevance)

12. Article 6(1)(b) of the Regulation (EU) 2016/679 of the European Parliament and of The Council of 27 April 2016 on the protection of natural persons with regard to the processing of personal data and on the free movement of such data, and repealing Directive 95/46/EC (General Data Protection Regulation) (Text with EEA relevance)

13. Article 6(1)(f) the Regulation (EU) 2016/679 of the European Parliament and of The Council of 27 April 2016 on the protection of natural persons with regard to the processing of personal data and on the free movement of such data, and repealing Directive 95/46/EC (General Data Protection Regulation) (Text with EEA relevance)

14. Article 8(1) of the Regulation (EU) 2016/679 of the European Parliament and of The Council of 27 April 2016 on the protection of natural persons with regard to the processing of personal data and on the free movement of such data, and repealing Directive 95/46/EC (General Data Protection Regulation) (Text with EEA relevance)

15. Article 9 of the Regulation (EU) 2016/679 of the European Parliament and of The Council of 27 April 2016 on the protection of natural persons with regard to the processing of personal data and on the free movement of such data, and repealing Directive 95/46/EC (General Data Protection Regulation) (Text with EEA relevance)

16. Article 25 of the Regulation (EU) 2016/679 of the European Parliament and of The Council of 27 April 2016 on the protection of natural persons with regard to the processing of personal data and on the free movement of such data, and repealing Directive 95/46/EC (General Data Protection Regulation) (Text with EEA relevance)

17. Article 35(1) of the Regulation (EU) 2016/679 of the European Parliament and of The Council of 27 April 2016 on the protection of natural persons with regard to the processing of personal data and on the free movement of such data, and repealing Directive 95/46/EC (General Data Protection Regulation) (Text with EEA relevance)

18. Article 36 of the Regulation (EU) 2016/679 of the European Parliament and of The Council of 27 April 2016 on the protection of natural persons with regard to the processing of personal data and on the free movement of such data, and repealing Directive 95/46/EC (General Data Protection Regulation) (Text with EEA relevance)

DSA

19. Recital 71 of Regulation (EU) 2022/2065 of the European Parliament and of the Council of 19 October 2022 on a Single Market For Digital Services and amending Directive 2000/31/EC (Digital Services Act) (Text with EEA relevance)

20. Article 14(3) of Regulation (EU) 2022/2065 of the European Parliament and of the Council of 19 October 2022 on a Single Market For Digital Services and amending Directive 2000/31/EC (Digital Services Act) (Text with EEA relevance)

21. Article 28(1) of Regulation (EU) 2022/2065 of the European Parliament and of the Council of 19 October 2022 on a Single Market For Digital Services and amending Directive 2000/31/EC (Digital Services Act) (Text with EEA relevance)

22. Article 28(2) of Regulation (EU) 2022/2065 of the European Parliament and of the Council of 19 October 2022 on a Single Market For Digital Services and amending Directive 2000/31/EC (Digital Services Act) (Text with EEA relevance)

23. Article 34(1)(d) of Regulation (EU) 2022/2065 of the European Parliament and of the Council of 19 October 2022 on a Single Market For Digital Services and amending Directive 2000/31/EC (Digital Services Act) (Text with EEA relevance)

UNPD

24. Consolidated text: Directive 2005/29/EC of the European Parliament and of the Council of 11 May 2005 concerning unfair business-to-consumer commercial practices in the internal market and amending Council Directive 84/450/EEC, Directives 97/7/EC, 98/27/EC and 2002/65/EC of the European Parliament and of the Council and Regulation (EC) No 2006/2004 of the European Parliament and of the Council (Unfair Commercial Practices Directive) (Text with EEA relevance)

25. Article 5(5) of Consolidated text: Directive 2005/29/EC of the European Parliament and of the Council of 11 May 2005 concerning unfair business-to-consumer commercial practices in the internal market and amending Council Directive 84/450/EEC, Directives 97/7/EC, 98/27/EC and 2002/65/EC of the European Parliament and of the Council and Regulation (EC) No 2006/2004 of the European Parliament and of the Council (Unfair Commercial Practices Directive) (Text with EEA relevance)

26. Part 28, Annex 1 of Consolidated text: Directive 2005/29/EC of the European Parliament and of the Council of 11 May 2005 concerning unfair business-to-consumer commercial practices in the internal market and amending Council Directive 84/450/EEC, Directives 97/7/EC, 98/27/EC and 2002/65/EC of the European Parliament and of the Council and Regulation (EC) No 2006/2004 of the European Parliament and of the Council (Unfair Commercial Practices Directive) (Text with EEA relevance)

Directive on Combating Sexual Abuse and Exploitation of Children

27. Directive 2011/93/EU of the European Parliament and of the Council of 13 December 2011 on combating the sexual abuse and sexual exploitation of children and child pornography, and replacing Council Framework Decision 2004/68/JHA

28. Articles 5(2) – (4) and 6 of the European Parliament and of the Council of 13 December 2011 on combating the sexual abuse and sexual exploitation of children and child pornography, and replacing Council Framework Decision 2004/68/JHA

Proposal for a Regulation to Prevent and Combat Child Sexual Abuse

29. Proposal for a Regulation of the European Parliament and of the Council laying down rules to prevent and combat child sexual abuse (Text with EEA relevance) (2022/0155 (COD))

30. Articles 3 – 15 of the Proposal for a Regulation of the European Parliament and of the Council laying down rules to prevent and combat child sexual abuse (Text with EEA relevance) (2022/0155 (COD))

D. De Cicco et al.

Cases

31. Bundesverband der Verbraucherzentralen und Verbraucherverbände - Verbraucherzentrale Bundesverband e.V. v Planet49 GmbH (Case C-673/17)
32. Meta Platforms Inc., formerly Facebook Inc., Meta Platforms Ireland Limited, formerly Facebook Ireland Ltd., Facebook Deutschland GmbH v Bundeskartellamt, intervener: Verbraucherzentrale Bundesverband e.V (Case C-252/21), Opinion of A-G Rantos on 20 September 2022, paragraph 51. https://eur-lex.europa.eu/legal-content/en/TXT/?uri=CELEX:620 21CC0252. Accessed 7 Feb 2023

Secondary

33. Article 29 Data Protection Working Party.: Guidelines on Data Protection Impact Assessment (DPIA) and determining whether processing is "likely to result in a high risk" for the purposes of Regulation 2016/679, p. 4, 9–12, 4 October 2017. https://ec.europa.eu/newsroom/article29/items/611236. Accessed 7 Feb 2023
34. Barros Vale, S., Berrick, D.: Reality check: how is the EU ensuring data protection in XR technologies?' (The Digital Constitutionalist, 25 January 2023. https://digi-con.org/reality-check-how-is-the-eu-ensuring-data-protection-in-xr-technologies/. Accessed 7 Feb 2023
35. British Toy & Hobby Association: Guidance Connected Toys. https://www.btha.co.uk/wp-content/uploads/2020/07/MT2P-connected-toys-social-media-posts.pdf. Accessed 7 Feb 2023
36. Commission Recommendation of 3.6.2021 on a common Union Toolbox for a coordinated approach towards a European Digital Identity Framework. https://digital-strategy.ec.europa.eu/en/library/trusted-and-secure-european-e-id-recommendation. Accessed 7 Feb 2023
37. Confidential Computing Consortium.: Confidential Computing: Hardware-Based Trusted Execution for Applications and Data, pp. 3–5. https://confidentialcomputing.io/wp-content/uploads/sites/85/2023/01/CCC_outreach_whitepaper_updated_November_2022.pdf. Accessed 7 Feb 2023
38. Council of the EU: DSA: Council gives final approval to the protection of users' rights online. https://www.consilium.europa.eu/en/press/press-releases/2022/10/04/dsa-council-gives-final-approval-to-the-protection-of-users-rights-online/#:~:text=The%20DSA%20defines%20clear%20responsibilities%20and%20accountability%20for,%28VLOPs%29%20and%20very%20large%20online%20search%20engines%20%28VLOSEs%29. Accessed 7 Feb 2023
39. Data Protection Commission: Decision of the Data Protection Commission made pursuant to Section 113 of the Data Protection Act, 2018 and Articles 60 and 65 of the General Data Protection Regulation. https://noyb.eu/sites/default/files/2023-01/DPCDecision_Facebook.pdf. Accessed 7 Feb 2023
40. EDPB: Guidelines 05/2020 on consent under Regulation 2016/679, pp. 7–29 https://edpb.europa.eu/sites/default/files/files/file1/edpb_guidelines_202005_consent_en.pdf. Accessed 7 Feb 2023
41. European Commission: Communication from the Commission to the European Parliament, the Council, the European Economic and Social Committee and the Committee of the Regions, Commission work programme 2023: A Union standing firm and united, 18.10.2022 COM (2022) 548 final, p. 6. com_2022_548_3_en.pdf (europa.eu). Accessed 7 Feb 2023
42. Vigkos, A., Bevacqua, D., Turturro, L., et al.: European commission, directorate-general for communications networks, content and technology. In: VR/AR Industrial Coalition: Strategic Paper. Publications Office of the European Union (2022). https://data.europa.eu/doi/10.2759/197536. Accessed 7 Feb 2023

43. European Commission: People, technologies & infrastructure – Europe's plan to thrive in the metaverse I Blog of Commissioner Thierry Breton, 14 September 2022. https://ec.europa.eu/commission/presscorner/detail/en/STATEMENT_22_5525. Accessed 7 Feb 2023

44. European Commission: Communication from the Commission to the European Parliament, The Council, The European Economic and Social Committee and the Committee of the Regions, A Digital Decade for children and youth: the new European strategy for a better internet for kids (BIK+). Brussels 11 May 2022. COM(2022) 212 final. https://eur-lex.europa.eu/legal-content/EN/TXT/PDF/?uri=CELEX:52022DC0212&from=EN. Accessed 7 Feb 2023

45. European Commission: Register of CommissionDocument, SEC(2023)2445. https://ec.europa.eu/transparency/documents-register/api/files/SEC(2023)2445_0/090166e5f75e5855?rendition=false. Accessed 7 Feb 2023

46. European Parliament: Loot boxes in online games and their effect on consumers, in particular young consumers. https://www.europarl.europa.eu/RegData/etudes/STUD/2020/652727/IPOL_STU(2020)652727_EN.pdf. Accessed 7 Feb 2023

47. Fiedler, T.: EU throws party in €387K metaverse—and hardly anyone turns up, Politico. https://www.politico.eu/article/eu-threw-e387k-meta-gala-nobody-came-big-tech/. Accessed 1 Feb 2023

48. Geppert, T., Deml, S., Sturzenegger, D., Ebert, N.: Trusted execution environments: applications and organizational challenges. Frontiers Comput. Sci., 3 (2022). https://www.frontiersin.org/articles/10.3389/fcomp.2022.930741/full. Accessed 7 Feb 2023

49. Gupta, A.: Dangers of smart or internet-connected toys you need to be aware of, TheWindowsClub. https://www.thewindowsclub.com/dangers-of-smart-or-internet-connected-toys. Accessed 7 Feb 2023

50. Huddleston, Jr. T.: This 29-year-old book predicted the 'metaverse'—and some of Facebook's plans are eerily similar, CNBC. https://www.cnbc.com/2021/11/03/how-the-1992-sci-fi-novel-snow-crash-predicted-facebooks-metaverse.html. Accessed 7 Feb 2023

51. ICO: Age appropriate design: a code of practice for online services, pp. 5–43. https://ico.org.uk/for-organisations/guide-to-data-protection/ico-codes-of-practice/age-appropriate-design-a-code-of-practice-for-online-services. Accessed 7 Feb 2023

52. ICO: Privacy Enhancing Technologies: Draft anonymisation, pseudonymisation and privacy enhancing technologies guidance, pp. 3–30. https://ico.org.uk/media/about-the-ico/consultations/4021464/chapter-5-anonymisation-pets.pdf. Accessed 7 Feb 2023

53. ICO: What are the rules about an ISS and consent? https://ico.org.uk/for-organisations/guide-to-data-protection/guide-to-the-general-data-protection-regulation-gdpr/children-and-the-uk-gdpr/what-are-the-rules-about-an-iss-and-consent/. Accessed 7 Feb 2023

54. ICO: What do we need to consider when choosing a basis for processing children's personal data? https://ico.org.uk/for-organisations/guide-to-data-protection/guide-to-the-general-data-protection-regulation-gdpr/children-and-the-uk-gdpr/what-do-we-need-to-consider-when-choosing-a-basis-for-processing-children-s-personal-data/#a2. Accessed 7 Feb 2023

55. Kabelka, L.: MEPs sceptical on EU proposal to fight online child sexual abuse, EURACTIV. https://www.euractiv.com/section/digital/news/meps-sceptical-on-eu-proposal-to-fight-online-child-sexual-abuse/. Accessed 7 Feb 2023

56. Lomas, N.: Europe wants to shape the future of virtual worlds with rules and taxes. TechCrunch, 14 September 2022. https://techcrunch.com/2022/09/14/eu-metaverse-virtual-worlds-tax/. Accessed 7 Feb 2023

57. Meta: What is the Metaverse? https://about.meta.com/what-is-the-metaverse/. Accessed 7 Feb 2023

58. di Pietro, R., Cresci, S.:Metaverse: security and privacy issues (2021). https://doi.org/10.1109/TPSISA52974.2021.00032

59. ProvsCons: Is Metaverse Owned by Facebook? https://provscons.com/is-metaverse-owned-by-facebook/#:~:text=Facebook%20%28Meta%29%20doesn%E2%80%99t%20own%20M etaverse.%20In%20fact%2C%20in,nobody%20owns%20and%20will%20ever%20own% 20the%20Metaverse. Accessed 7 Feb 2023
60. Ravenscraft, E.: What Is the Metaverse, Exactly? Wired. https://www.wired.com/story/what-is-the-metaverse/. Accessed 7 Feb 2023
61. Stolton, S.: Vestager: Metaverse poses new competition challenges, Politico. https://www.pol itico.eu/article/metaverse-new-competition-challenges-margrethe-vestager/. Accessed 7 Feb 2023 and EU's Vestager wants free movement between virtual worlds, Politico Pro Alert, 21 March 2023
62. UNICEF: What is the UN Convention on Child Rights. https://www.unicef.org.uk/what-we-do/un-convention-child-rights/. Accessed 7 Feb 2023
63. UNCTAD: Guidelines for Consumer Protection. https://unctad.org/topic/competition-and-consumer-protection/un-guidelines-for-consumer-protection. Accessed 7 Feb 2023
64. Walker, D.: Hackers can 'talk to your children' through connected toys. https://www.itpro.co.uk/security/29941/hackers-can-talk-to-your-children-through-connected-toys. Accessed 7 Feb 2023
65. Wiles, J.: What Is a Metaverse? And should you be buying in? https://www.gartner.com/en/articles/what-is-a-metaverse. Accessed 7 Feb 2023
66. The Metaverse has the option to introduce differing thresholds for the age at which an individual is deemed a child

Indirect References

67. ENISA definition cited from ICO: Privacy Enhancing Technologies: Draft anonymisation, pseudonymisation and privacy enhancing technologies guidance, p. 4
68. Gentile, D., Swing, E., Lim, C., Khoo, A.: Video game playing, attention problems, and impulsiveness: evidence of bidirectional causality. Psychology of Popular Media and Culture, 1 as cited in European Parliament: Loot boxes in online games and their effect on consumers, in particular young consumers (2012). https://www.europarl.europa.eu/RegData/etudes/STUD/2020/652727/IPOL_STU(2020)652727_EN.pdf. Accessed 7 Feb 2023
69. King, D.L., Delfabbro, P.H.: The convergence of gambling and monetised gaming activities. Current Opin. Behav. Sci. 31, 32–36 (2020). As cited in European Parliament.: Loot boxes in online games and their effect on consumers, in particular young consumers (2020). https://www.europarl.europa.eu/RegData/etudes/STUD/2020/652727/IPOL_STU(2020)652727_EN.pdf. Accessed 7 Feb 2023
70. Lobel, A., Engels, R.C., Stone, L.L., Burk, W.J., Granic, I.: Video gaming and children's psychosocial wellbeing: a longitudinal study. Journal of youth and adolescence 46(4), 884–897. As cited in European Parliament.: Loot boxes in online games and their effect on consumers, in particular young consumers. https://www.europarl.europa.eu/RegData/etudes/STUD/2020/652727/IPOL_STU(2020)652727_EN.pdf. Accessed 7 Feb 2023
71. Sunstein, C.R.: Probability neglect: emotions, worst cases, and law. Yale Law J. 112(1), 61–107 (2002). As cited in European Parliament: Loot boxes in online games and their effect on consumers, in particular young consumers. https://www.europarl.europa.eu/RegData/etudes/STUD/2020/652727/IPOL_STU(2020)652727_EN.pdf. Accessed 7 Feb 2023
72. Zendle, D., Meyer, R., Over, H.: Adolescents and loot boxes: links with problem gambling and motivations for purchase. Roy. Soc. Open Sci. 6(6), 190049 (2019). As cited in as cited in European Parliament: Loot boxes in online games and their effect on consumers, in particular young consumers. https://www.europarl.europa.eu/RegData/etudes/STUD/2020/652727/IPOL_STU(2020)652727_EN.pdf. Accessed 7 Feb 2023

Home Alone? Exploring the Geographies of Digitally-Mediated Privacy Practices at Home During the COVID-19 Pandemic

Kim Cheetham[1] and Ola Michalec[2]([✉])

[1] Bristol, England
[2] Bristol Cyber Security Group, University of Bristol, Bristol, England
ola.michalec@bristol.ac.uk

Abstract. During the COVID-19 pandemic, digital technologies have enabled work, education, community activity, and access to healthcare to be situated within our homes. These emerging applications call for a renewed focus on the geographies of online privacy. Thus, this research aims to **explore the geographies of digitally-mediated privacy practices at home during the COVID-19 lockdown** through the method of qualitative in-depth interviews with the lay-users of the Internet. Using Social Practice Theory, the paper explores contextual, collective and spatial dimensions of privacy. In particular, the paper explores how increased use of digital technologies at home during the COVID-19 lockdown has reconfigured practices of self-disclosure, data-sharing and protection of private spaces. First, the paper argues that the use of new work tools, the re-purposing of work tools for social means, and the use of personal devices for work functions, have all affected people's ability to maintain boundaries between their work and personal lives. Second, the paper uncovers how public health concerns during the pandemic mobilised the collective dimensions of privacy, countering the popular belief that privacy is an individualistic concern. Taken together, these findings point at reorienting digital geographies of privacy towards the people and spaces 'behind' the screen.

Keywords: Privacy · Social Practice Theory · Lockdown · digital mundane · work from home

1 Introduction

The global COVID-19 pandemic—dubbed a 'great accelerator' of digital transformation [3]–has lead to the adoption of numerous emerging technology trends. Social distancing and 'lockdown' measures have created the need for home accessibility, leading to people interacting with online 'universities of the future' and

---

K. Cheetham—Independent Researcher.
Supported by the REPHRAIN National Research Centre on Privacy, Harm Reduction and Adversarial Influence Online.
Paper type: Full paper, original research, student paper.

K. Rannenberg et al. (Eds.): APF 2023, LNCS 13888, pp. 109–141, 2024.
https://doi.org/10.1007/978-3-031-61089-9_6

work-from-home 'officeless firms', maintaining health and well-being through 'eHealth systems', receiving policy updates from social-media posts of 'digital governments', and logging day-to-day activities using contact tracing systems [20,23,25,71]. The proponents of this shift to digitally-mediated services have reported benefits in work efficiency, citizen engagement, and entrepreneurial inclinations [12,30]. However, others stress that although COVID-19 has offered a glimpse of a possible digital future, crisis management is not equal to 'time travel' and the adoption of digital technologies at home may reconfigure society in ways we cannot yet envision [14]. Cross-disciplinary work finds that the COVID-19 pandemic has amplified existing risks and harms associated with digital technologies including the 'digital divide', criminal opportunities, and market failures (such as 'price gouging' from hand sanitizer merchants on Amazon) [6,49,56]. This paper serves as an exploratory study of the digitally-mediated privacy practices performed in the home during the COVID-19 lockdown. Theoretically, it brings attention to the spatial, contextual and collective dimensions of privacy, pointing at the people and spaces behind the digital screens.

The home is protected as a private space in traditional privacy legislation across Europe. The European Convention on Human Rights asserts that 'everyone has the right to respect for his private and family life, his home and his correspondence' [16]. Yet, since the introduction of electronic and digital technologies to homes, the home has served as a focal point for the interaction between technology and privacy—from the wiretapping of phone conversations in the early 1960s [52] to the contemporary issues of Intimate Partner Violence threats in 'smart homes' [63,68]. Situating sensing, quantifying and monitoring technologies within the home results in an increased capacity to observe actions regarded as private, listen in on conversations thought to be private, collect and exchange information thought to be private, and interpret physiological responses viewed as private [52]. Furthermore, there is the potential for organisations providing digital tools to derive power from their panoptic access to an individual's histories, activities, communications, thoughts, and proclivities [52]. This is a cause for alarm when users are consenting to giving these private things away unknowingly, or through an all-or-nothing and non-autonomous choice [5].

Internet technologies positioned within the home—whether for work, education, commerce, health, well-being, or entertainment—routinely require users to make choices about their informational privacy. The character of these everyday choices is different from those addressed in previous off-line privacy research, due to the volume of data collection opportunities and people's capacity to meaningfully consent to a privacy setting [69]. Any change to the number and variety of privacy decisions that users are having to make is of interest because privacy concern is *adaptive* and once an intrusion becomes part of the common fabric of our daily lives, we become less concerned about it [22]. Lockdowns have highlighted a conflict between the need to maintain a flourishing life and the need to protect public health. This conflict necessitates an understanding of to what extent these needs have led to the adoption of new technology practices and how these practices are reconfiguring the notion of privacy [2].

As such, the research tackles the following questions:

- How has the COVID-19 pandemic impacted people's privacy protective practices?
- How has the COVID-19 pandemic impacted people's self-disclosure practices?
- How has the COVID-19 pandemic impacted people's data-sharing practices?

Through a qualitative analysis based on 18 semi-structured interviews with internet lay-users, this research aims to **explore the geographies of digitally-mediated privacy practices at home during the COVID-19 pandemic**. The use of Social Practice Theory (SPT) [60] enabled the identification of privacy practices as well as the associated methods and meanings.

2   Conceptual Discussions

The following section will present a brief overview of the concept of privacy; highlighting multiple definitions and key research questions concerning scholars over several decades. Following the conventions of qualitative social sciences [32], the aim of the literature review is to present a history of "turns" within the field, i.e., how definitions of privacy changed over time. The authors conducted the review by engaging with the foundational papers on privacy across disciplines, paying attention to theoretical outputs offering novel frameworks. One of the first conceptualisations of privacy in relation to everyday technologies goes back to the 1890s when Warren [73] considered the camera, and its potential for instantaneous photographs, as a reason to grant a legal right to privacy—the 'right to be let alone' [73]. Philosophical debates have centred around the questions: 'what is privacy?'; 'is it a necessary human value?'; if so, 'is it a human value that is inherently distinct from other human values?'; if so, 'why is it so valuable?'.

Schoeman [57] considers the three questions above in depth in his 1984 anthology *Philosophical Dimensions of Privacy*. Considering the question 'what is privacy?': depending on the academic discipline, Schoeman writes that privacy can be understood as a *claim, entitlement* or *right* of an individual to determine what information about themselves may be communicated to others [57]. Alternatively, the measure of *control* that an individual has over: information about themselves; intimacies of personal identity; or who has sensory access to them [1, 75]. These conceptualisations all have their respective criticisms centering around their static nature in the face of changing privacy planes. In order to transcend the definitional debates and focus on empirical experiences of privacy, this paper takes the approach of Solove to consider privacy pluralistically. In this understanding, privacy is simultaneously collective, contextual and spatial [4, 24, 65]. This approach is flexible enough to accommodate the evolving debate on privacy in the light of COVID-19-induced adoption of digital technologies.

2.1   Privacy is Collective

Privacy is a collective concept in two senses: the interpersonal and the political [42]. With regards to the interpersonal dimension, privacy is key to social interactions [1], its understandings are products of our own social and cultural development [41], and, finally, privacy is an attribute not only of individuals but also of groups and organisations [52]. Moreover, privacy is a political concept for three reasons [42]: people have a common right to privacy [52], privacy supports and is supported by democratic political systems [52], privacy is a societal good because it is increasingly difficult for any one person to have privacy unless everyone is granted a similar minimum level of privacy [42]. These emerging collectivist conceptualisations counter the popular notion that privacy is an individualised concern and cannot be mobilised in a way to build communities or enact political change [9].

2.2   Privacy is Contextual

The collective nature of privacy means that privacy management is not just negotiated at an individual level, but between many individuals, often at a group or community level, in a variety of social and practical contexts. To further that argument, scholars such as Altman, Margulis and Solove [1,40,65] believe that privacy is so dependent on a specific context that it is impossible to develop a one-size-fits-all conceptualisation [64]. What is considered sensitive, and therefore worthy of protection, obfuscation or concealment, varies depending on a range of contextual factors. These could relate to the information usage, spatial setting, and the relationship between the receiver and the sender of the information [45]. For example, situational increases in privacy concern may be triggered by external cues that signal a lack of privacy such as targeted advertisements [33] and situational decreases in privacy concern may occur in response to technological protections such as private browsing mode [27]. Furthermore, privacy has temporal contextuality in that the sensitivity of information may change over time, such as an individual's willingness to disclose their age [45]. Collectively held practices of defining, preserving and subverting sensitivity evolve over time, in response to historical, cultural and geographic influences. Nissenbaum's theory of contextual integrity posits that information technologies violate privacy when the information flows cease to conform with contextual information norms [48]. Using this contextual perspective, privacy can be understood as a process of managing boundaries across different social contexts, which may shift, collapse or reemerge as social circumstances change [76]. Who has the power to make these boundaries visible and negotiable is an inherently political question, therefore worthy of exploration for critical social scientists, including digital geographers.

2.3   Privacy is Spatial

So far, the literature on privacy has emphasised the need to investigate this concept as a collective phenomenon situated in a social context [15,43,48]. As the notion of 'social context' has spatial attributes, it benefits from a cross-disciplinary reading involving human geography theorists. Geography brings attention to the social construction, fluidity and instability of places, spaces and boundaries between them [35]. Operating across a range of scales, from investigating the mundane activities inside smart homes [36,54], the discourses of smart cities [44,53], to the local embeddedness of seemingly global cyberspace(s) [19], geographers question assumptions held about the relationships between people and places. Within the context of digital privacy, geography offers three core contributions. First, that the private-public distinction is not a reflection of a 'natural order', rather, it is an expression of power [35]. Private-public is not a clear-cut binary; rather: "a [private/public] space only gets meaning in context: in relation to the people in it and in relation to its outside; 'home' and 'public space' are therefore two sides of a coin" [35, p. 45]. Second, social identities are constructed in spatial settings [35]. Understanding privacy as a freedom to shape one's identity in a given context (e.g. work, school, domestic) allows making a distinction between researching private practices and private spaces. Finally, geographers argue that researching privacy concerns in spatial settings (e.g. smart homes, smart cities) should move beyond procedural concerns ('is the connection encrypted? Are datasets anonymised?') and, instead, ask: 'whose interests and logics are materialised by the creation of 'smart' spaces?', 'who has the power negotiate the boundaries of digital privacy and publicity?' [39]. Here one should note that although the theoretical critiques of 'smart' spaces are ample across critical social sciences, they still lack solid grounding in lay-user experiences [31]. As such, the enmeshing of cyber and physical spaces calls for further research on embodied experiences of lay-users [13].

2.4   Privacy in the Pandemic

Widespread fears of loneliness, contagion and illness are affecting the ways we interact with technologies, and technology is being used adaptively to alleviate stress and anxiety [34]. [46] Nabity-Grover et al. have found that people are engaging in self-disclosure on social media to stay connected with others during the pandemic. They theorise that during the COVID-19 pandemic, perceptions of which disclosures serve the public good and which are considered socially inappropriate have altered [46]. For example, the sharing of medical data, traditionally regarded as sensitive, is being encouraged, while disclosing information on social gatherings has shifted to the private realm over the course of lockdown restrictions. To explain this shift, they use the term *'inside-out, outside-in'* and attribute its existence to the performance of *social calculus* (making decisions based on the perceptions of others) in addition to *privacy calculus* (making decisions based on perceived personal benefits) [46].

There is a growing body of work researching the privacy of contact tracing apps. [37] report the widespread acceptance of contact tracing in the UK and suggest that acceptance increases when measures are specifically time-limited and come with opt-out clauses or other assurances of privacy. Furthermore, Vitak and Zimmer [70] use violation of contextual integrity to explain why the contact tracing proposals of Apple and Google were largely considered acceptable by users, whereas the initial suggestions of a centralised and government-led approach were met with strong negative attitudes.

3   Conceptual Framework

This paper draws on Social Practice Theory (SPT) to conceptualise digitally-mediated privacy practices in the time of COVID-19 [60]. A practice can be defined as the integration of elements resulting in a structured arrangement of what people do in a given context. Drawing on Shove [60], these elements fall into one of three empirically helpful categories: *materials* (including things, technologies, and tangible physical entities), *competences* (including skill, know-how and techniques) and *meanings* (including symbolic meanings, ideas and aspirations). A focus on practice allows a researcher to do more than just determine what participants are thinking, facilitating consideration of how practice elements circulate, and how skills are being continually deferred and re-framed, resulting in an interactive, complex and dynamic process that is continually performed [66]. Dourish et al. [15] perceive privacy as a continual accomplishment that is perpetually being produced and reproduced, rather than a static need that can be 'set up' through a control panel and then left alone. They also characterise it as a pervasive element of everyday settings, which extends beyond the boundaries of any technology system and incorporates organisational arrangements and practices as well as the physical environment [15].

When used within the context of technology, SPT decenters technology and stresses that technology is just a piece of a bigger story [66]. This is particularly relevant when considering the concept of privacy as it far out-dates the modern technologies that are our current concerns (consider Warren [73] being alarmed about the privacy of early cameras). In the view of Dourish [15], technology is just a site at which social meaning can be produced. Thus technology is something that plays a part in helping or hindering our desires for privacy, but privacy does not originate from technology, and this decentering is a key motivation for the use of SPT.

In this view, pro- or anti-privacy actions are not seen as the result of people's attitudes, values and beliefs, constrained by various contextual 'barriers', but as embedded within and occurring as part of social practices [72]. In turn, the performance of various social practices is seen as part of the routine accomplishment of what people take to be 'normal ways of life' [58]. Individuals are removed from centre stage and instead become the 'carriers' of social practices [51]. Importantly, SPT raises a series of radically different questions about how best to protect privacy. The focus shifts to understanding how people maintain and routinise practices in temporal and spatial dimensions.

Social Practice Theory (SPT) has been broadly applied by scholars across geography and sociology as a means to move beyond 'behaviourist' accounts of planet-friendly living [59]. Acknowledging that social practices form at the intersection of material affordances, social meanings and competences, scholars like Shove [60], Watson [74] and Evans [17] counter the popular belief of pro-environmental actions solely resulting from individual rational attitudes and choices. The past two decades have been witness to "a practice turn" in social theory [11], with SPT applied to a range of geographical settings, from water and energy consumption practices [28,67], cycling [8] or grassroots activism [21].

This article presents an opportunity to apply social practice theory in a novel context of digitally-mediated experiences of privacy.

4 Methods

4.1 Research Design: Semi-structured Interviews

A set of semi-structured interviews were conducted with 18 UK-based participants listed in Table 1 during February and March of 2021. The inclusion criteria required that the participant is an internet 'lay-person', defined for this specific purpose as a person with a minimum capability of being able to use an internet search engine, but who is not an IT professional. A proportion of the interviews (n = 11) were transcribed by the first author and the remaining (n = 9) were transcribed by a professional transcription service. This project received internal ethical approval from the University of Bristol research committee (reference number 97842).

Table 1. Interview participant demographics

Participant	Age	Gender	Location	Occupation	Education
Rachel (pilot)	62	F	Nottinghamshire	Administration	Undergraduate
Michael	20	M	Leicestershire	Student (Design)	Undergraduate
Jordan	22	M	Nottinghamshire	Student (Engineer)	Undergraduate
Margaret	78	F	Essex	Retired (Teacher)	Postgraduate
Ruth	55	F	Leicestershire	Homemaker	Undergraduate
Greg	21	M	Bristol	Student (Computer Science)	Undergraduate
Edward	22	M	Nottinghamshire	Student (Law)	Undergraduate
Claire	52	F	Berkshire	Technical Writer	Undergraduate
Phillip	81	M	Essex	Retired (Chemist)	High School
Lois	23	F	Cardiff	PhD Student (Biology)	Postgraduate
Luke	21	M	Bristol	Student (Maths)	Undergraduate
Emily	22	F	Derby	Marketing	Undergraduate
Julie	59	F	Essex	Administration	High School
Simon	21	M	Bristol	Student (Medic)	Undergraduate
Archie	20	M	Bristol	Student (Computer Science)	Undergraduate
Sarah	56	F	Nottinghamshire	Homemaker	Postgraduate
Miranda	22	F	Bristol	Student (Vet)	Undergraduate
Joe	21	M	Bristol	Student (Biology)	Undergraduate
Hollie	32	F	Nottingham	Teacher	Undergraduate

The interview participants constitute a non-random and non-representative sample with recruitment being performed in a purposive [55] and snowball [26] manner; i.e., through a digital poster displayed via university social media and word-of-mouth recommendations. The sample was purposive because although participants were chosen on a basis of convenience, it was balanced on a range of variables and participants were purposely selected as information-rich and able to yield insights and in-depth understanding rather than empirical generalisations [50]. Snowball sampling occurred in that the participants were asked to identify individuals that they knew that they thought could meaningfully add to the discussion topic. Due to the exploratory nature of the study, we make no claims to generalisability and recommend further comparative research investigating privacy practices at home across various demographics (e.g., professions or age groups).

The interviews were performed *actively*, meaning that the interviewer and respondent can both be considered as active agents in the construction of the content of the interview [55]. Examples of this included: helping participants better understand their own answers by rephrasing their answers back to them; offering interviewer's thoughts and feelings on privacy in order to create an environment conducive to intimate disclosure; and providing participants' with scenarios that the interviewer thought might test their position on an issue, to better understand the limits of their situational understanding. Framing the interviews in this way elicited more latent themes and allowed a deeper understanding of the participants responses [55] but required careful facilitation to minimise bias. Furthermore, respondents were not corrected when they gave incorrect or incoherent information or did not produce an answer that was an obvious fit with the research question. This aided in setting the participant at ease and the misconceptions, misunderstandings, and general musings of participants were a useful basis for latent analysis. Interviews ranged in duration from 50 min to 1 h 40 min and were conducted using Voice Over Internet Protocol (VOIP) tools.

Development of interview questions began with the overarching research aim: **"to explore the geographies of digitally-mediated privacy practices at home during the COVID-19 pandemic"**. To make sense of the complex nature of practices, social practice theorists argue that analysts must investigate the four tenets of: materials, competences, meanings and connections [66]. These four tenets became the main areas of inquiry and were expanded into topics of interest which, could then be further developed into interview questions (for further details, please see Appendix C). The final topic guide covered the following (for further details, please see Appendix A):

1. The participant's current internet tool usage and usual information disclosure patterns at home.
2. Changes in the participant's internet tool usage and information disclosure patterns that have occurred during the COVID-19 pandemic.
3. Actions that the participant takes to protect their privacy since the outbreak of the pandemic.
4. The relative importance of privacy to the participant when compared to other actions in the context of the COVID-19 pandemic.

4.2   Data Analysis: Thematic Analysis

Thematic analysis, 'a method for identifying, analysing, and reporting patterns (themes) within data' [7], was used. It involved organising and describing the data set in rich detail, using themes. Thematic analysis facilitates exploration of a thematic range and the analysis of a social group's knowledge of it, rather than finding a core category and developing theory. The thematic analysis performed was both 'deductive' and 'inductive' [7]. The analysis was driven by a theoretical interest in the area, coding was performed to match the research question, and significant input for codes was taken from previous researchers' work on privacy and formulated before the thematic analysis began (deductive coding). However, new codes were also generated as thematic analysis was performed (inductive coding). A code book with example codes is attached in Appendix B

5   Results and Discussion

5.1   The Blurring of the Work-Life Divide

The first theme of this research concerns participants' experiences of their work-life divide, and the privacy-related discomfort of working from home. Although the practice of working from home is not new, the COVID-19 pandemic restrictions have provided many with a novel opportunity (or, indeed, a requirement) to work from home. The interview data shows that the use of new digital tools, the repurposing of these tools for social means, and the use of personal devices for work functions, has affected participants' privacy practices and led them to conclude that the divide between their work life and their home life has blurred. In addition, when attempting to address these concerns, participants were experiencing privacy stigma.

Negotiating New Tools? The key technologies of concern amongst the participants were found to be business communication platforms and Voice Over Internet Protocol (aka. conference call software). Participants were concerned about the potential for surveillance, disclosure errors and misuse by third-parties. Although neither these tools nor these concerns are new to public debate, for our participants, they presented a novel opportunity to gain first-hand experience of home working or education and associated privacy practices.

Business Communication Technologies. A number of communication technologies were introduced during the COVID-19 pandemic to ensure fluid interactions between employees while working from home. Slack is the most commonly used business communication technology amongst the participants and of the four participants that reported regular use, three had never used this tool before. Some participants express difficulty using the tool, leading to errors, and inhibiting use. Participant Lois reports that she feels "really uncomfortable with using Slack" because the different levels of communication ('channels', organised by team or project, 'threads', for organised side-conversations within channels, and direct-messaging functionality [62]) make it difficult to understand the spatial bounds and persistence of communication. The overlapping of different communication contexts obscures who has access to posts and messages (colleagues? management? HR?), where they can access them, and for what period of time. This uncertainty causes Lois not to use Slack unless she has to (although this is still "nearly every day"). The confusing interactions with the tool also create an environment conducive to mistakes. Participant Emily shared a story about the time that she accidentally sent a message to the wrong Slack channel:

> We have a channel dedicated for non-work related stuff, called The Water Cooler, or something, as a bit of a joke ... and we were talking about something really menial like ice-cream flavours and I accidentally posted "dude, it has got to be mint choc chip" to my project team instead of The Water Cooler chat... I have never been so embarrassed in my life.

The discomfort that Emily feels as a result of this mistake is because the wrong people were the recipients of her self-disclosure, which despite being "menial" information, is more intimate than the norms of a work relationship demand. The context of the information flow—a joke post on a 'for fun' Slack channel to co-workers with which she had a friendly relationship—is altered, leading to a violation of contextual integrity and resultant feelings of discomfort and embarrassment. The absence of a social script (should Emily delete the message? Laugh it off? Ignore it?) in these novel situations makes it particularly challenging to adapt and flourish in a remote workplace.

Participants are also suspicious of surveillance while using business communication technologies. For example, both Lois and Emily are unaware of whether their bosses can see their communication in group channels and private messages and admit that this creates a chilling effect when using the tool (Emily: "I have to watch what I say"). Emily is also conscious that potential data violations by coworkers such as screen-shots and copy-and-pasting mean that the audience of her Slack posts might be wider than she can be aware of. Tools like Slack have been in use for a number of years across workplaces, however, they are far from widely adopted communication platforms. When an organisation assigns a new default informational infrastructure in haste, it misses out on an opportunity to re-establish the ground rules of workplace communication and work-life boundaries.

Indeed, Emily and Lois express that business communication technologies have made them more contactable outside of work hours, reducing the separation between their work- and home-lives, making them more likely to work beyond hours and have a poor work-life balance. As comparatively junior staff members (aged 21 and 22), they feel like they have little choice in the use of these tools. This highlights that employers are yet to fully acknowledge workers' agency (or the lack of such) in the co-creation of digital workplaces. One way to advance this debate would be to shift away from questioning 'how to make lay-users aware of digital privacy?' to 'how can we create environments where lay-users feel empowered to raise privacy concerns?'

Voice Over Internet Protocol. In comparison with business communication technologies, participants appeared more comfortable interacting via VOIP. Participant Joe who explains that it is "just like Facetiming six of my mates at the same time". Despite participants expressing a higher level of familiarity with the tool, they were still keen to share their privacy concerns. These centre around not wanting professional contacts to get a view into their personal lives, and (in the case of participants whose jobs involve offering professional services) wanting to maintain the privacy of their clients. Participants take a number of privacy protective actions such as ensuring that their background is clear when using camera functionalities, and ensuring they are in a private location where they can not be disturbed or overheard.

Participant Hollie feels that, as a primary school teacher, she has to be especially careful in maintaining her work-life divide. The reasons she cites for this are child safeguarding, her own well-being, and the children's educational needs. She sees privacy as a defining component of a student-teacher relationship and explains that it is "something that you are taught about extensively in teacher training". As well as taking steps outside the bounds of the pandemic such as using her middle name instead of her family name on her Facebook profile, she also takes care to ensure that there are no personal items in her background while she is teaching Zoom classes and has moved her desk to give a completely empty screen. Participant Simon, a medical student, has situations in which he has to deal with patient contacts from his room in his shared student house using Microsoft Teams. As a medical professional, he feels the need to take steps to protect his patients' privacy. Simon only takes meetings using headphones, always faces the camera to prevent being overheard, and uses alphanumerical pseudonyms when writing notes that are visible to others. He asserts that he performs these actions because it is "the right thing to do" and because medicine is built on trust, rather than because there is any immediate consequence within his medical school. In addition, Simon expresses a desire to protect his own privacy and is uncomfortable with the idea of his classmates and patients seeing his bedroom:

> *I don't like the fact that people are in my private space... Whenever I am using my camera, I am obviously in my bedroom because that is where my desk is ... That is where I sleep, that is where I relax and therefore there is no privacy ... We actually have to show our beds on camera when we are pretending to interact with replica patients. I completely mind.*

As well as having concerns grounded in identity management (Simon: "I don't want anyone to think I am untidy"), he perceives his bedroom (and more acutely his bed) as a part of his most intimate and private sphere and is uncomfortable sharing these on camera with people with whom he does not hold a close intimate relationship. However, because of the nature of his vocation, he feels unable to action his personal privacy concerns. Furthermore, he feels that any request for more privacy would be met with an unsympathetic "deal with it" response from his medical school. Yet again, an accelerated transition into home-based employment and education seemingly closed down the possibility to negotiate what constitutes a 'good' digital workplace.

Technology Exaptation. The research found that a number of tools and technologies participants previously used for work have been repurposed for social means during the COVID-19 pandemic. This phenomenon is defined here as *technology exaptation*, taking inspiration from the manufacturing use of the term as the ability of a technology to pivot from one use to another without a costly redevelopment process [38]. A prime example of this is the use of Zoom for social events, such as band rehearsals and escape rooms. Lack of access to work equipment has also meant that personal devices such as phones and computers are also being used for work purposes.

All of the participants use VOIP tools for social purposes, and 15 of these had originally used them for work or education purposes. Although Zoom socials have been an integral part of maintaining social connections and mental well-being [34], our paper also suggests that this further blurring of the work-life divide has led to privacy problems such as accidental disclosure. Two respondents (Edward and Luke) reported that they had occasionally accidentally joined professional or educational Zoom meetings with their name still appearing as a nickname from a previous Zoom social—for Luke this was "L-Dog" and for Edward, this was something more "NSFW"[1]. Both participants felt that they had sufficient rapport with their professional connections to laugh this off but were very aware of the potential consequences of actions that they felt were appropriate within a social context but were not in line with their workplace information sharing norms.

One participant, Emily (who works for a small marketing firm) expresses discomfort regarding her personal devices being repurposed for work. She has concerns that this is encroaching on her privacy and well-being. Emily has been using her home devices for work purposes when working from home during the pandemic. Emily chooses to use her work device (a desktop computer) for most tasks but, in cases where this has been unavailable, she has then used her personal device instead. When interacting with clients, the necessity to screen share has exposed her personal browser bookmarks (including indications of what she feels are potentially embarrassing teenage hobbies), as well as her screensaver (a personal photo of her family). Emily feels that it is the responsibility of the company she works for to change its policy to prevent the use of home devices. Although there is no company requirement for her to use her personal device in these circumstances, because there is no ban on the use of these devices, Emily feels obliged to use them if no other equipment is available.

Privacy Stigma. A common thread throughout participants' responses on the theme of work-life divide was of what we term *privacy stigma*. This was evident

---

[1] Internet slang meaning "not suitable for work", used to denote content that is inappropriate for the workplace, usually associated with pornography or violence.

when expressing concerns about the use of new tools (including business communication tools and VOIP) as well as about the repurposing of home devices for work purposes. Although participants often had privacy concerns regarding the way that they are having to perform their work and education during the COVID-19 pandemic, they did not often feel comfortable voicing these concerns to their superiors or education coordinators.

For example, Michael doesn't feel comfortable expressing his privacy concerns to his university in case he is seen as a "bit of a Karen"[2]. Emily fears privacy stigma, believing that her boss would tell her to "suck it up" were she to express concerns over using her personal devices for work purposes.

Some participants were resentful of this privacy stigma. For example, Emily expresses her concern about her employers letting privacy fall by the wayside, saying that "it is a really dangerous road to start going down". However, she reflects that the pandemic situation means that she needs her job and wants her career to progress and therefore isn't about to challenge the status quo.

Although the internet has been awash with recommendations [18] and the NCSC [47] and ICOL [29] have stepped in to provide guidance around security and the protection of client data during the COVID-19 pandemic, this work suggests that not enough consideration is being given to workers' and students' privacy. Since participants are not raising privacy concerns because of their worry about privacy stigma, this research argues that companies and educational institutions transitioning to digital activities have not sufficiently considered their implications for privacy, whether for employees, clients or the environment they work and study from. Going forward, highlighting the adaptive, contextual and collective dimensions of digital privacy will be helpful in addressing it as an ongoing socio-technical negotiation between the concerned stakeholders.

5.2   Collective Dimensions of Privacy in Times of Pandemic

The second central theme of this research concerns the impact that the COVID-19 pandemic has had on privacy practices because of changing collective norms. There has also been a movement towards participants making privacy decisions based on collective, rather than individual, benefits.

Self-disclosure Norms. The COVID-19 pandemic poses a challenge to interpersonal and community interactions [61] and, indicative of this, all of the participants have lost significant access to their usual in-person methods for socialisation and social connection. This research has already suggested that this change has led to the repurposing of work tools for social means (see 5.1). In addition it has also had an effect on self-disclosure. The lack of usual social contact has led to a shift towards sharing more *opinion based content*. Furthermore, there has been a significant change in what topics are now considered socially acceptable

---

[2] Defined by dictionary.com as a pejorative slang term for an obnoxious, entitled middle-aged women who use their privilege to get their way (https://www.dictionary.com/e/slang/karen/).

and not socially acceptable to disclose, for which Nabity Grover [46] coin the phrase *inside-out, outside-in.*

Opinion-Based Content. This research suggests that, during the pandemic, participants are increasingly using social media platforms to post opinion-based content. Participant Claire explains that the Facebook group she is a part of has felt "closer" over the pandemic and she explains that this is because of the opinion-based content that members are sharing. She explained that this opinion sharing gives her a feeling of community membership as well as exposing her to the relationships that she feels she is lacking while being in lockdown in a difficult home situation.

> *It is people really airing their dirty washing ... I am posting stuff on there that I wouldn't want to share with close family ... It is great to get a second opinion and support with issues, as well as really good discussion about all sorts of things, when I have such a lack of diversity of opinion at home.*

However, Joe speaks much more negatively about the increase in opinion-based content that he perceives from his connections on social media.

> *Say if you were watching a sporting event ... instead of emotionally fueled conversations about the referee decisions happening in person, now people take to social media to air their opinions and that can cause some major issues. The stuff I see posted from some of my Facebook friends, directed at [sports professionals] ... No one wants to see that.*

Joe is also critical of opinion-based content outside the bounds of the pandemic, so his reaction to it is not novel to the situation. He finds social media a really uncomfortable place when his connections are sharing opinion-based content, to the point where he takes steps to make himself more comfortable by 'unfriending' friends, colleagues and family who he thinks share too much opinion-based content. However, when asked why he didn't feel the need to post opinion-based content on social media during the pandemic, Joe conceded that he is lucky not to be separated from those friends with whom he can have varied and informative opinion-based discussions. This suggests that the context of a person's home environment might be affecting the degree to which they feel the need to share opinions on social media. People like Joe, whose shared living arrangements gives them varied social contact, may not feel the need to seek online opinion-based discussions. Amongst the participants, 10 are students who have had comparatively busy and varied social setups during the pandemic, and few of them express a need to share opinions online. In contrast, Lois, who as a result of the pandemic is separated from her close family and friends, believes that she is re-posting more opinion-based content than usual to her Instagram Story.

> *With all the political stuff going on in the summer[3], I, like a lot of other people, posted various stories and opinions on my Instagram story because*

---

[3] In reference to action from Black Lives Matter, Extinction Rebellion and womens' safety activists

I think it is a really important issue and I wanted to use my platform. But I can't lie, it probably was partly because everyone was ... Sharing the same stories as the people you are close to kind of feels like indirect communication like a kind of "I see you and agree with you" thing going on that you wouldn't need if you were communicating in person.

Inside-Out, Outside-In. As presented in 2.4, [46] Nabity Grrover et al. suggest that during the COVID-19 pandemic there has been an 'inside-out' shift, with things that did not use to be socially appropriate becoming socially appropriate, and an 'outside-in' shift with things that used to be socially appropriate now being met with vitriol. They posit that this is in part because individuals are performing 'social calculus' [46], i.e. considering the perspectives of others when evaluating the costs and benefits of sharing information [10].

This work provides some evidence for this theory. The participants report that they are increasingly sharing information that they would not normally share, including medical information. For example, Lois disclosed for the first time on social media that she has a rare chronic medical condition, in order to establish a COVID-19 advice sharing platform for people with the same condition. Ruth and Claire are also both part of closed Facebook groups which, although intended for other hobbyist purposes, have become platforms where individuals are discussing their symptoms and vaccination status. This research also shows some evidence of the topic of support shifting 'inside-out', with individuals increasingly offering support to their connections and wider community via self-disclosure on social media. The two instances of this were confined to closed online social groups, such as Ruth posting offers of help to collect food for isolating individuals on her community WhatsApp group chat.

The second consideration is the aspects of self-disclosure that have moved 'outside-in'. Nabity-Grover, Thatcher and Cheung suggest that this may include the sharing of activities such as visiting crowded venues because of fear of a negative reaction from connections [46]. Among our participants, Ruth expressed a change in self-disclosure reminiscent of 'outside-in'. She feels uncomfortable sharing her home situation indiscriminately on social media. She explains that she does not want to appear self-entitled and would be uncomfortable if her disclosure was to be seen by connections who did not share her fortune:

I feel like I can't post about things like [my university age children] being at home at the moment as I know so many people haven't been so lucky and I don't want to seem like I am pushing it in anybody's face.

However, in contrast to the suggestions of Nabity-Grover, Cheung and Thatcher, a number of participants explain that the reason that they are not following their normal interaction pattern of sharing information about their activities is because they have "nothing to share", rather than because they are wary of a negative reaction. This makes the 'outside-in' aspect of the theory difficult to validate using the research data. Instead, the data suggests that the lack of disclosure surrounding activities is less a change in social norms, and more a practical implication of lockdown lifestyle.

Societal Benefit. This second sub-theme considers changes to people privacy practices because of perceived benefits to society. The most prevalent example of this is the downloading of COVID-19 monitoring technologies. Participants, in and out of the bounds of the pandemic, are increasingly attempting to wield their data for social good, and some are making an attempt to meaningfully choose recipients of their data based on the perceived effect and contribution that the recipient organisation makes to society.

COVID-19 Monitoring Technologies. The two main COVID-19 monitoring technologies investigated in this work are the NHS COVID-19 app[4] and the ZOE COVID-19 Symptom Tracker[5] There is widespread acceptance and uptake of the NHS COVID-19 app amongst the participants with 16 using the app. Use of the ZOE Symptom Tracker is less widespread, but of the 12 that are aware of the app, 10 are users. This research suggests that there are different reasons for using each of these apps. The 8 participants who are regular users of the ZOE Symptom Tracker all gave reasons for use that revolve around its capacity to help other people and achieve societal benefit (Sarah: "It feels like I am actually doing something"). Although a proportion of the participants are also using the NHS COVID-19 app for its potential for societal benefit, this was more likely to be performed begrudgingly because of feelings of duty and obligation (Michael: "It is the bare minimum you should do, as a social duty"). Furthermore, 6 of the participants provided reasons for use of the NHS COVID-19 app that were more individualistic, such as Luke admitting "I downloaded it so that I was allowed in to the pub".

There were also differences in the way that people interact with these two apps. Users of the ZOE Symptom Tracker explain that they are happy to disclose sensitive medical information that they would not normally disclose, as well as a number ($n = 5$) committing to reporting these symptoms daily which, over a year, is a significant commitment as well as a large quantity of data. Of those participants using the app, six explained that they would disclose this data to any medical study, whereas two said they would only do it in a health emergency that was similar in nature to COVID-19. In comparison, four participants explain that although they have downloaded the NHS COVID-19 app, they rarely urn their Bluetooth on, or have downloaded the app but never interact with it. This suggests that although some individuals are willing and able to download the app, their commitment to its use is not that strong. The contrast between the two tools is evident in Lois's response:

ZOE feels like I am proactively doing something that helps people ... I only remember about [the NHS app] after realising I've had my Bluetooth off for two weeks, it is just not on my radar until I am somewhere with a QR code.

---

[4] A voluntary contact-tracing app provided by the NHS for use in England in Wales (see https://covid19.nhs.uk/).

[5] Epidemiological research app developed by researchers in King's College London (see https://covid.joinzoe.com/).

The different levels of commitment to sharing personal data that these technologies invoke may be due to how participants perceive their potential for societal good. A further factor influencing whether participants chose to download these apps was their level of trust in the parties that run them, rather than perceptions of personal or societal gain. The organisation behind the ZOE symptom tracker is known to be a medical and educational institution (Claire: "It might make me a bit of a snob but I trust it because it is a university"), whereas the distrust of some individuals towards government, was evident in some participants perception of the tracker as a government control mechanism (Edward: "I just don't think the government should have that role").

Vitak and Zimmer attribute the widespread acceptance of the NHS COVID-19 app to its maintenance of contextual integrity. They posit that contextual integrity is not violated because participants see contact tracing apps as having the same information flow as other non-COVID-related surveillance apps such as navigation and fitness trackers. This research suggests that although there is wide-spread acceptance of the NHS COVID-19 app, a number of participants were highly concerned about it and perceived it as very different from these other suggested technologies. Thus their decision to download the app was often strongly against their privacy concerns and due to a sense of civic duty, rather than because they did not have privacy concerns. These concerns revolved around the aforementioned perceptions of the 'correct' role of government and the potential for expanded and continued use post-pandemic. Those participants with strong privacy concerns surrounding the app were able to 'trade' these off against the social needs to save lives, and to prevent unnecessary national economic loss. This exposes a gap between individuals privacy attitudes and actions which, without knowledge of the underlying social context, may appear paradoxical. Michael typifies this decision-making process when he explains:

Literally no other circumstance would make me do this. But my privacy has to be nothing in the face of lives ... That is not a hard decision.

Despite steps being taken to make the second version of the NHS COVID-19 app much more protective of its users privacy, the participants were often unaware of the technicalities of the app, meaning that concern surrounding the version 1 app often continued into concern surrounding the version 2 app, with Lois worrying "well it is still a government thing, right?". Thus although these participants concerns were sometimes unfounded (Julie: "I don't want Boris[6] seeing me go to the shop"), their perceptions of the information flow, whether these were correct or not, violated their perceptions of privacy as contextual integrity.

---

[6] The UK's Prime Minister at the time of writing.

6 Future Research and Conclusions

6.1 Further Research and Practice Recommendations

It is vital to understand the privacy impact of the interchangeable use of personal and company devices, as well as the lack of agency by people to negotiate privacy boundaries between them and their employers. Following the COVID-19 lockdowns, it is becoming a common practice for companies to allow remote working and enable Bring-Your-Own-Device. The effects on the right to privacy of those practices is an important matter to consider.

We hope this work moves beyond a conceptual remit and will have practical applications. An improved understanding of privacy practices can prompt employers and educators to draw better boundaries between work and personal life and aid privacy engineers with considering novel privacy-preserving features. We outline three key recommendations:

- Both software developers and employers should introduce privacy-preserving mechanisms in workplace/education ICT, which enable protection of employees' and students physical environments, personal identities and relationships outside of work/education.
- Workplaces ought to introduce policies establishing boundaries of communication at work, setting expectations regarding appropriate response time and meeting scheduling.
- Policymakers ought to monitor the development of remote working trends and the associated tracking technologies, so that the provision for workers' rights reflects the adoption of contemporary ICT.

We also recommend that further research explores the evolving technological and legal context of home working and education, i.e. the emergence of worker surveillance tech and obfuscation mechanisms. Finally, future research could validate our initial findings by conducting a comparative survey of privacy practices at home, highlighting similarities and difference across ages, professions and cultures.

6.2 Conclusions

The paper concludes that the 2020 COVID-19 lockdown prompted a re-framing of privacy practices at home: privacy emerged as a collective right as people's perception of privacy is influenced by their relationship with employers, fellow employees, and their respective perspectives on the use of the technology.

Below, we summarise the findings as responses to our initial research questions:

- *How has the COVID-19 pandemic impacted people's privacy protective practices?* While participants took effort to learn and negotiate new ICT tools, they had limited agency over their privacy and experienced privacy stigma while discussing their concerns.

- *How has the COVID-19 pandemic impacted people's self-disclosure practices?* In the absence of social script or employer's guidance, the events of accidental or inappropriate disclosure led to embarrassment and pose a significant barrier to professional fulfillment.
- *How has the COVID-19 pandemic impacted people's data-sharing practices?* Participants were overall happy to share personal data when they regarded it as civic duty.

We offer number of theoretical and empirical contributions to the field of digital geography vis-a-vis privacy research. First, we adds to the patchwork of cross-disciplinary literature seeking to understand the role of the COVID-19 pandemic in shaping our society. Second, we argue that an exploration of privacy practices within the novel context of COVID-19 will enrich the debates on collective and spatial dimensions of privacy. This is an important dimension to explore, as the majority of privacy studies consider the technology (network or device) or individual's cognition (attitudes, perceptions or biases) as a unit of analysis.

In exploring the digitally-mediated privacy practices of Internet lay-users during COVID-19 pandemic, this paper offered a number of empirical findings. First, there is an emerging evidence that the pervasiveness of digital communication technologies as well as technology exaptation in our everyday work and social lives has raised new privacy concerns surrounding the blurring of the work and life boundaries. Second, we posit that these novel concerns are not yet addressed due to the privacy stigma experienced by employees who do not have the capability to negotiate privacy boundaries with their managers. Third, we uncovered the collective motivations for participants' privacy-protective and self-disclosure practices, countering a popular notion that privacy is a matter of an individualist trade-off.

The technological, social and political change caused by the pandemic has led to the situation of many of our public interactions within the private home, creating opposing social contexts that need to be navigated. Therefore this work seeks to contribute to a broad understanding of digital privacy, not simply as a technical phenomenon but as a concept embedded in collective and spatial contexts. Going forward, we hope that this cross-disciplinary integration of ideas across Social Practice Theory, Digital Geography and Computer Science literature will aid in cultivating environments where lay-users are empowered to raise privacy concerns and, collectively with practitioners, work on co-creating 'good' digital workplaces, educational settings and domestic spaces.

A   Interview Questions

A.1   Introduction

"The theme of this interview is information privacy. I am interested in the kinds of information that you choose to disclose while using internet technologies as well as your thoughts and feelings around the collection, use and dissemination of this data by third parties. I am especially interested in how the information that you share about yourself has changed during a global pandemic and whether any of your thoughts and feelings around the use of your data have been impacted by any conflicting priorities such as the need for social interaction, the need to access education or work or the need to support initiatives to aid public health."

A.2   Information Disclosure

1. What sort of internet tools do you regularly use?
2. What kind of information do you disclose on the internet?
   - Why do you choose to disclose this information? What factors impact your decision?
   - How does this compare to the data that the people around you disclose?
   - What are the consequences of not disclosing this data?
   - What are the consequences of disclosing this data?

A.3   Changes in Information Disclosure

1. Tell me about the change in the internet tools you use as a result of the pandemic?
2. Has this resulted in any change in the amount, or type, of information that you share?
   - Why do you feel this change has occurred?

A.4   General Privacy Practices

1. What sort of steps to you take to protect your data privacy?
   - Do you feel suitably protected by the actions you take?
   - What level of competency is required to perform these actions? i.e. what skills have you developed to perform these tasks and how easy/hard do you find them?
   - How did you become aware of this method? i.e. who introduced you to it, was it a social or educational setting?
2. What other further steps could you be taking to protect your privacy?
3. To what extent do you feel responsible for protecting your privacy?

A.5   The Importance of Privacy

1. To what extent do you feel information privacy is important in the current climate of covid-19?
   - Social interaction
   - To make a living
   - To access amenities
   - To protect public health
   - Are there any other further factors that you have had to prioritise over privacy in the current climate?

A.6   Internet Tools for Fighting COVID-19

1. Have you downloaded any apps that have been specifically developed to help fight COVID-19?
   Whether this was to prevent the spread (e.g. NHS contact tracing) or to document symptoms for scientific research (e.g. ZOE Symptom Tracker).
   - What part did privacy play in informing this decision?
   - Do you feel these apps will sufficiently protect your information privacy?
   - How comfortable were you in inputting the data that the app asks for? Would you happily have inputted this data into a service that is not attempting to fight a pandemic?
2. What level of privacy sacrifice would you be willing to make in order to aid a public health crisis?

A.7   Wrap-Up

- Thank you again - your contribution will be invaluable
- I think I have everything I need here but would I be okay to contact you via email if I have any further questions?
- Is there anyone you can recommend who might be willing and able to talk to me over the next 2 weeks or so?

B   Code Book

See Table 2.

Table 2. Final code book

Code	Inclusion Statement	Examples
Accidental self-disclosure - occurrence	x accidentally discloses information about themselves that they did not intent to disclose	"I opened up a Zoom meeting and my nickname was still L-Dog"
Accidental self-disclosure - concern	x is concerned that they may accidentally disclose information about themselves that they did not mean to disclose	"The channels in Slack are so hard to use, I'm worried I am going to use it wrong"
Competency - awareness of threats	x expresses an awareness of privacy threats	"I know with all of these things that there is always the potential for information to get into the wrong hands"
Competency - business practices	x is aware of common business data practices	"I mean, Google collects all of these things about you anyway"
Competency - spatial bounds of internet	x expresses an understanding/lack of understanding of the spacial bounds of the internet	"I am careful not to post things that I don't want even one person not seeing as I know how far these things can get"
Competency - persistence of the internet	x expresses an understanding/lack of understanding of the temporal bounds of the internet	"I had no idea that they would still have this stuff from 10 year ago that I swear I deleted"
Contact tracing - misconceptions	x expresses a perception about contact tracing apps that is not true	"I don't want Boris seeing me go to the shop"
Contact tracing - perceptions	x expresses an opinion surrounding contact tracing	"Well we all know contact tracing hasn't worked quite like they intended"
Contact tracing - reasons	x expresses a reason for using contact tracing	"It is a social duty"
Contact tracing - usage	x gives supplementary information about their usage of contact tracing apps	"My Bluetooth is never switched on so I doubt it is doing anything"
Contextual integrity - maintenance	x expresses that they have no privacy concerns as the information flow is as they expected	"You come to expect to have to give your data to these things therefore it doesn't concern you"

(continued)

Table 2. (*continued*)

Code	Inclusion Statement	Examples
Contextual integrity - violation	x expresses (often latently) that they have privacy concerns because the information flow is not as they expected	(latent) feelings of discomfort at the wrong people the recipient of a communication
Consumer choice	x exercises their data meaningfully as a consumer	"I deliberately click on the affiliate advertising of content creators that I like because they do provide this entertainment for free"
Device repurposing	x is using a device for a purpose for which it was not originally intended	"I having to use my personal phone to take work calls"
Escapism	x shares that they have turned to internet tools as an escape from their daily reality	"TikTok is a good distraction from everything, like a really unhealthy meditation method"
Friends and family data misuse - concern	x is concerned that friends and family might misuse their data	"a friend might screenshot and share it"
Home environment	x's home environment is affecting their privacy practices	"I don't have diversity of opinion here so I post more online"
Identity - junior staff member	x identifies as a junior staff member	"I am pretty junior compared to my co-workers"
Identity - poor computer literacy	x perceives themselves as not having a very high level of computer literacy	"You know me, I have no idea what goes on with computers"
Identity management - concern	x is concerned about maintaining their identity amongst connections	"I don't want anyone to think I am untidy"
Inside-out - occurrence	x perceives/engages in disclosing information of particular topic that they would not normally disclose	"everyone has been posting about their vaccination status on there"
Involuntary disclosure - occurrence	x has disclosed information about themselves involuntarily e.g. because of coercion or obligation	"As part of work, I have to give out my personal mobile number to clients"
Loss of access - social	x expresses that they have lost access to their usual methods of socialisation	"We haven't been able to go out and see anyone at the moment"

(*continued*)

Table 2. (*continued*)

Code	Inclusion Statement	Examples
Loss of access - amenities	x expresses that they have lost access to their usual methods of amenities e.g. shopping and healthcare	"I am technically shielding so I haven't just been able to pop to the shop"
New tools	x is using a new tool in the course of the COVID-19 pandemic	"I started using TikTok last summer"
Nothing to share	x expresses that they have nothing of note to share on social media	"We haven't done anything is why I am not posting anything"
Opinion-based disclosure - occurrence	x is perceiving, or engaging in opinion-based disclosure	"It was strange with the US election because people were posting their opinions about it"
Opinion-based disclosure - perception	x provides a perception of opinion-based disclosure	"no-one wants to see that"
Other values	x expresses that there are other values they are more concerned about than privacy	"It is far more important to try and save lives"
Outside-in - occurrence	x perceives/engages in not disclosing a particular topic that they would normally be comfortable disclosing	"I don't want to post that my adult children are home ... this feels entitled"
Privacy of alternatives	x is aware that there are options with more privacy and this changes their attitude or action	"With the NHS app, there were ways to achieve the same result without collecting that level of data"
Privacy paradox - evidence	x shows a difference between their privacy concerns and privacy actions	"I am pretty concerned about it but I am not about to do anything about it"
Privacy paradox - explanation	x provides an (often latent) explanation for the privacy paradox	"It doesn't matter how concerned I am because what I do has no impact"
Privacy stigma - concern	x expresses that they are concerned they may experience privacy stigma, but have not actually experienced it	"I am pretty sure they would just tell me to suck it up"
Privacy stigma - occurrence	x expresses that they have experienced privacy stigma	"They told us not to bother complaining about it"

(*continued*)

Table 2. (*continued*)

Code	Inclusion Statement	Examples
Proctoring practicalities	x expresses concern around the practicalities of proctoring ahead of privacy concerns	"From the sounds of it, you are not able to access water for hours on end"
Proctoring privacy	x expresses concern around the privacy of proctoring ahead of the practicalities	"A random person is just there watching me sitting an exam"
Pseudonym	x uses a pseudonym to protect their privacy	"I use my middle name as my surname on Facebook"
Surveillance - concern	x expresses concern regarding surveillance capabilities	"I don't like that lectures are able to take attendance and see who attends lectures"
Role of government	x expresses privacy concerns because of their perceived role of government	"I just don't think the government should have that role"
Social calculus	x makes a privacy decision based on the perceptions of others	"People want to be perceived as doing the right thing"
Societal benefit	x makes a privacy decision based on the good of someone other than themselves	"If we can save lives and prevent massive economic loss then that is good"
Support system - established	x has an established support system in place	"We haven't been alone, [neighbour] has been helping us out"
Symptom tracker - perceptions	x expresses an opinion about the ZOE Symptom Tracker	"I think it is such a good initiative"
Symptom tracker - reasons	x expresses a reason for using the ZOE Symptom Tracker	"It feels like I am proactively doing something that helps people"
Symptom tracker - usage	x gives supplementary information around how they use the ZOE symptom tracker	"I have been inputting my symptoms into it every day since about April"
Technology repurposing - occurrence	x is using a technology for a purpose which it was not originally intended	"Like everybody, I am now using Zoom for social stuff, as well as work stuff"
Technology repurposing - concern	x is (not) concerned about using a technology for a purpose which it was not originally intended	"Zoom for social is no different than Zoom for work for my privacy"
Tool disuse - action	because of privacy concerns, x stops using a tool	"I had to un-download the Google Play store app"

(*continued*)

Table 2. (*continued*)

Code	Inclusion Statement	Examples
Tool use - business communication	x uses a tool for the purpose of business communication	"We tend to use Slack to communicate"
Tool use - VOIP	x uses a tool for the purpose of video communication	"I have been using Zoom for my meetings with clients"
Tool use - proctoring	x uses a tool for the purpose of exam proctoring	"We have all had to download a proctoring tool for our exams"
Trust	x makes a privacy-related decision based on trust of platform or information recipient	"It might make be a bit of a snob but I trust it because it is a university"
Unfriending - action	x takes privacy action to 'unfriend' their connections	"I had to unfriend my mum as she kept posting too many pictures of me and my brother"
Vocational privacy	x expresses privacy concerns or requirements as a results of their vocation	"I have to protect the privacy of my patients"
Work background - concern	x is concerned about their work background when they are working with their camera enabled	"I don't like that my class-mates can see my bedroom"
Work background - action	x takes action to alter their work background because of privacy concerns	"I have moved my desk to give an empty wall behind me"
Work background - reasons	x provides a reason for the action/inaction they take in relation to their work background	"The process is already confusing enough already without having to think about a virtual background"
Work-life divide - decreased	x expresses that they feel that their work-life divide has decreased (may be latent)	"I feel like my work life and my home life are getting too close"

C Interview Question Formulation

This appendix illustrates how Social Practice Theory shaped the process of interview question formulation (Figs. 1, 2, 3 and 4).

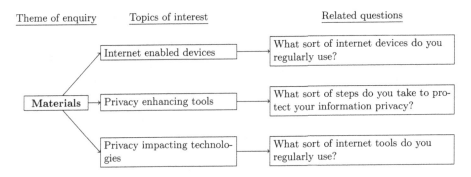

Fig. 1. Questions related to practice elements: Materials

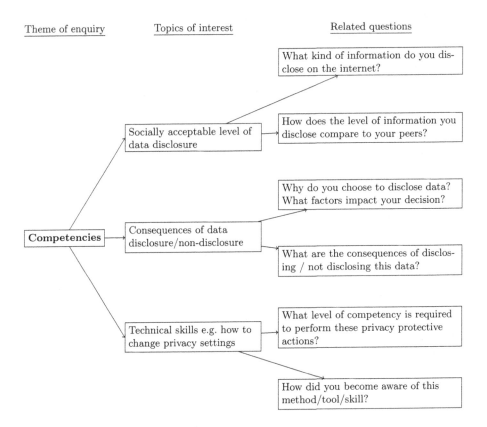

Fig. 2. Questions related to practice elements: Competencies

Theme of enquiry   Topics of interest   Related questions

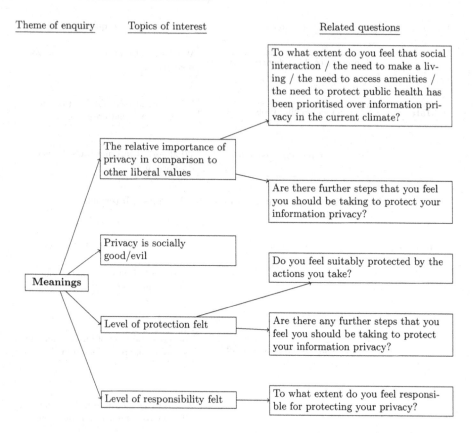

Fig. 3. Questions related to practice elements: Meanings

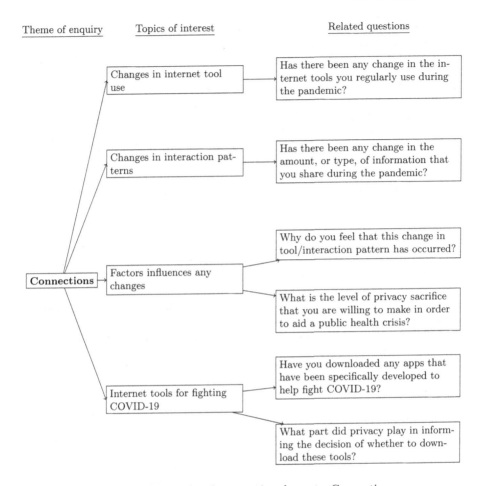

Fig. 4. Questions related to practice elements: Connections

References

1. Altman, I.: The Environment and Social Behaviour: Privacy, Personal Space, Territory, Crowding. Brooks/Cole Publishing Company, Monterey, CA (1975)
2. Apthorpe, N., Shvartzshnaider, Y., Mathur, A., Reisman, D., Feamster, N.: Discovering smart home internet of things privacy norms using contextual integrity. In: Proceedings of the ACM on Interactive, Mobile, Wearabloe and Ubiquitous Technologies, pp. 1–23 (2018). https://doi.org/10.1145/3214262
3. Armano, D.: COVID-19 will be remembered as the 'great accelerator' of digital transformation (2020). https://www.forbes.com/sites/davidarmano/2020/09/09/covid-19-will-be-remembered-as-the-great-accelerator-of-digital-transformation/
4. Baruh, L., Popescu, M.: Big Data analytics and the limits of privacy self-management. New Media Soc. **19**(4), 1–18 (2015). https://doi.org/10.1177/1461444815614001

5. Betkier, M.: Privacy Online, Law, and the Effective Regulation of Online Services. Intersentia, Cambridge (2019)
6. de Bolle, C.: Pandemic profiteering: how criminals exploit the COVID-19 crisis. Technical report, Europol, The Hague, The Netherlands (2020)
7. Braun, V., Clarke, V.: Using thematic analysis in psychology. Qual. Res. Psychol. **3**(2), 77–101 (2006). https://doi.org/10.1191/1478088706QP063OA
8. Bruno, M., Nikolaeva, A.: Towards a maintenance-based approach to mode shift: comparing two cases of Dutch cycling policy using social practice theory. J. Transp. Geogr. **86**(C) (2020). https://doi.org/10.1016/j.jtrangeo.2020.102772
9. Brunton, F., Nissen, H.: Privacy's trust gap: a review. Yale Law J. **126**(4), 908–1241 (2017)
10. Buller, D.B., Burgoon, J.K.: Interpersonal deception theory. Commun. Theor. **6**(3), 203–242 (1996). https://doi.org/10.1111/j.1468-2885.1996.tb00127.x
11. Cetina, K.K., Schatzki, T.R., von Savigny, E.: The Practice Turn in Contemporary Theory. Routledge (2005)
12. Chen, Q., Min, C., Zhang, W., Wang, G., Ma, X., Evans, R.: Unpacking the black box: how to promote citizen engagement through government social media during the COVID-19 crisis. Comput. Hum. Behav. **110** (2020). https://doi.org/10.1016/j.chb.2020.106380
13. Cohen, J.E.: Configuring the networked citizen. In: Imagining New Legalities, pp. 129–153. Stanford University Press (2020)
14. Coldicutt, R.: Infrastructure not time travel (2020). https://glimmersreport.net/report/insight
15. Dourish, P., Anderson, K.: Collective information practice: exploring privacy and security as social and cultural phenomena. Hum. Comput. Interact. **21**(3), 319–342 (2009). https://doi.org/10.1207/s15327051hci2103_2
16. European Convention: Charter of fundamental rights of the European union. Technical report, OJ C 326 (EN) (2012)
17. Evans, D., McMeekin, A., Southerton, D.: Sustainable consumption, behaviour change policies and theories of practice (2012)
18. Evans, J.: 12 security tips for the 'work from home' enterprise (2020). https://www.computerworld.com/article/3532352/12-security-tips-for-the-work-from-home-enterprise.html
19. Ferreira, D., Vale, M.: From cyberspace to cyberspatialities? Fennia-Int. J. Geogr. **199**(1), 113–117 (2021). https://doi.org/10.11143/fennia.100343
20. Florida, R.: The uncertain future of corporate HQs (2020). https://hbr.org/2020/09/the-uncertain-future-of-corporate-hqs
21. Foden, M.: Everyday consumption practices as a site for activism? Exploring the motivations of grassroots reuse groups. People Place Policy Online **6**(3) (2012). https://doi.org/10.3351/ppp.0006.0003.0004
22. Francis, L.P., Francis, J.G.: Privacy: What Everyone Needs to Know. Oxford University Press, New York, NY (2017)
23. Freeguard, G., Shepheard, M., Davies, O.: Digital government during the coronavirus crisis. Technical report Institute for Government, London, UK (2020)
24. Galič, M.: Surveillance and privacy in smart cities and living labs: conceptualising privacy for public space. Optima Grafische Communicatie, Rotterdam (2019)
25. Goh, L.: The future is now: imagining university life post-COVID (2021). https://www.universityworldnews.com/post.php?story=20210224140632590
26. Goodman, L.A.: Snowball sampling. Ann. Math. Stat. **32**(1), 148–170 (1961)

27. Habib, H., et al.: Away from prying eyes: analyzing use and understanding of private browsing. In: Proceedings of the Fourteenth Symposium on Usable Privacy and Security, pp. 159–175. USENIX Association, Baltimore, MD (2018)

28. Hoolohan, C., Browne, A.L.: Design thinking for practice-based intervention: co-producing the change points toolkit to unlock (un) sustainable practices. Des. Stud. **67**, 102–132 (2020). https://doi.org/10.1016/j.destud.2019.12.002

29. Information Commissioner's Office: The ICO's updated regulatory approach in response to the coronavirus pandemic (2021). https://ico.org.uk/media/2617613/ico-regulatory-approach-during-coronavirus.pdf

30. Ipsen, C., van Veldhoven, K., Kirchner, K., Hansen, J.P.: Six key advantages and disadvantages of working from home in Europe during COVID-19. Int. J. Environ. Res. Pub. Health **18**(4), 1826 (2021). https://doi.org/10.3390/ijerph18041826

31. Jameson, S., Richter, C., Taylor, L.: People's strategies for perceived surveillance in Amsterdam smart city. Urban Geogr. **40**(10), 1467–1484 (2019). https://doi.org/10.1080/02723638.2019.1614369

32. Jesson, J.K., Lacey, F.M.: How to do (or not to do) a critical literature review. Pharm. Educ. **6**(2), 139–148 (2006)

33. Kim, T., Barasz, K., John, L.K.: Why am i seeing this ad? The effect of ad transparency on ad effectiveness. J. Consum. Aff. **45**(5), 906–932 (2018). https://doi.org/10.1093/jcr/ucy039

34. Kiraly, O., Potenza, M.N., Stein, D.J., Kind, D.C., Hodgins, D.C., Saunders, J.B.: Preventing problematic internet use during the COVID-19 pandemic: consensus guidance. Compr. Psychiatry **100**, 152–180 (2020). https://doi.org/10.1016/j.comppsych.2020.152180

35. Koops, B.J., Galič, M.: Conceptualizing Space and Place: Lessons from Geography for the Debate on Privacy in Public. Edward Elgar Publishing, Cheltenham (2017)

36. Leszczynski, A.: Digital methods iii: the digital mundane. Prog. Hum. Geogr. **44**(6), 1194–1201 (2020). https://doi.org/10.1177/0309132519888687

37. Lewandowsky, S., et al.: Public acceptance of privacy-encroaching policies to address the COVID-19 pandemic in the united kingdom. PLOS ONE **16**(1) (2021). https://doi.org/10.1371/journal.pone.0245740

38. Liu, W., Beltagui, A., Ye, S.: Accelerated innovation through repurposing: exaptation of design and manufacturing in response to COVID-19. R&D Manage. (2021). https://doi.org/10.1111/radm.12460

39. Maalsen, S., Sadowski, J.: The smart home on fire: amplifying and accelerating domestic surveillance. Surveill. Soc. **17**(1/2), 118–124 (2019). https://doi.org/10.24908/ss.v17i1/2.12925

40. Margulis, S.T.: Conceptions of privacy: current status and next steps. J. Soc. Issues **33**(3), 5–21 (1977). https://doi.org/10.1111/j.1540-4560.1977.tb01879.x

41. Margulis, S.T.: Privacy as information management: a social psychological and environmental framework. Technical report, U.S. Department of Commerce, National Bureau of Standards, Washington, DC (1979)

42. Margulis, S.T.: Privacy as a social issue and behavioural concept. J. Soc. Issues **59**(2), 243–261 (2003)

43. Margulis, S.T.: Three theories of privacy: an overview. In: Trepte, S., Reinecke, L. (eds.) Privacy Online, pp. 9–17. Springer, Heidelberg (2011). https://doi.org/10.1007/978-3-642-21521-6_2

44. Michalec, A.O., Hayes, E., Longhurst, J.: Building smart cities, the just way. A critical review of "smart" and "just" initiatives in Bristol, UK. Sustain. Cities Soc. **47** (2019). https://doi.org/10.1016/j.scs.2019.101510

45. Morton, A., Sasse, M.A.: Privacy is a process, not a pet: a theory for effective privacy practice. In: Proceedings of the 2012 New Security Paradigms Workshop (2012). https://doi.org/10.1145/2413296.2413305
46. Nabity-Grover, T., Cheung, C.M.K., Thatcher, J.B.: Inside out and outside in: how the COVID-19 pandemic affects self-disclosure on social media. Int. J. Inf. Manage. **55**, 102–188 (2020). https://doi.org/10.1016/j.ijinfomgt.2020.102188
47. National Cyber Security Centre: Home working: preparing your organisation and staff (2020). https://www.ncsc.gov.uk/guidance/home-working
48. Nissenbaum, H.: Privacy in Context: Technology, Policy and the Integrity of Social Life. Stanford University Press, Redwood City, CA (2009)
49. Palmer, A.: Amazon sellers fined for price gouging hand sanitizer amid coronavirus pandemic (2020). https://www.cnbc.com/2020/11/17/amazon-sellers-fined-for-coronavirus-price-gouging-hand-sanitizer.html
50. Patton, M.Q.: Two decades of developments in qualitative inquiry: a personal, experiential perspective. Qual. Soc. Work. **1**(3), 261–283 (2002). https://doi.org/10.1177/1473325002001003636
51. Reckwitz, A.: Toward a theory of social practices: a development in culturalist theorizing. Eur. J. Soc. Theor. **5**(2), 243–263 (2002). https://doi.org/10.1177/2F13684310222225432
52. Regan, P.: Legislating Privacy: Technology, Social Values, and Public Policy. University of North Carolina Press, Chapel Hill, NC (1995)
53. Sadowski, J., Bendor, R.: Selling smartness: corporate narratives and the smart city as a sociotechnical imaginary. Sci. Technol. Hum. Values **44**(3), 540–563 (2019). https://doi.org/10.1177/0162243918806061
54. Sadowski, J., Strengers, Y., Kennedy, J.: More work for Big Mother: revaluing care and control in smart homes. Environ. Plan. A Econ. Space **56**, 0308518X2110223 (2021)
55. Schwandt, T.A.: The SAGE Dictionary of Qualitative Inquiry. Sage, London (2007)
56. Seifert, A.: The digital exclusion of older adults during the COVID-19 pandemic. J. Gerontol. Soc. Work **63**(6–7), 674–676 (2020). https://doi.org/10.1080/01634372.2020.1764687
57. Shoeman, F.D.: Philosophical Dimensions of Privacy: An Anthology. Cambridge University Press, Cambridge (1984)
58. Shove, E.: Changing human behaviour and lifestyle: a challenge for sustainable consumption. In: The Ecological Economics of Consumption, pp. 111–131 (2004). http://citeseerx.ist.psu.edu/viewdoc/download?doi=10.1.1.124.7935&rep=rep1&type=pdf
59. Shove, E.: Beyond the ABC: climate change policy and theories of social change. Environ Plan A **42**(6), 1273–1285 (2010). https://doi.org/10.1068/a42282
60. Shove, E., Pantzar, M., Watson, M.: The Dynamics of Social Practice: Everyday Life and How It Changes. Sage, London (2012)
61. Singh, J., Singh, J.: COVID-19 and its impact on society. Electron. Res. J. Soc. Sci. Humanit. **2**, 102–106 (2020)
62. Slack Help Center: What is a channel? (2021). https://slack.com/intl/en-gb/help/articles/360017938993
63. Slupska, J.: Safe at home: towards a feminist critique of cybersecurity. St. Antony's Int. Rev. **15**(1), 83–100 (2019)
64. Smith, H.J., Dinev, T., Xu, H.: Information privacy research: an interdisciplinary review. MIS Q. **35**(4), 989–1015 (2011). https://doi.org/10.2307/41409970
65. Solove, D.J.: Understanding Privacy. Harvard University Press, Cambridge, MA (2008)

66. Sovacool, B.K., Hess, D.J.: Ordering theories: typologies and conceptual frameworks for socio-technical change. Soc. Stud. Sci. **47**(5), 703–750 (2017). https://doi.org/10.1177/0306312717709363

67. Strengers, Y.: Peak electricity demand and social practice theories: reframing the role of change agents in the energy sector. In: The Global Challenge of Encouraging Sustainable Living. Edward Elgar Publishing (2013)

68. Strengers, Y., Kennedy, J., Arcari, P., Nicholls, L., Gregg, M.: Protection, productivity and pleasure in the smart home: emerging expectations and gendered insights from Australian early adopters. In: Proceedings of the 2019 CHI Conference on Human Factors in Computing Systems, pp. 1–13 (2019). https://doi.org/10.1145/3290605.3300875

69. van de Waerdt, P.J.: Information asymmetries: recognizing the limits of the GDPR on the data-driven market. Comput. Law Secur. Rev. **38**, 105436 (2020). https://doi.org/10.1016/j.clsr.2020.105436

70. Vitak, J., Zimmer, M.: More than just privacy: using contextual integrity to evaluate the long-term risks from COVID-19 surveillance technologies. Soc. Media Soc. **6**(3), 44 (2020). https://doi.org/10.1177/2056305120948250

71. Wang, W., Sun, L., Lui, T., Lai, T.: The use of e-health during the COVID-19 pandemic: a case study in China's Hubei province. Health Sociol. Rev. **31**, 215–231 (2021). https://doi.org/10.1080/14461242.2021.1941184

72. Warde, A.: Consumption and theories of practice. J. Consum. Cult. **5**(2), 131–153 (2005). https://doi.org/10.1177/1469540505053090

73. Warren, S.D., Brandeis, L.D.: Right to privacy. Harv. Law Rev. **4**(5), 193 (1890). https://doi.org/10.2307/1321160

74. Watson, M., Browne, A., Evans, D., Foden, M., Hoolohan, C., Sharp, L.: Challenges and opportunities for re-framing resource use policy with practice theories: the change points approach. Glob. Environ. Chang. **62**, 102072 (2020). https://doi.org/10.1016/j.gloenvcha.2020.102072

75. Westin, A.F.: Privacy and Freedom. Athenum, New York, NY (1968)

76. Wu, P.F., Vitak, J., Zimmer, M.T.: A contextual approach to information privacy research. J. Am. Soc. Inf. Sci. **71**(4), 485–490 (2020). https://doi.org/10.1002/asi.24232

Modelling Perceptions of Privacy

From Dark Patterns to Fair Patterns? Usable Taxonomy to Contribute Solving the Issue with Countermeasures

Marie Potel-Saville[1]([✉]) and Mathilde Da Rocha[2]

[1] Amurabi, Legal Innovation Studio, Paris, France
marie@amurabi.eu

[2] Cognitive Ergonomics and UX Designer, Human-Centered Design, Lyon, France

Abstract. Dark patterns are deceptive or manipulative interfaces that can lead users to act against their preferences or best interests. They are widely spread in the digital environment and there is multi-disciplinary evidence of the individual and structural harms that they cause. In this article, we synthesize evidence of the prevalence of dark patterns, evidence of their harms, and the legal framework addressing them. Then, we propose a complementary area of research: a new taxonomy to contribute to solving the issue. We detail existing taxonomies, their main respective purposes, and we provide a gap analysis bridging human-centered principles and practitioners needs. Based on that analysis, we propose a new taxonomy to provide a usable, accessible, and sustainable tool to empower all stakeholders to take action and fight against dark patterns. In this taxonomy, we introduce the notion of fair pattern as a way to shift from a problem-oriented to a problem-solving perspective. Finally, the advantages and limitations of this taxonomy, such as the perspectives it opens as a countermeasure to solve the issue, are discussed.

Keywords: dark patterns · deceptive patterns · taxonomy · resolution method · fairness by design · autonomy enhancing measures · fair patterns

1 Introduction

Dark patterns - deceptive or manipulative interfaces in innumerable corners of the digital environment that can lead users to act against their preferences or best interests - have been the subject of a great deal of research for the past 13 years or so. They have been identified in various interfaces ranging from social media platforms to websites, video games, mobile applications, etc. and there is multi-disciplinary evidence of the individual and structural harms that they cause. Platforms such as Brignull's Deceptive Design website features the infamous 'hall of shame', an online repository of examples documenting the evidence of dark patterns in our world [1].

In this article, we firstly provide a robust literature framework and synthesize existing work to define the concept, assess their prevalence, evidence of their harms, as well as the legal framework addressing them. Then, we propose a complementary area of research:

a new taxonomy to contribute to solving the issue. We detail existing taxonomies, their main respective purposes, and we provide a gap analysis bridging human-centered principles and practitioners needs. Based on this analysis, we propose a new taxonomy that provides a usable, accessible, and sustainable tool to empower all stakeholders to take action and fight against dark patterns by focusing not only the problems which they pose, but also the methods which can solve them. This is why the proposed new taxonomy introduces the notion of 'fair patterns' as a way to shift from a problem-oriented to a problem-solving perspective. Finally, the advantages and limitations of this taxonomy, such as the perspectives it opens as a countermeasure to solve the issue, are discussed.

2   Current State of Play on Dark Patterns: Prevalence, Evidence of Harms and Legal Framework

2.1   Definitions and Prevalence

For over a decade, there has been rich academic literature on the definitions of dark patterns. This term was coined in 2010 by Harry Brignull, UX designer and PhD in cognitive sciences, referring to "tricks used in websites and apps that make you do things that you didn't mean to, like buying or signing up for something" [1].

Dark and Deceptive Patterns. Since then, some authors such as Brignull [1] and King [2] have used the term "deceptive patterns" to avoid any misunderstanding as to any negative connotation associated with the term "dark". We fully adhere to this precaution, however since recent legislation and regulatory publications have used the term "dark pattern", we will use it in this article for legal precision purposes.

Definitions. There are several definitions of dark patterns in the various literature [3–9]. Most of the definitions include notions of deception, manipulation, coercion, or exploitation in the design and wording of user interfaces, exploitation of humans' cognitive biases and leading users to make decisions unknowingly, against their preferences or against their best interests.

Deceptive by Design. Across the various definitions, Mathur et al. [10], finds the commonality of dark patterns in scientific literature is that they "modify the choice architecture presented to users".

They do so either by modifying the set of choices available to users by making some choices more burdensome, or less appealing than other choices (usually the most privacy protective or the cheapest for the users), or manipulating the information flow to users by making protective information more difficult to find, more difficult to understand, or even providing false information [9].

Exploitation of Cognitive Biases. Either way the deception occurs, dark patterns exploit cognitive biases [9] and, in particular, seek to trigger Kahneman's "System 1" thinking, which requires automatic, fast, intuitive decisions with low cognitive effort, rather than "System 2" thinking, which includes deliberative, conscious and effortful decision-making [4, 11].

Therefore, dark patterns defeat the purpose of consent, tricking users into "accepting" terms that they would not knowingly accept, or substantively altering their preferences, making the concept of consent meaningless and irrelevant [12].

Dark Patterns and Data Privacy. The influence of design on user empowerment, and conversely, its capacity to trick users, has been clearly identified by the CNIL's innovation laboratory, the LINC, which created a non-extensive typology of potentially deceptive design practices in relation to personal data in 2019 [13].

Specifically addressing the issue of dark patterns in social media, the European Data Protection Board issued draft guidelines in 2022 defining privacy dark patterns as "interfaces and user experiences implemented on social media platforms that lead users into making unintended, unwilling and potentially harmful decisions in regards to their personal data" [14].

There has also been rich research regarding the use of dark patterns to collect and process ever more personal data and obfuscate privacy protective options. Sadly, perhaps the most famous research is "Privacy Zuckering", which details tricking users into sharing more personal data than they intended to share [1]. But dozens of privacy dark patterns were identified in 2018 by the Norwegian Consumer Council, a government-funded consumer protection body [15], in the account creation and management settings of Facebook, Google, and Windows 10.

Following a workshop on dark patterns in 2022, the Federal Trade Commission published a Staff Report on dark patterns in 2022 [16], announcing further enforcement and identifying "design elements that obscure or subvert privacy choices", whether they do not allow consumers to definitively reject data collection or use, repeatedly prompt consumers to select settings they wish to avoid, present confusing toggle settings leading consumers to make unintended privacy choices, purposely obscure consumers' privacy choices and make them difficult to access, highlight a choice that results in more information collection, while graying out the option that enables consumers to limit such practices, or include default settings that maximize data collection and sharing.

Thus, it is obvious that there are many different types of privacy-related dark patterns and dark pattern strategies that affect users' data privacy choices and the level of protection of their personal data.

High Prevalence of Dark Patterns Around the World. Significant research efforts have been made to identify the prevalence of dark patterns, beyond privacy-specific ones. The OECD Report on dark patterns identifies a large number of studies by researchers, regulatory authorities, and consumer protection bodies [9].

In 2018, the Norwegian Consumer Protection Council analyzed the account creation and management settings of Facebook, Google and Windows 10 and identified dozens of "privacy intrusive" interfaces that lead users to share more personal data than they would have consciously done [15].

In 2022, the European Commission study on dark patterns found that 97% of 75 popular e-commerce websites and apps in the EU contained at least one dark pattern [17].

In early 2023, the European Commission and the national consumer protection authorities of 23 Member States, Norway, and Iceland (CPC Network), screened 399 retail websites and identified that nearly 40% of retail websites contain at least one consumer-protection related dark pattern [18].

Mathur et al. [6] identified that 11.1% of around 11 000 popular e-commerce websites that were examined featured dark patterns.

The Chilean consumer protection authority [19] found that 64% of 103 Chilean e-commerce websites that were examined featured at least one dark pattern.

The International Consumer Protection Enforcement Network [20] identified that 24% of 1754 e-commerce websites/apps investigated featured "dark nudges".

Di Geronimo et al. [21] found that 95% of a sample of 240 popular apps contained at least one dark pattern.

Gunawan et al. [22] found that all 105 of the most popular online services in the Google Play Store that featured both an app and website format contained at least one dark pattern.

Even more astounding, Radesky et al. [23] found that 80% of popular children's apps contained at least one manipulative design feature.

While the precise prevalence varies, mostly depending on the method used to identify them, most researchers agree that dark patterns pose serious harms, particularly in regard to privacy.

2.2 Evidence of Serious Individual and Structural Harms

The European Commission's 2022 study on dark patterns points out that the harmful consequences for consumers have been widely documented in recent years [17]. These consequences include financial losses, impairment of autonomy and privacy, cognitive burdens, and in some cases mental health impairment (addictions, etc.), these are in addition to the risks of impairment of competition, reduced price transparency, and ultimately loss of confidence in markets.

The study also shows that dark patterns particularly affect vulnerable consumers. One third of Internet users worldwide are minors, who are officially vulnerable and need greater protection under the GDPR (General Data Protection Regulation), among other things [24]. Dark patterns generate two main types of harms, individual harm and structural harm.

Individual Harms. Unsurprisingly, there is evidence that dark patterns harm an individual's autonomy [10] as they trick users into deciding against their preferences, denying their choice, or making their choice more difficult. In addition, they harm consumers' welfare by generating a financial loss [25]. Dark patterns also create significant privacy harms as they lead users to share more personal data than intended.

For example, a survey of Australian consumers showed that one (1) in four (4) consumers shared more personal data than they intended due to dark patterns [26]. They have also been shown to cause a psychological detriment and time loss by generating frustration, shame, and increasing our cognitive burden [10]. The European Commission even found that dark patterns increase the heart rate, cause anxiety, and alertness [17].

Structural Harms. Beyond affecting individuals, dark patterns also weaken or alter competition. They prevent price comparison [27], they enable firms to increase their sales, or the volume of their personal data collected, all this without offering better services or products. In this respect, dark patterns give companies that employ these techniques an undue competitive advantage [9].

Concerns have also been voiced that dominant firms can use dark patterns to neutralize a competitive threat by including them in their default settings, or by nagging, or by collecting data to offer services in a way rivals cannot [9, 28–30]. To the extent dark patterns impede consumers' ability to select the best firms on the merits of their product offerings, the market use of dark patterns can also distort the competitive process as a whole [30, 31], where firms are competing through the "efficiency" of their dark patterns rather than on their merit.

Dark patterns also lead to less consumer trust and engagement as much of the consumers' behavior towards online businesses is based on trust, which has been defined as expectations that businesses will behave in a favorable and predictable manner [12]. Unsurprisingly, many researchers found that dark patterns alter consumers' trust in sites and apps that employ their services. For example, almost 50% of consumers exposed to scarcity and social proof dark patterns on hotel booking sites distrusted these sites as a result [32–36].

The harms generated by dark patterns are so serious that it can even call into question whether the market economy is still the system that provides the greatest benefits for consumers [9, 37]. The lack of trust resulting from dark patterns may lead consumers to lose faith in markets and market forces causing them to disengage [7].

2.3 Legal Framework

Numerous acts at the European level and in the United States are already applicable to dark patterns, as unfair practices, contrary to the protection of personal data, or even anti-competitive practices [38]. Given the seriousness of the harms generated by dark patterns and their prevalence, which has shown that the existing legislative framework is not sufficient, new texts have emerged to expressly prohibit them, as "dark patterns".

The California Privacy Rights Act (hereafter "CPRA"), passed in 2020, is considered to be the first legislation to provide a definition of dark patterns: "a user interface designed or manipulated with the substantial effect of subverting or impairing user autonomy, decision-making, or choice, as further defined by regulation". The CPRA provides that "consent obtained through dark patterns does not constitute consent" [39].

Similar amendments to privacy laws have been introduced in other states in the US or are under consideration. Similarly, Canada introduced a bill in 2022, the Digital Charter Implementation Act (Bill C-27) [40], to prohibit and invalidate consent obtained through deception or manipulation. Without expressly mentioning the term, it nevertheless covers dark patterns [2].

In the EU, it is clear that privacy-related dark patterns breach a number of principles and provisions of the GDPR [41]. Deceptive or manipulative interfaces breach the principle of fairness as per Article 5 of the GDPR. According to this overarching principle, data processing cannot be "detrimental, discriminatory, unexpected or misleading" to users.

Privacy-related dark patterns also must be assessed in the light of three other key principles: accountability, transparency and data protection by design. In terms of accountability (art. 5-2 GDPR), it is for the data controller (and data processor) to prove that it complies with GDPR. Thus, the user interface and user journeys can be assessed to determine whether users actually understand the data protection information, whether they have freely given their consent or not, whether they can easily exercise their rights, etc. In terms of transparency (articles 5-1 and 12 GDPR), many of the dark patterns contravene the obligation to provide information in a "concise, transparent, intelligible and easily accessible form, using clear and plain language". Dark patterns are contrary to Article 25 of the GDPR that deals with data protection by design and default, which requires users to be given "the highest degree of autonomy to make their own choices" regarding their personal data, requiring a "power balance", requiring "no deception", requiring information and options to be provided in an objective and neutral way, avoiding any deceptive or manipulative language or design, and requiring "truthfulness" [14].

In addition, the Digital Services Act (the "DSA") [42] lays out the transparency obligations of online platform providers and defines a dark pattern as 'online interfaces of online platforms are practices that materially distort or impair, either on purpose or in effect, the ability of recipients of the service to make autonomous and informed choices or decisions.' 'Those practices can be used to persuade the recipients of the service to engage in unwanted behaviors or into undesired decisions which have negative consequences for them' (recital 67). Article 25(1) expressly prohibits dark patterns: 'Providers of online platforms shall not design, organize or operate their online interfaces in a way that deceives or manipulates the recipients of their service or in a way that otherwise materially distorts or impairs the ability of the recipients of their service to make free and informed decisions.'

The DSA entered into force on 16 November 2022, but most of the obligations in the regulation will apply from 17 February 2024. It's important to note that article 25 applies only if the GDPR or the Unfair Practices Directive don't.

Further, most of the major recent texts that somehow involve the collection of personal information, which have been adopted or are in the process of being adopted at the time or writing, prohibit dark patterns in their respective fields.

For example, the Digital Markets Act includes an "anti-circumvention" provision for the main prohibitions imposed on gatekeepers, in practice the GAFAM (Google, Apple, Facebook, Amazon and Microsoft), notably through "interface design" (Article 13). The draft Regulation on Artificial Intelligence [43] also prohibits dark patterns, as artificial intelligence practices contrary to the values of the Union, under 5.2.2 of its Explanatory Memorandum. The following artificial intelligence practices are prohibited: the placing on the market, putting into service or using an artificial intelligence system that uses subliminal techniques below the threshold of a person's awareness to substantially alter their behavior in a way that causes or is likely to cause physical or psychological harm to that person or to a third party; and the placing on the market, putting into service or use of an artificial intelligence system that exploits possible vulnerabilities due to age or physical or mental disability of a given group of persons in order to substantially alter the behavior of a member of that group in a way that causes or is likely to cause physical or psychological harm to that person or to a third party.

Recital 34 of the Proposal for the Data Act [72], states that 'dark patterns are design techniques that push or deceive consumers into decisions that have negative consequences for them. These manipulative techniques can be used to persuade users, particularly vulnerable consumers, to engage in unwanted behaviors, and to deceive users by nudging them into decisions on data disclosure transactions or to unreasonably bias the decision-making of the users of the service, in a way that subverts and impairs their autonomy, decision-making and choice'. The proposed Data Act goes further to provide specifically that it should be easy for a user to discontinue access to certain data by the third party as it was to authorize access to said data. Article 6(a) of the proposed Data Act specifically prohibits third parties to use dark patterns: 'coerce, deceive or manipulate the user in any way, by subverting or impairing the autonomy, decision-making or choices of the user, including by means of a digital interface with the user.'

The question is whether these new acts, in their respective fields, will be sufficient to tackle dark patterns and whether the regulatory authorities will have the means to enforce the existing and the new prohibitions.

In any event, in parallel (or in advance) of the evolution of the regulations, it is key to frame and categorize what needs to be fought against. That's why literature has proposed a rich variety of taxonomies over the past decade.

3 Usable Taxonomy to Empower All Stakeholders to Take Action and Fight Against Dark Patterns

3.1 Related Work

Examples of Privacy Dark Patterns in the Wild. Overall, there are numerous studies, reports, and guidelines that have identified privacy-specific dark patterns:

- "Privacy Zuckering", where users are tricked into sharing more personal data than they intended to [1], also identified in a more sober way by the CNIL's innovation laboratory [13]
- Designs that deliberately increase the user's workload [3]
- Forced registration [4]
- Hidden legalese [4]
- Immortal accounts [4]
- Attempts to block users from accessing online services when TOR anonymizer technology is detected [44]
- Privacy intrusive default settings [15]
- Illusion of giving users control over their personal data [15]
- Distracting users from making privacy-protective choices [13, 15], somewhat similar to "Skipping": designing the interface or user experience in a way that the users forget or do not think about all or some of the data protection aspects [14]
- Making privacy-protective choices more difficult [15]
- Designs that influence consent for instance, a site might give certain options visual or interactive precedence over others [5]
- Designs that create friction on data protection action [13]

- Website design choices that make it confusing or difficult for users to delete data or opt out of email communications and targeted advertising [45],
- Dark patterns in cookie banners [2, 46],
- Dark patterns deployed by social media platforms to frustrate users' attempts to delete their accounts [47, 48] and this list is probably not extensive as new forms of dark patterns probably emerge every day.

Several Types of Taxonomies, Beyond Privacy-Specific Dark Patterns. In the last decades, academic research into dark patterns has evolved in three main waves [7]. The first wave was aimed at defining and categorizing the different types of dark patterns. The second wave was focused on their prevalence and identifying the basis for regulation. Finally, the third wave was aimed at assessing the harms to consumers by quantifying the effectiveness of dark patterns techniques.

The first wave of research is particularly important as a basis for the ones that follow. Indeed, user manipulation can take different forms and the first challenge to fight dark patterns is to be able to detect them. Many articles proposed classifications of dark patterns in various fields [2, 4–7, 13–15, 49, 50], while regulators, agencies or institutions such as the European Commission, the Federal Trade Commission, the Competition & Market Authority and the OECD [9, 13, 15–28] also proposed their own classifications, partially building on scholarship. These taxonomies are all different, either in their focus area, in the number of categories, or in the level of details; but they all aim at mapping existing dark pattern techniques and identifying the different ways to deceive or manipulate users.

For example, one of the widely acknowledged categorization are the 12 types of deceptive patterns described by Brignull, way beyond privacy [2]:

- Trick questions: a form is made so that the user's answer does not reflect what she/he intended (e.g., language is confusing, checkboxes are alternatively used to opt in or out).
- Sneak into basket: Extra products are added to the cart without actions from the user (e.g., trip insurance automatically added when the user books a hotel).
- Roach motel: A design that makes it easy to get into but hard to get out (ex. delete the account by sending a mail to the support; harder to unsubscribe than it is to subscribe).
- Privacy Zuckering: the user is tricked into publicly sharing more personal information than intended.
- Price comparison prevention: information available does not allow to compare the price of an item with another item (e.g., a kilo of apples with the price presented per kilo and six apples with the price presented per unit).
- Misdirection: The design is made to attract the user's attention and distract the user's attention from specific items.
- Hidden costs: Extra charge added without user demand (e.g., 'free shipping' argued on the website but charging handling costs; or online booking fees).
- Bait and switch: The user performs an action but a different, undesirable result happens instead.
- Confirm shaming: Make the user feel guilty for not opting for the proposed option.
- Disguised ads: Adverts are disguised as other kinds of content.

- Forced continuity: Charging a user for membership without warning or reminder (ex. free trial before charging).
- Friend Spam: using the user's email or social media permissions, the product sends emails to the contacts without the user's consent.

Other taxonomies are more oriented towards the underlying manipulation technique used by the different types of dark patterns. Gray et al. [5] sorted Brignull's types of dark patterns into five distinct categories: nagging (redirection of expected functionality that persists beyond one or more interactions), obstruction (making a process more difficult than it needs to be, with the intent of dissuading certain actions), sneaking (attempting to hide, disguise, or delay the divulging of information that is relevant to the user), interface interference (manipulation of the user interface that privileges certain actions over others), and forced action (requiring the user to perform a certain action to access or continue to access certain functionality).

Bösch et al. [4] identified eight "dark privacy strategies": maximize, publish, centralize, preserve, obscure, deny, violate, and fake.

Beyond privacy, Bongard-Blanchy et al. [50] classified dark patterns into 11 categories: High-demand message, limited-time message, confirm shaming, trick question, loss gain framing, pre-selection, false hierarchy, hidden information, auto play, bundled consent and forced consent, while additional criteria are also cited in several taxonomies such as 'Urgency' and 'Scarcity' [6, 7].

More recently, Jarovsky proposed a taxonomy derived from the four causes of invalidity of contracts in European contract law: mistake, fraud, threat and excessive benefit/unfair advantage; that she transposed for personal data collection into 'pressure', 'hinder', 'mislead' and 'misrepresent' [49].

Among organizations and regulators, the Norwegian Consumer Council categorization [15] focuses on five forms of dark patterns: 'default settings,' 'ease,' 'framing,' 'rewards and punishment,' and 'forced action and timing'. In CNIL's approach [13], the categories of dark patterns in privacy are 'enjoy', 'seduce', 'lure', 'complicate' and 'ban'. Each of them can either 'push the individual to accept sharing more than what is strictly necessary,' 'influence consent,' 'create friction on data protection actions' or 'divert the individual'. The European Data Protection Board [14] proposed a classification on two levels with six categories that contain 14 types of dark patterns:

- Overloading: high volume of requests, information, options or possibilities, to prompt users to share more data or unintentionally allow personal data processing against their expectations.
- Stirring: appealing to users' emotions or using visual nudges to affect users' choices.
- Hindering: making it more difficult or impossible for users to be informed on their privacy options or to manage their data.
- Fickle: inconsistent and unclear design, making it hard for users to navigate the different data protection control tools and to understand the purpose of the processing.
- Left in the dark: design that hides information or data protection control tools or that leaves users unsure of how their data is processed and what kind of control they might have over it regarding the exercise of their rights.

This led to fragmented typologies, focused on specific domains. For example, there are some privacy-focused taxonomies [4, 13, 14], while other taxonomies include privacy-related dark patterns and wider consumer-related dark patterns [1, 15, 50]. This means that there is currently no extensive taxonomy. In addition, some taxonomies overlap, but name the type of dark patterns differently. For example, Brignull's "roach motel" is named "obstruction" under Mathur et al.'s taxonomy, but also has the same effect as "dead end" under EDPB's privacy-focused taxonomy [14].

Gaps to Fill

All these taxonomies are very interesting and each one covers a need from a specific point of view. However, there are several gaps in the existing taxonomies.

First, none of the existing taxonomies can be used as a definitive and complete state of the dark pattern types. As explained above, they sometimes overlap without one single taxonomy being extensive. In addition, the taxonomies differ in the level of details proposed. For example, Brignull's dark pattern "price comparison prevention" applies to a very specific e-commerce environment [2]. On the contrary, some categories proposed are very broad, such as 'Misrepresent' [8] that may include a wide diversity of dark pattern strategies.

Second, existing taxonomies often focus on a specific area of application (privacy, regulation, e-commerce, etc.). The recent OECD report states that none of the taxonomies can be extensive as they reflect their authors' objectives [9].

We can distinguish four major areas in the existing taxonomies: researchers in privacy [4, 7, 8, 50], user Experience design [2], computer sciences [5, 6, 10, 46], regulators or consumer protection bodies [9, 13, 15–28].

In the existing taxonomies, the categories proposed are oriented towards the area of application. For example, the dark pattern types proposed by Bösch et al. [4] are less focused on the dark pattern's techniques that can be used in an e-commerce buying funnel, as they mainly cover the dark pattern used to retrieve more personal data protection.

Third, current typologies are categorizing existing dark patterns and can potentially miss the future ones. Having a 'future proof' taxonomy is particularly important as new forms of dark pattern strategies are emerging more and more rapidly with new technologies and the increasing personalization possibilities [9]. Luguri et al.'s [7] statement that the "scale of dark patterns, their rapid proliferation, the possibilities of using algorithms to detect them, and the breadth of the different approaches that have already emerged" highlights the current need of a sustainable taxonomy.

Finally, and perhaps more importantly, these taxonomies can be difficult to use for practitioners seeking to detect dark patterns in order to avoid or correct them. Some of the taxonomies are fairly complex and too unspecific to be directly applied to a development or design process. For example, a designer will need to use several taxonomies to check an entire website (from cookie banner to e-commerce buying funnel through subscription). Moreover, even if the existing taxonomies can help to detect the dark patterns and to understand the issue, they do not provide clues on how to fight dark patterns. In their article, Bösch et al. [4] initiated the idea of a correspondence between dark strategies and privacy strategies using Hoepman's framework [51]. This shift from a problem-focused approach to dark patterns to a taxonomy that is solution oriented is necessary for digital players to practically take action and have a direct impact on combating dark patterns.

3.2 Proposal of a Usable Taxonomy

Based on these findings, we propose a fourth wave of taxonomy, one that builds on previous taxonomies but contributes to solving the issue. Building on the first waves of taxonomies, the proposed taxonomy aims at fighting dark patterns and solving the issues they raise by providing a usable framework for practitioners while taking into account the different areas of application.

In order to build this new taxonomy, several activities were led with a cross functional team composed of designers, lawyers, cognitive science experts, and digital project managers.

The following activities were performed during several collective work sessions: mapping existing items from the different taxonomies, discussing each item by identifying underlying strategies to manipulate users and cognitive biases used, identifying redundant concepts and grouping them, performing a global analysis of the different groups in terms of internal homogeneity and distinction to ensure consistency, defining each group and characterized in terms of risks and practical detection criteria, specifying Fair patterns as a countermeasure for each category, defining Fair patterns and detailing the success criteria to be met.

First, starting from the existing taxonomies [2, 4, 6–10, 13, 15–17, 28–50], a mapping was done to group similar categories (see Fig. 1).

As shown in Fig. 1, several categories are overlapping between taxonomies. For specific categories, they are grouped based on the underlying strategy to manipulate users and cognitive biases used as a trigger. The goal is to stay at a macro level to ensure that the new categories will be applicable to several areas of application and future-proof (i.e., independent of a specific form currently taken by dark patterns).

The groups formed are analyzed in terms of internal homogeneity and distinction to ensure that the new categories are consistent and different from each other. For each group, a reflection has been conducted on the risks for users and underlying cognitive biases involved to define corresponding fair patterns.

Resulting from this process, a taxonomy of seven dark pattern types with associated fair patterns are proposed (see Table 1).

The new taxonomy proposed is not intended to achieve consensus or cover all needs in a definitive or extensive way. However, the goal was to bridge the gaps existing in current taxonomies to create a usable, actionable, and sustainable taxonomy.

As regards usability, under ISO norm 9241-11 [73], it is the extent to which a product or service can be used by specified users to achieve specified goals with effectiveness, efficiency, and satisfaction in a specified context of use. In this case, users include designers, developers, digital marketers, lawyers, researchers, regulatory bodies, and judges, all with common and specific needs. Common needs consist in easily and rapidly understanding the type of dark pattern at stake. This is achieved through self-explanatory names of categories for example "more than intended" or "maze". As regards specific needs: for example judges or regulators need to clearly identify overlaps between regulators and scientific taxonomies, as the legal framework sometimes refers to both, which

Fig. 1. Mapping of the proposed taxonomy for dark patterns on previous classifications of reference. Under a Creative Commons license.

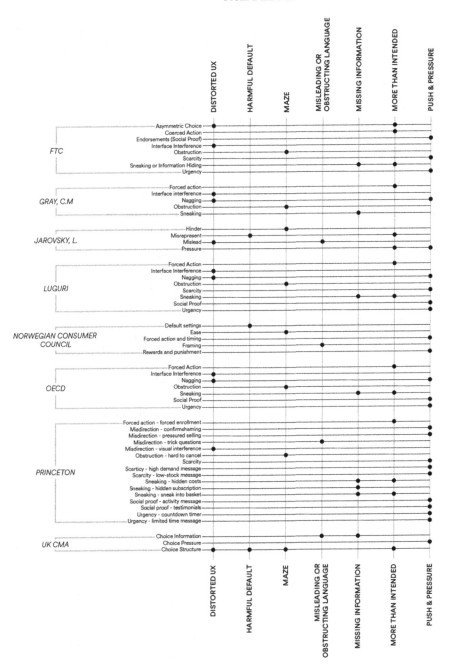

Fig. 1. (*continued*)

Table 1. Proposal of a usable taxonomy of dark patterns with corresponding fair patterns. In the same way as dark patterns used in combination have a cumulative effect, optimal results are obtained combining several fair patterns.

Dark pattern	Fair pattern
Harmful default Default settings are against the interest of the user	**Protective Default** Privacy-protective options and consumer-friendly options are set as defaults. Positive consumer outcomes or positive society outcomes (for example climate friendly) and data protection by design are used to define "protective" defaults
Missing information Selective disclosure of information	**Adequate Information** Sufficient information for the users' intended action e.g. consequences of choices, while avoiding information overload. Additional suggestions clearly identify as such
Maze Make the user tasks, path to information, preferences, or choices unnecessarily complex or long	**Seamless path** Ensure users' tasks, path to information, preferences or choices are as easy when they are in the user's interest than when they are in the company's interest. This includes equivalent salience of buttons and text, same number of clicks and plain and empowering language
Push & Pressure Emotional, social, time or other triggers to induce/push a given behavior	**Non-intrusive information** Absence of trigger to push a behavior not initiated by the user. Exceptions can be considered when pushed information provides best outcomes for consumers (e.g. savings plan) or society (e.g. climate change)
Misleading or Obstructing Language Language is confusing, manipulating or impeding	**Plain and Empowering Language** Language is so clear that users easily find what they need, understand it upon first reading, and understand the consequence of their choices. In addition, language is designed for accessibility and usability, e.g. small portions of text at the right time of the user journey. When certain legalistic terms are mandatory, an information bubble in plain language is provided

(continued)

Table 1. (*continued*)

Dark pattern	Fair pattern
More than intended Sequence of events, clicks, or flows that force the user to do or give more than they intended	**Free action** Empower users to understand the consequences of their choices (especially in terms of spending more or sharing more personal data), while avoiding information overload
Distorted UX Visual interface is trapping users	**Fair UX** Visual interface respects users' intended actions and choices, e.g. place, shape, size and salience of buttons, meaning of buttons and icons

is achieved through the correspondence table. Designers will need practical guidance as to how to avoid creating dark patterns but also how to solve them, which is achieved through the clear-cut definition of each dark pattern and the associated fair pattern.

As regards actionability, this taxonomy also seeks to trigger action by shifting from a problem-focused to a problem-solving approach. The goal is to encourage a move beyond the identification of dark patterns and towards remedying them with fair patterns. Proposing corresponding fair patterns helps practitioners to act in a concrete way to get rid of dark patterns and foster user sovereignty: empowering users to make enlightened and free choices.

As regards sustainability, this taxonomy is namely based on the main cognitive biases manipulated through each dark pattern type, which makes it more robust to include future forms of dark patterns which will inevitably appear, beyond the currently described categories.

On the merits of the categories, with respect to the first category, i.e. the harmful default of dark patterns versus the protective default under fair patterns, this position aligns with the data protection by default principle under Article 25 of the GDPR which requires that only personal data which are necessary for each specific purpose of the processing are processed- essentially, that user service settings are data protection friendly by default. For minors in particular, protective defaults take this into consideration their cognitive limitations by virtue of their age, and their right to an additional protection, as provided by the GDPR [24]. Hence, the default will not be merely to offer them an opportunity to consent freely about decisions relating to their data, but to protect them from choices which lean in the favour of the data controller.

Under the second category, missing versus adequate information under dark and fair patterns respectively, the proposed fair pattern entails providing sufficient information which users need take action at the appropriate time and in the right context, while identifying additional suggestions as such. This stance was acknowledged as a best practice by the EDPB in its 03/2022 Guidelines on Deceptive Design Patterns. The Guidelines also emphasise the presentation of information in an easily comprehensible manner and not simply one that is exhaustive, as more information does not necessarily mean better information [14].

The third category, which is a maze, versus a seamless path as a fair pattern, the fair pattern simplifies the process of accessing information which is beneficial to users rather than hiding them or shrouding them in jargon incomprehensible to the average user. This entails placing the information needed within the right context as needed (the right information at the right time). This also aligns with the obligation provided under Article 12 (1) of the GDPR, which states that the relevant information relating to data processing (particularly those specified under Articles 13–15, 22, and 34) should be put in an intelligible, concise, transparent, and easily accessible form [41].

In the fourth category, plain and empowering language stands in contrast to the dark pattern of misleading or obstructing language which is confusing, manipulating or impeding. It means that in the fair pattern, the information given is so clear that users easily find what they need, understand it upon first reading, and understand the consequence of their choices. In addition to that, it involves information being presented in a layered manner which considers the technical background of the data subject [41].

Free action, on the other hand, empowers users by informing them sufficiently and clearly about the implications of their actions in language which is easy to understand. Lastly, fair UX refers to visual interfaces that respect users' intended actions and choices. This entails interfaces designed to be consistent and clear for users which present choices to be made in a clear and easy to understand manner.

Finally, the depth of this taxonomy was set at a macro-level (e.g., by anchoring the categories on cognitive biases) to be more robust against new forms of dark patterns which will inevitably appear. The intention is to encompass wider categories, not strictly based on types of design or types of language, to propose a sustainable and future-proof taxonomy.

4 Discussion

In this taxonomy, fair patterns are juxtaposed to the deceiving and misleading dark patterns, all the while providing users with the knowledge and tools to preserve their autonomy, which is a central human attribute. The positioning is neutral and shifts away from consent or nudging users towards privacy- or consumer-friendly options. It builds on the concepts of "bright" or "light" patterns [2, 52, 53] and on Jarovsky's [49] "autonomy enhancing measures" and "privacy enhancing design". The idea is that influencing the decisions of individuals or groups towards "good choices" implies giving up on humans' capacity to make their own informed choices online (see Fig. 2). Given the ever-increasing prevalence of digital in our lives, it seems all the more dangerous.

This taxonomy stems from a human-centered design approach, taking into account the characteristics of the context of use. According to the ISO definition [55], human-centered design implies: a design team with multidisciplinary skills and perspectives, a design based on the context of use (users, tasks, and environments), users involvement throughout design and development, an iterative process, a design addressing the whole user experience, and user-centered evaluation to refine solutions. While creating and using the taxonomy (as in projects as practitioners), we followed these principles. The

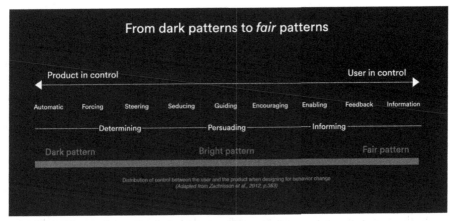

Fig. 2. Distribution of control between the user and the product when designing for behavior change, adapted from Zachrisson et al. [54].

team involved was composed of designers, digital projects managers, and privacy experts. Potential users of the taxonomy were involved during conception in an iterative way.

The point is to ensure that the design of each fair pattern takes into account the capacities and limitations of the users [50]. Indeed, for the same dark pattern strategy, if the user is a child or a highly informed adult, the impact will not be the same. Similarly, regarding the environment, it has been shown that mobile is far more problematic in terms of prevalence and risk. For example, hidden information dark pattern strategies were found to be much more effective on smaller screens such as smartphones as opposed to bigger screens such as desktop monitors [56]. This should be taken into account when weighing the risks of dark patterns and for designing fair patterns.

Regarding the consideration of the whole user experience, as mentioned above, existing taxonomies have targeted different dark patterns depending on the authors' field of work. In this new taxonomy that we propose, we do not solely focus on the dark patterns affecting data protection or commercial strategies. The different exposures to dark patterns in data protection or commercial strategies occur in the same experience at different times (e.g. cookie banner, buying funnel, subscription) from a user's point of view. Thus, our proposed taxonomy addresses the whole user experience in a human-centered design process.

In the next steps, an evaluation of the effectiveness of this taxonomy, the proposed fair patterns and their application, will be conducted. Independent expert review of the concept of fair patterns and our current 23 fair patterns prototypes is being conducted at the time of writing. Iteration is then planned, as well as user testing in the EU and the US and beyond. Continuous improvement of fair patterns will also be required.

Moreover, fighting dark patterns and empowering users requires a global approach which combines different strategies. As described by Bongard Blanchy [50], a holistic framework is required including actions on education, design techniques, and regulations to protect users from dark patterns.

5 Conclusion

It is now clear through multi-disciplinary evidence that dark patterns are a crucial contemporary issue in the digital economy on a global level. The current state of research demonstrates the individual and structural harms and the regulations regarding dark patterns are ever evolving [9]. Dark patterns are a topic that impacts several stakeholders, such as, designers, developers, digital marketers, lawyers, researchers, regulatory bodies, judges, sociologists, economists, etc. In order to contribute to solving this issue, it is important to equip all the stakeholders with usable and actionable tools.

After several waves of research aimed at defining and categorizing dark patterns, while gauging their prevalence and effectiveness, our research question was "how to fight against dark patterns?", which led us to bridge the gap between a problem-oriented to a problem-solving vision.

In this sense, we proposed a taxonomy of dark patterns with corresponding fair patterns as countermeasures. This taxonomy groups the categories from the existing taxonomies making them easily usable and resistant to change. Complementary to the taxonomy, we propose fair patterns as an alternative that creates interfaces which do not manipulate users and respect the legal and regulatory framework.

References

1. Brignull, H.: Types of Deceptive Design (2010). https://www.deceptive.design. Accessed 23 Jan 2023
2. King, J., Stephan, A.: Regulating privacy dark patterns in practice- drawing inspiration from California Privacy Rights Act. Georgetown Law Technol. Rev. **5**(2), 250–276 (2021)
3. Conti, G., Sobiesk, E.: Malicious interface design: exploiting the user. In: Proceedings of the 19th International Conference on World Wide Web, pp. 271–280 (2010, April)
4. Bösch, C., Benjamin, E., Kargl, F., Kopp, H., Pfattheicher, S.: Tales from the dark side: privacy dark strategies and privacy dark patterns. Proc. Privacy Enhanc. Technol. **2016**(4), 237–254 (2016). https://doi.org/10.1515/popets-2016-0038
5. Gray, C., Kou, Y., Battles, B., Hoggatt, J., Toombs, A.: The dark (patterns) side of UX design. In: CHI 2018, pp. 1–14. CHI, Montréal (2018). https://doi.org/10.1145/3173574.3174108
6. Mathur, A., Acar, G., Friedman, M., Lucherini, E., Mayer, J., Chetty, M., et al.: Dark patterns at scale: findings from a crawl of 11k shopping websites. ACM Hum.-Comput. Interact. **3**, 81–113 (2019). https://doi.org/10.1145/3359183
7. Luguri, J., Strahilevitz, L.: Shining a light on dark patterns. J. Legal Anal. **13**(1), 43–109 (2021). https://doi.org/10.1093/jla/laaa006
8. Jarovsky L.: Dark patterns in personal data collection: definition, taxonomy and lawfulness. SSRN 1–51 (2022). https://doi.org/10.2139/ssrn.4048582
9. OECD: Dark Commercial Patterns (2022)
10. Mathur, A., Mayer, J., Kshirsagar M.: What makes a dark pattern... dark? design attributes, normative considerations, and measurement methods. In: CHI Conference on Human Factors in Computing Systems (CHI 2021), pp. 1–27. ACM, New York (2021)
11. Kahneman, D.: Judgment Under Uncertainty: Heuristics and Biases. Cambridge University Press, New York (1982)
12. Waldman, A.E.: Cognitive biases, dark patterns, and the 'privacy paradox. Curr. Issues Psychol. **31**, 1–11 (2020). https://doi.org/10.1016/j.copsyc.2019.08.025

13. Commission Nationale de l'informatique et des Libertés (CNIL). Shaping choices in the digital world: from dark patterns to data protection: the influence of ux/ui design on user empowerment. (2019)
14. European Data Protection Board (EDPB). Guidelines 3/2022 on deceptive design patterns in social media platform interfaces: how to recognise and avoid them (2023)
15. Forbrukerrådet (The Norwegian Consumer Council). Deceived by design: how tech companies use dark patterns to discourage us from exercising our rights to privacy (2018)
16. FTC Bureau of Consumer Protection. Bringing dark patterns to light (2022)
17. European Commission (EC). Behavioral study on unfair commercial practices in the digital environment: dark patterns and manipulative personalization- final report (2022)
18. European Commission Press Corner. https://ec.europa.eu/commission/presscorner/detail/en/ip_23_418. Accessed 03 Feb 2023
19. SERNAC. https://www.sernac.cl/portal/619/w3-article-62983.html. Accessed 03 Feb 2023
20. Organization for Economic Cooperation and Development (OECD). Roundtable on Dark Commercial Patterns Online: Summary of Discussion (2021). https://www.oecd.org/officiald ocuments/publicdisplaydocumentpdf/?cote=DSTI/CP(2020)23/FINAL&docLanguage=En
21. Di Geronimo, L., Braz, L., Fregnan, E., Palomba, F., Baccheli A.: UI dark patterns and where to find them: a study on mobile applications and user perception. In: CHI 2020, pp. 1–14. ACM, New York (2020). https://doi.org/10.1145/3313831.3376600
22. Gunawan, J., Choffnes, D., Woodrow, H., Wilson, C.: Towards an understanding of dark pattern privacy harms. In: CHI 2021, pp 1–15. ACM, New York (2021)
23. Radesky, J., et al.: Prevalence and characteristics of manipulative design in mobile applications used by children. JAMA Netw. Open 5(6), 1–11 (2022). https://doi.org/10.1001/jamanetwo rkopen.2022.17641
24. Potel-Saville, M., Talbourdet, E.: Empowering children to understand and exercise their personal data rights. In: Legal Design Perspectives. Theoretical and Practical Insights from the Field, pp. 253–276. Ledizioni, Milano (2021). https://doi.org/10.5281/zenodo.5710845
25. Blake, T., Moshary, S., Sweeney, K., Tadelis, S.: Price salience and product choice. Mark. Sci. 40(4), 619–636 (2021). https://doi.org/10.1287/mksc.2020.1261
26. Consumer Policy Research Centre (CPRC). Duped by Design. Manipulative Online Design: Dark Patterns in Australia (2022)
27. Rasch, A., Thöne, M., Wenzel, T.: Drip pricing and its regulation: experimental evidence. J. Econ. Behav. Organiz. 176(1), 353–370 (2020). https://doi.org/10.1016/j.jebo.2020.04.007
28. Competition and Markets Authority. Online Choice Architecture: How Digital Design Can Harm Competition and Consumers (2022)
29. Slaughter, R.K.: Opening remarks of acting chairwoman Rebecca Kelly Slaughter at "Bringing dark patterns to light" workshop. In: FTC 'Bringing Dark Patterns to Light' Workshop, pp. 1–2
30. Kemp, K.: Concealed data practices and competition law: why privacy matters. Eur. Compet. J. 16(2), 628–672 (2020). https://doi.org/10.1080/17441056.2020.1839228
31. Day, G., Stemler, A.: Are dark patterns anti-competitive? Alabama Law Rev. 72(1), 2–45 (2020). https://doi.org/10.2139/ssrn.3468321
32. Shaw, S.: Consumers Are Becoming Wise to Your Nudge. https://behavioralscientist.org/con sumers-are-becoming-wise-to-your-nudge/
33. Maier, M., Harr, R.: Dark design patterns: an end-user perspective. Hum. Technol. 16(2), 170–199 (2020)
34. Voigt, C., Schlögl S., Groth, A.: Dark patterns in online shopping: of sneaky tricks, perceived annoyance and respective brand trust. In: HCI International, pp. 1–12. HCI, Washington, D.C. (2021). https://doi.org/10.48550/arXiv.2107.07893
35. Robbert, T., Roth, S.: The flip side of drip pricing. J. Prod. Brand Manag. 23(6), 413–419 (2014). https://doi.org/10.1108/JPBM-06-2014-0638

36. Totzek, D., Jurgensen, G.: Many a little makes a mickle: why do consumers negatively react to sequential price disclosure? Psychol. Mark. **38**(1), 113–129 (2020). https://doi.org/10.1002/mar.21426

37. OECD. OECD Recommendation of the Council on Consumer Protection in E-Commerce (2016)

38. Potel-Saville, M.: Dark patterns: l'étau législatif se resserre (enfin?) sur les interfaces manipulatrices ou trompeuses. Revue pratique de la Prospective et de l'Innovation **2**(6), 41–47 (2022)

39. California Privacy Rights Act, 2020: CPRA/Cal. Civ. Code § 1798.140(l)

40. Digital Charter Implementation Act (Bill C-27)

41. Regulation (EU) 2016/679 of the European Parliament and of the Council of 27 April 2016 on the protection of natural persons with regard to the processing of personal data and on the free movement of such data, and repealing Directive 95/46/EC (General Data Protection Regulation)

42. Regulation of the Parliament and of the Council on an internal market for digital services (Digital Services Legislation) and amending Directive 2000/31/EC. (Digital Services Act)

43. Proposal for a Regulation laying down harmonized rules on artificial intelligence, COM (2021) 206 final, 21 April 2021

44. Fritsch, L.: Privacy dark patterns in identity management. In: Roßnagel, H., Hühnlein, D. (eds.) Open Identity Summit 2017, pp. 93–105. Gesellschaft für Informatik, Bonn (2017)

45. Habib, H., Li, L., Young, E., Cranor, L.: "Okay, whatever": an evaluation of cookie consent interfaces. In: CHI Conference on Human Factors in Computing Systems, pp 1–27. ACM, New York (2022). https://doi.org/10.1145/3491102.3501985

46. Gray, C., Santos, C., Bielova, N., Toth, M., Clifford, D.: Dark patterns and the legal requirements of consent banners: an interaction criticism perspective. In: 2021 CHI Conference on Human Factors in Computing Systems, pp. 1–18. ACM, New York (2021). https://doi.org/10.48550/arXiv.2009.10194

47. Kelly, D., Rubin, V.: Dark pattern typology: how do social networking sites deter disabling of user accounts? In: 12th International Conference on Social Media and Society (#SMSociety), pp. 1–5. EasyChair, Online (2022). https://doi.org/10.13140/RG.2.2.14087.47528

48. Schaffner, B., Lingareddy, N.A., Chetty, M.: Understanding account deletion and relevant dark patterns on social media. PROC. ACM Hum.-Comput. Interact. **6**(417), 1–27 (2022). https://doi.org/10.1145/3555142

49. Jarovsky, L.: Improving consent in information privacy through autonomy-preserving protective measures (APPMs). EDPL **4**(4), 447–458 (2018). https://doi.org/10.21552/edpl/2018/4/7

50. Bongard-Blanchy, K., Rossi, A., Rivas, S., Doublet, S., Koenig, V., Lenzini, G.: "I am definitely manipulated, even when I am aware of it. It's ridiculous!" – dark patterns from the end-user perspective. In: Designing Interactive Systems Conference, pp. 1–10. ACM, New York (2021). https://doi.org/10.1145/3461778.3462086

51. Hoepman, J.H.: Privacy design strategies. In: Cuppens-Boulahia, N., Cuppens, F., Jajodia, S., Abou El Kalam, A., Sans, T. (eds.). IFIP Advances in Information and Communication Technology (SEC 2014), vol. 428, pp. 446–459 Springer, Heidelberg (2014). https://doi.org/10.1007/978-3-642-55415-5_38

52. Graßl, P., Schraffenberger, H., Borgesius, F., Buijzen, M.: Dark and bright patterns in cookie consent requests. J. Digit. Soc. Res. **3**(1), 1–38 (2021). https://doi.org/10.33621/jdsr.v3i1.54

53. Nouwens, M., Liccardi, I., Veale, M., Karger, D., Kagal, L.: Dark patterns after the GDPR: scraping consent pop-ups and demonstrating their influence. In: CHI 2020, pp. 1–13. ACM, Honolulu (2020). https://doi.org/10.1145/3313831.3376321

54. Zachrisson, J., Storrø, G., Boks, C.: Using a guide to select design strategies for behavior change: theory vs. practice. In: Matsumoto, M., Umeda, Y., Masui, K., Fukushige, S. (eds.) Design for Innovative Value Towards a Sustainable Society, pp. 362–367. Springer, Dordrecht (2012). https://doi.org/10.1007/978-94-007-3010-6_70
55. International Organization for Standardization. 2019. ISO 9241-210:2019. Ergonomics of Human-System Interaction - Part 210: Human-Centered Design for Interactive Systems (2019). https://www.iso.org/fr/standard/77520.html
56. Strahilevitz, L.: Comments at US FTC workshop "Bringing Dark Patterns to Light" (2021)
57. Ahuja, S., Kumar, J.: A framework for ethics education in persuasive UX design. In: International Conference on Interfaces and Human Computer Interaction 2022; and Game and Entertainment Technologies (2022)
58. Ahuja, S., Kumar, J.: Conceptualizations of user autonomy within the normative evaluation of dark patterns. Ethics Inf. Technol. **24**(52), 1–18 (2022). https://doi.org/10.1007/s10676-022-09672-9
59. Berbece, S.: Let there be Light!: Dark Patterns Under the Lens of the EU Legal Framework. KU Leuven (2019)
60. Borberg, I., Hougaard, R.., Rafnsson, W., Kulyk, O.: "So I Sold My Soul": Effects of Dark Patterns in Cookie Notices on End-User Behavior and Perceptions. In: Usable Security and Privacy (USEC) Symposium, pp. 1–11. Usable Security and Privacy, San Diego (2022). https://doi.org/10.14722/usec.2022.23026
61. Chang, D., Krupka, E., Adar, E., Acquisti, A.: Engineering information disclosure: norm shaping designs. In: CHI 2016, pp. 1–11. ACM, San Jose (2016). https://doi.org/10.1145/2858036.2858346
62. Dinner, I., Goldstein, D., Johnson, E., Liu, K.: Partitioning default effects: why people choose not to choose. J. Exp. Psychol. Appl. **17**(4), 332–366 (2011). https://doi.org/10.1037/a0024354
63. Jeulin, P.: "Dark pattern": comment le droit se saisit-il de l'exploitation de nos biais cognitifs. https://www.village-justice.com/articles/dark-patterns-comment-droit-saisit-exploitation-nos-biais-cognitifs.39971.html. Accessed 23 Jan 2023
64. Kollmer, T., Eckhardt, A.: Dark patterns: conceptualization and future research directions. Bus. Inf. Syst. Eng. **64**(6), 1–8 (2022). https://doi.org/10.1007/s12599-022-00783-7
65. Li, D.: The FTC and the CPRA's regulation of dark patterns in cookie consent notices. Univ. Chicago Bus. Law Rev. **1**(1), 561–590 (2022)
66. Michaels, J.: Pathways to the light: realistic tactics to address dark patterns. Rutgers Comput. Technol. Law J. **49**(1), 176–205 (2023)
67. Nousiainen, K., Potel-Saville, M., Perdomo Ortega, M.: Online contracting, fair patterns and business sustainability. EDFS 309: Scholarly Personal Narrative Writing (in Press 2023)
68. Klein, T.: The true colors of dark patterns. https://www.oxera.com/insights/agenda/articles/bits-of-advice-the-true-colours-of-dark-patterns/. Accessed 23 Jan 2023
69. Rieger, S., Sanders, C.: Dark patterns: regulating digital design; how digital design practices undermine public policy efforts & how governments and regulators can respond. https://www.stiftung-nv.de/sites/default/files/dark.patterns.english.pdf. Accessed 23 Jan 2023
70. Truong, H., Dalbard, A.: Bright Patterns as an Ethical Approach to Counteract Dark Patterns: A Closer Investigation of The Ethics of Persuasive Design. Jönköping University (2022)
71. United Kingdom Competition and Markets Authority. Appendix Y: Choice Architecture and Fairness by Design. (2019)
72. Proposal for a Regulation of the European Parliament and of the Council on Harmonised Rules on Fair Access to and Use of Data (Data Act) COM/2022/68 Final, 23rd February 2022
73. International Organization for Standardization. ISO 9241-11:2018. Ergonomics of human-system interaction — Part 11: Usability: Definitions and concepts (2018). https://www.iso.org/obp/ui/#iso:std:iso:9241:-11:ed-2:v1:en

A Singular Approach to Address Privacy Issues by the Data Protection and Privacy Relationships Model (DAPPREMO)

Nicola Fabiano[1,2][✉]

[1] Studio Legale Fabiano, Rome, Italy
nicola@fabiano.law
[2] University of Ostrava, Ostrava, Italy

Abstract. We describe the Data Protection and Privacy Relationships Model (DAPPREMO), which is based on the set theory and high mathematics, considering that both the data protection and privacy regulation and Ethics principles in those domains belong to a set. DAPPREMO is a new, singular, and innovative solution to adopt a model in data protection and privacy activities. DAPPREMO, through the analysis of reality, allows identifying objects often ignored or unknown. From a data protection and privacy perspective, DAPPREMO reveals itself as an innovative approach to having a broad overview of all the objects related to a specific case or more cases. Moreover, by DAPPREMO, it is possible to identify better the roles of individuals (as data subjects), Institutions (as a controller or processors), and professionals (as Data Protection Officers - DPO or advisors). Thus, we describe DAPPREMO as a solution for a multidisciplinary approach to address any data protection and privacy issue and its future development by applying Machine Learning and Deep Learning to realize a complete artificial intelligence system.

Keywords: Data Protection · Privacy · Relationships · Model

1 Introduction

Our confrontation with the protection of personal data and privacy is a constant note in our daily life. We cannot do without it (even when we face exceptions that exclude the applicability of the specific legislation, such as the hypothesis of state secrecy or something else). No aspect of our lives should be assessed regarding the impact on privacy and data protection. During the spring/summer 2020 health emergency, we saw this that disrupted our lives and questioned our privacy and personal data protection.

Their importance is unquestionable, so much so that they are the subject of internal and European legislation which aims to ensure the primacy of fundamental rights relating to the confidentiality and protection of individuals about processing personal data.

K. Rannenberg et al. (Eds.): APF 2023, LNCS 13888, pp. 166–181, 2024.
https://doi.org/10.1007/978-3-031-61089-9_8

However, some contexts - particularly digital ones - seem governed by specific dynamics. Let us look, for example, at an Internet of Things (IoT) system: on closer inspection, it could be qualified only by focusing on the architecture, the technological solutions adopted, and the devices used. In an IoT system, the technical component, precisely the specificity of communication between objects, is the only dominant and qualifying element. As we highlighted at the beginning of this chapter, we can describe IoT architecture as an "ecosystem" within which several components coexist, including protecting personal data and privacy.

That IoT system (and here we would like to recall our arguments presented in other scientific fora briefly) is relevant in the protection of personal data (or privacy) topic because it becomes an essential part of the ecosystem. Data protection (or privacy) affects the entire ecosystem since the latter aspect is incredibly important. An IoT ecosystem without the data protection component does not perform all its functions correctly and is, therefore, imperfect.

The same consideration concerns any public or private context: the performance of ordinary activities - with or without the aid of technology - must be carried out in compliance with the protection of personal data and privacy regulations. One thinks, for example, of a public office that must carry out bureaucratic activities or a private office that carries out sales activities, regardless of the use of IT tools. Indeed, the typical activities of each sector make up the core. Still, in both cases (public and private), relations with other contexts, such as the processing of personal data and confidentiality, can also be achieved. It is clear that even here, confidentiality and protection of personal data continue to play a fundamental role because the data controller must comply with the rules in force.

In essence, confidentiality and the protection of personal data are of such importance that they significantly affect the context and are fundamental elements.

Given these premises, it is possible to reflect on the possibility of using logical-mathematical analysis to qualify individual areas or domains. We use the term "domain" to refer to a specific sector, such as, for example, the core business of an activity, the complex processes of a Public Administration office, or even a single software development project.

It is also possible to make a leap and identify a precise model that is useful for in-depth analysis and study, on the one hand, and forecasting activities, on the other. It is necessary to proceed with mathematical logic, observing each sector's activities and proposing a logical-mathematical reading. Each area corresponds to the whole (domain); objects are part of the entire (static or dynamic elements such as activities that constitute processes).

Here is an example: a public administration office must carry out specific activities in that sector, and each can be considered the whole object.

Let's make another example similar: in a private company in the single business field, each activity can be considered an object that, together with the others (i.e., as a whole, all the actions), contribute to form a whole.

At this point, we can close the circle and superimpose this logical-mathematical observation considering the impact of the rules on the protection of personal data in each area, which from now on, we can classify as a whole.

The starting point is to ask whether the confidentiality and protection of individuals concerning the processing of personal data can also constitute an ecosystem as a whole. From our perspective, the answer is yes because they are both based on legal and ethical rules, which can form the objects of a system of the whole. However, this set is not an end in itself and cannot generate activities. Still, its existence is necessary and functional to other sets (i.e., different contexts) with which it must relate. Indeed, a set of legal rules, although sector-specific, does not autonomously involve the performance of activities except through their concrete application. Regarding the protection of personal data, the provisions of the GDPR, therefore, autonomously do not involve the performance of activities. Still, in each case, the subjects, according to their respective roles, will be required to comply with this sector discipline.

Indeed, the protection of personal data is more than just respecting and applying rules (this would be a minimal and limited view). In reality, data protection represents a real system, defined according to the mathematically oriented perspective, as a homogeneous set of objects (the single norms). Those objects could also coexist with others not present within the normative body of the sector (concerning the protection of personal data, not expressly contained in a legal norm) of different natures (e.g., ethics) to constitute a heterogeneous whole [see below].

2   Application of the Set Theory

In reality, there are almost daily interactions between systems, domains, or themes (e.g., the Internet of Things "system" interacts with the data protection one, or the Public Administration "system" interacts with the data protection one, and so on). In essence, schematically, it is possible to identify several sets, each belonging to a specific sector and composed of objects. These sets can express "one-to-one" or "one-to-many" relations between or among them and present possible sub-relations between the objects containing them. Therefore, they are dynamic phenomena, not static, which involve continuous relationships and related effects.

It is essential to understand the mathematical explanation of relationships.

In mathematics, given two sets A and B, where both A and B are not the empty set, if we say that the set A consists of objects that we state by $a, b, c, d, e, \ldots$ then we will denote $A = \{a, b, c, d, e, \ldots\}$, while if we say that the set B may consist of totally different elements that we state by $x, y, s, t, u, v, \ldots$, then we will denote $B = \{x, y, s, t, u, v, \ldots\}$.

If we consider the following two sets:

$$A = \{a, b, c, d, e, \ldots\} \qquad \text{and} \qquad B = \{x, y, s, t, u, v, \ldots\}$$

Any relation between A and B is usually denoted by writing notations such as $A\mathcal{R}B$, or $A\mathcal{E}B$, or even $A \sim B$ or with other symbols interposed between A and B. To define a relation between two sets in Mathematics, however, we must consider the Cartesian product between two sets A and B. This is, by definition, the new set indicated by the symbol $A \times B$ made by all the possible ordered pairs whose first coordinate is any element of A and whose second coordinate is whichever element of B. For example, if $A = \{1, 2, 3, 4\}$ and $B = \{x, y\}$, then the Cartesian product $A \times B$ is the following set:

$$A \times B = \{(1, x), (1, y), (2, x), (2, y), (3, x), (3, y), (4, x), (4, y)\}$$

Whose elements are all ordered pairs (c_1, c_2), where c_1 is any element of A (so $c_1 = 1$, or $c_1 = 2$, or $c_1 = 3$, or $c_1 = 4$) and c_2 is any element of B (so $c_2 = x$, or $c_2 = y$).

Having acquired the notion of Cartesian product between two sets A and B, we can define the notion of *relation* between A and B. A *relation* between A and B is defined as any subset of the Cartesian product $A \times B$ in Mathematics.

Therefore, if A and B are the two sets in the example just illustrated, an example of *relation* between A and B is given by the set:

$$\mathcal{R} = \{(1, x), (1, y), (3, x)\}$$

In this relation, the element $1 \in A$ is related to both x and y, the latter being elements of B. The element $3 \in A$ is only related to x. Elements $2 \in A$ and $4 \in A$ are not related to anything (it is possible to assign relations in which one or more elements of the first set A are "orphans", i.e., are not related to anything). The relation

$$\mathcal{R} = \{(1, x), (1, y), (3, x)\}$$

We can have a suggestive graphical representation if we use Venn diagrams and indicate the ordered pairs of elements in relation by arrows, as in the following figure (Fig. 1).

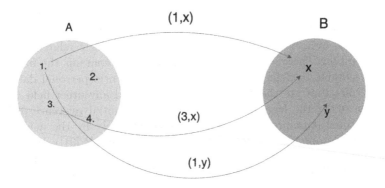

Fig. 1. Venn diagram: the ordered pairs of elements in relation by arrows

Given any relation $\mathcal{R}$ between two sets A and B, the fact that the pair (a, b) belongs to $\mathcal{R}$, i.e., which is the same, the fact the elements $a \in A$ and $b \in B$ are related by $\mathcal{R}$, is usually denoted by simply writing $a\mathcal{R}b$.

On the other hand, if we have more than two sets, for example, a family of n sets $(S_1, S_2, S_3, \ldots S_n)$, we will say that two of them, for example, S_i and S_j are *connected* if there is a relation of any kind between them; we denote this configuration by $S_i \sim S_j$. In other terms, given a family of n sets $(S_1, S_2, S_3, \ldots S_n)$ we have that:

$$S_i \sim S_j \iff \text{there exists a relation } \mathcal{R} \text{ such that } S_i \mathcal{R} S_j$$

Below is an image of the relation between several sets (one-to-many) (Fig. 2):

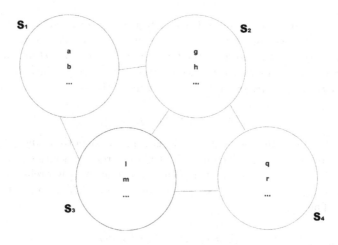

Fig. 2. Relation between several sets (one-to-many)

One set, say S_1, can be connected to several different sets simultaneously. In this case, you have a one-to-many relationship.

That said, more specifically, we can describe the context related to data protection as a set of objects that are the legal rules of the sector in addition to other entities, even non-homogeneous (e.g., ethics), closely related to the context in question. Therefore, the "data protection" set contains the fundamental elements suitable to define the specific area. In essence, personal data protection has rules that are the norms for the sector and any other field worthy of protection under the legal system. Therefore, the initial reference of the sector of personal data protection is constituted precisely by the field laws (for example, in Europe, the EU Regulation 2016/679 - GDPR [31]). However, even the hermeneutic survey of legal rules can reveal other essential aspects, such as ethics. These elements, legal norms, and other entities constitute a real'personal data protection' ecosystem that we can define as a whole. The 'data protection' set is identified by a characteristic property that unites all and only the elements.

Therefore, objects of a set, such as ethics and legal norms, have the characteristic property expressed as their applicative effect in common. Thus, ethics is not described in any data protection law - it is an element of the whole because it has the same characteristic property as the other elements (the legal rules) regarding their enforcement effect. The interaction with other sets continues after a simple and, in any case, necessary verification of regulatory compliance. Still, it constitutes the initial impulse of an osmotic, exchange, and dynamic process that proceeds from analyzing the specific context, identifying all its attributes, and providing the necessary elements for the correct hermeneutic approach.

3 The Relationships Between Objects and Those Between Subassemblies

The above description constitutes a part - the initial one - which concerns the relations. Indeed, it is possible that, in addition to the connections between sets, there may also exist those between individual objects in a set, according to the following example scheme (Fig. 3).

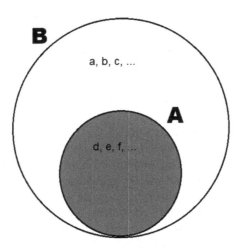

Fig. 3. Connections between individual objects in a set

Considering this image and assuming that set A is the one related to privacy (or to the protection of personal data), it is evident not only what the regime of relations between sets may be but also what the significant impact of the subject matter covered by this volume with many other areas is. Indeed, any area generates a relationship with that relating to the protection of personal data and privacy. Identifying relationships by applying mathematics is a necessary added value to provide a broad and precise approach.

The mentioned diagram shows the Eulero-Venn inclusion report which can be denoted by

$$A \subset B$$

Set A relates to privacy (or protection of personal data) and the set B describes a different area (or field or sector). It emerges that set A is always present in the diverse relationships among sets since we cannot dismiss the rules on the protection of personal data. It is an example of *subset*, where, as the number of objects in the set "privacy" in common with another set varies, the impact of the legal discipline and, therefore, the rules to be respected will vary accordingly. This graphic representation, expressed mathematically by the formula reproduced above, makes it possible to have a definite impact on the rules for the protection of personal data in each area, sector, or area.

The inversion of the scenario just described shows how the set A is that one related to the protection of personal data (or privacy) and broader than the smaller set B. It appears feasible only in the hypothesis that exogenous elements or external objects (e.g., ethics) concerning the legal regulations on privacy are dominant and must also have in common with the smaller set or content. In particular, we said that the whole "protection of personal data" (or privacy) is mainly made up of legal regulations, is not an end in itself, and, above all, does not enjoy autonomous operation but is characterized by dynamic interaction with other sets.

By analyzing the relationships, it is also possible that one may be created between sets and, in particular, and specifically between the one containing the legal rules on the protection of personal data and another domain, another area. A union of non-empty sets may come true depending on each set's content (of the objects).

Turning back to the considerations of the beginning, we point out the fact that since the notation of inclusion, $A \subset B$ implies that all elements of A are also elements of B when such an assumption is used in a context such as the one above, it implies that all legal and/or regulatory or operating/administrative rules of a specific sphere are also rules of privacy or ethics; in general, this may be too strong a claim and overly restrictive. Therefore, it might be helpful to express a similar concept but in a weaker, and thus broader, form, as follows. Let us denote by P and E the following sets:

$$P = \{\text{privacy rules}\} \quad \text{and} \quad E = \{\text{ethical principles}\}$$

Thus, setting $B = P \cup E$, it can be said that whatever the set A of norms of a particular area of public life is, there is always some appropriate subset $A' \subset B$ which is related to A according to the above sense of set relation. In formula:

$$\text{it exists } A' \subset B \text{ such that } A \mathcal{R} A'$$

Suppose, for example, A indicates the set of all the rules of regulation and behavior that - for example - regulate the functioning of a collegiate body. In that case, it is not necessarily the case that the element of A are also data protection or privacy and Ethics rules, as the notation $A \subset B$ would suggest. Instead, it may be that the elements of A are related to appropriate norms of data protection or privacy and Ethics. The latter eventually depend on the elements of A and constitute the subset A' of B to which A is related.

There is yet another way by which it is possible to interpret the whole framework. The following Figure is the Eulero-Venn diagram representing intersections of sets (Fig. 4):

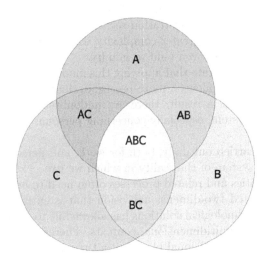

Fig. 4. Eulero-Venn diagram representing intersections of sets

Whose intersection relations are expressed mathematically as:

$$A \cap B \cap C, \quad A \cap C, \quad B \cap A, \quad C \cap B$$

Suppose one of the three sets, for example, A, is the data protection (or privacy) set. The diagram represents an intersection between domains, one of which is the one related to the protection of personal data (or privacy), and it shows how it is possible to identify common areas constituted precisely by the intersections and, therefore, the relationships between sets and objects of each set or domain.

However, a clarification is necessary. Even graphically, what is proposed and described may seem represented on a two-dimensional plane. In reality, the complexity of the relationships must also be analyzed on a three-dimensional or multidimensional plane since, in this way, it is possible to obtain a broader vision that is much closer to reality.

As it is evident, even in this brief exposition of the relations between sets, one or more connections between different domains with a specific role related to the protection of personal data (or privacy) can occur.

4   Description of a Complex Multidimensional Model

The summary of the proposals described in the previous paragraphs leads to some reflections.

We said that the proposed model is based on set theory, where each area (e.g., privacy, personal data protection, Internet of Things, Public Administration sectors, private sectors, etc.) constitutes a set, and that is a domain. In everyday activities, there are always relationships between areas or domains. Indeed, the "protection of personal data" (a domain) has a relationship - for example - with that of a specific Public Administration sector, an IoT ecosystem, or a private sector. The model assumes greater complexity where the relationships between domains increase and may even tend to infinity.

The aim is to demonstrate that applying this model, allowing a much broader view of the phenomena, allows a more precise evaluation of domains and individual relationships. As a result, there are undoubtedly beneficial effects for the entire analysis system, especially concerning personal profiles, as illustrated later.

The activities carried out daily, both for work, and personal needs, are part (processes) of the system of the reality in which we live.

However, activities and related processes often need to be correctly observed due to a short-sighted two-dimensional vision that is entirely reductive. Using the most modern technological solutions has allowed us to see the so-called "augmented reality", i.e., multidimensional contexts. Therefore, if we observed phenomena not on a two-dimensional plane but a three-dimensional or multidimensional one, we would have the possibility to perceive any with greater precision any component.

For example, the request for a document to the Public Administration consists of two different processes: the application by a person and the appropriate activities by the competent Office who have to handle it. The applicant and the Office carry out their actions on a single plane or level of observation. If one imagines using zoom and thus enlarging the field of view, the point of observation changes with the possibility of having an overall look from both the applicant's and the Office's side.

If we use the same method to analyze scenarios relating to the relationship between the personal data protection (or privacy) domain and other domains, we would have a broader view and the opportunity to benefit from a completely different perception.

The complexity of the model proposed is precisely characterized by the innumerable and unpredictable number of domains to be considered for relations, considering that, in theory, the number of domains (i.e., sets) is potentially infinite.

In its graphic representation, the model appears very close to that of a multidimensional distributed network system. Each point of intersection represents a set (a domain), and the relationship is the union of the different points (which represents the sets). We should evaluate the representation not so much on a two-dimensional plane but in multidimensional terms as a link between sets. One of the essential elements is multidimensionality because we imagine different planes in space as if they were layers of a single system (Fig. 5).

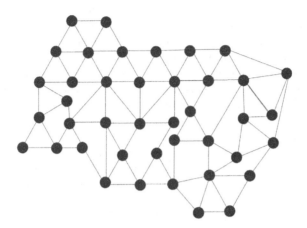

Fig. 5. Distributed network system

At a first brief investigation, it emerges that the system of relations here presented could find some similarities with a complex structure, borrowed from advanced mathematics, known as the "fiber bundle set", which would seem to be able to account for the interactions and connections that occur both between individual elements and between sets of elements.

In development, that is the first and innovative approach to the mathematical interpretation of the multidimensional inter-relational framework. Still, our model has the merit of providing a unifying and abstract vision of a scenario of high complexity, such as the one on which we intend to focus our study investigation.

The complexity of the "**fiber bundle**" makes its description not simple. Still, we can illustrate it as a brush (see figure below) where the shaft represents, in our case, the data protection set. The individual bristles constitute the relationships and connections between sets and objects of each other set[1].

We can also illustrate the "**fiber bundle**" with another image of a book open 360° where the covers joined. That could give an idea of the complexity of the phenomenon.

Intersecting lines represent the relationships between the single words on the pages.

The proposed model, representing the links between sets, can be a potent tool for a global and systemic approach.

The model, therefore, is based on the links between sets. The objects belonging to the data protection (or privacy) domain comprise the legislation in force and other external (exogenous) contexts to the legal discipline, neither typical

---

[1] This representation can be found on Wikipedia under "Fiber bundle".

nor predetermined. The data protection set is related to the others, providing from time to time valuable attributes for the qualification of the single scenario and, therefore, the most suitable tools. It is impossible to generalize and pre-determine the quality and quantity of attributes helpful to the individual case in a single scenario. These are sure enough dynamic and variable contexts that as much can differ from each other as, on the contrary, each one can achieve a standard in terms of approach and operation.

The complexity of the model, at times, can make the dynamic aspect escape and lose sight of it, leaving space to focus only on the static part of the core that corresponds to the regulations in force. The regulatory discipline is not and cannot be an end in itself. Still, we must evaluate it as contributing to analyzing a complex and dynamic context.

The attributes of ecosystem data protection are numerous, some precise and identified, and others indefinite and indeterminable. Among the specific fundamental objects, there is undoubtedly ethics, which is a crucial and essential element for analyzing every single scenario. Ethics can seem an exogenous factor, extraneous to the set of rules governing the matter of the protection of personal data. In reality, this is not the case because the reference to ethics emerges from the principles contained in the whole body of rules. Thus, ethics is very close to the effects of the other elements of the whole (the legal norms) regarding the same characteristic property that unites them.

The proposed model, called DAPPREMO, the acronym for "Data Protection Relationships Model", can be expressed mathematically through the concept of equivalence relationships (Fig. 6).

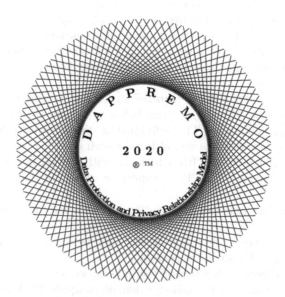

Fig. 6. DAPPREMO Logo^{TM}®

Analyzing the results of the links and the relationships, the roles of the subjects, and the activities on personal data, it is clear that many consequences arise from this model. Here we wanted to present the DAPPREMO model, although with the clarification that it is still the subject of further study and any updates will be contained in future publications.

5 The Model and the Role of the Subjects

As described, the DAPPREMO model allows an extensive view of the relations between domains with the definite possibility of a detailed analysis and possible appropriate and specific solutions or interventions, much more precise than they commonly are.

Knowledge of the issues to be addressed and their full awareness are the basis of a correct approach to any scenario. In essence, the proposed model undoubtedly is a more intelligent approach.

Being the case, what could be the effects of using this model for individual persons (let's call them "agents") involved in the data protection domain?

The first significant effect is on the supervisory authorities since using the model-based approach described gives a comprehensive view of the individual phenomenon and those related to it. Imagine that a supervisory authority has to face a preliminary investigation on a specific issue that, at first glance, is independent but is indeed strictly related to other domains.

An investigation, even if only exploratory, for example, on the effects of an app, through the model-based approach, allows the supervisory authority to have a much broader view of any existing relationship (software development domain, Internet of Things, data transfer, etc.). If, on the other hand, the supervisory authority has to decide on a complaint, it is possible - through the proposed model-based approach - to have a comprehensive overview of each existing relationship with the case under examination.

In essence, it is a tool that offers the opportunity of an approach consistent with the "new" privacy, which must consider not only the regulatory part but any context that can be related to the phenomenon - even purely bureaucratic - under examination.

Regarding the data controller and data processor, the use of the model will offer undoubted advantages in terms of analysis of the links of its core business with any other domain with which there is a connection.

In this way, the complex activity of adaptation and compliance with the legal rules on the "protection of natural persons with regard to the processing of personal data" will be facilitated and, above all, much more precise, knowing well in the analysis phase which types of principles to implement and the consequent interventions to be carried out.

It will also benefit the person concerned by using the model in terms of a different approach than merely consulting and applying legal rules. Knowing existing relationships regarding one's personal data allows one to exercise one's rights more consciously and correctly.

6   DAPPREMO's Concrete Applications for Individuals and Institutions, and Future Developments: The Use of Artificial Intelligence

DAPPREMO, as described before, represents an innovative data protection and privacy approach. Indeed, some organizations already consider and adopt it in their data protection and privacy processes, so we already have a few concrete applications.

Thinking that DAPPREMO is only a theoretical new approach or does not represent a practical data protection and privacy solution is a rushed, rough, and wrong conclusion. No doubt about applying DAPPREMO in practice, although it may appear complex.

Considering DAPPREMO's complexity, we are deepening the model further by improving and enhancing it. We aim to put so much effort on it to become "DAPPREMO 2: the evolution". We are working to create an artificial intelligence system capable of analyzing reality and carrying out some outcomes to help people address data protection and privacy issues.

The application of the model (DAPPREMO) makes it possible to identify the entire data protection context very precisely and, more specifically, individual processes. In this way, it is possible to identify the roles of the "agents" clearly: individuals and organizations involved in each data protection and privacy process.

From the perspective of individuals, DAPPREMO enables them to have much more transparent data protection processes so that the entire context is more precise concerning the rights of data subjects, whether the processing respects the information provided by the controller, referring mainly to the purposes, and whether it complies with the law.

In addition, DAPPREMO allows any Institution (as a controller or Supervisory Authority) or professionals (as a Data Protection Officer - DPO or advisors) to carry out an assessment more accurately in identifying "objects" strictly relevant to the analyzed case or context that, instead, very often are overlooked because they are ignored or not considered intentionally or unintentionally.

Declining DAPPREMO entirely is indeed complex and challenging. It is necessary to proceed by realizing UML models that describe specific contexts more precisely according to the concrete application of DAPPREMO.

Considering that the objects described in DAPPREMO tend to be infinite, we decided to initially focus on the relationships among individuals, Public Administration, and Institutions. A first analysis highlights unexplored points representing objects in the DAPPREMO's ontology.

In summary, the approach we adopted to investigate a solution was to start creating datasets, whose activities are very demanding for finding credible data sources and analyzing their results, to prepare the basis for Machine Learning and Deep Learning application.

The ambitious and complex project requires technical and legal knowledge. We are putting all our effort into it.

We aim to deepen the interactions between individuals (agents) and Public Entities (those who should deal with individuals' instances) by identifying the unknown or ignored relevant objects.

In this way, DAPPREMO will be improved and refined with the support of artificial intelligence, and its practical application will be more effective.

7 Conclusions

DAPPREMO is an innovative and powerful relational personal data protection and privacy model.

DAPPREMO also includes Ethics, which is a crucial element in the approach and analysis of any scenario.

In conclusion, DAPPREMO is the tool to analyze reality with a highly innovative approach.

We realized its structure and essence, being fully aware - all should be - that we have long since entered a new era of personal data protection and privacy.

Any analysis in these areas must allow for insights accurately adhering to current contexts.

With outdated conceptions and approaches, one cannot approach and operate in personal data protection and privacy today.

The evolution of DAPPREMO will be an artificial intelligence system through the application of Machine Learning and Deep Learning.

References

1. 40th International Conference of Data Protection and Privacy Commissioners, Declaration on Ethics and Data Protection in Artificial Intelligence (2018). https://globalprivacyassembly.org/wp-content/uploads/2018/10/20180922_ICDPPC-40th_AI-Declaration_ADOPTED.pdf. Accessed Mar 2023
2. 42nd Closed Session of the Global Privacy Assembly - GPA. Resolution on accountability in the development and use of Artificial Intelligence (2020). https://globalprivacyassembly.org/wp-content/uploads/2020/11/GPA-Resolution-on-Accountability-in-the-Development-and-Use-of-AI-EN.pdf. Accessed Mar 2023
3. 38th International Conference of Data Protection and Privacy Commissioners. Artificial Intelligence, Robotics, Privacy and Data Protection (2016). https://edps.europa.eu/data-protection/our-work/publications/other-documents/artificial-intelligence-robotics-privacy-and_en. Accessed Mar 2023
4. Atabekov, A.: Artificial intelligence in contemporary societies: legal status and definition, implementation in public sector across various countries. Soc. Sci. **12**, 178 (2023). https://doi.org/10.3390/socsci12030178
5. Charter of Fundamental Rights of the European Union (2016). https://eur-lex.europa.eu/legal-content/EN/TXT/?uri=celex%3A12016P%2FTXT. Accessed Mar 2023
6. Council of Europe. Recommendation CM/Rec(2020)1 of the Committee of Ministers to member States on the human rights impacts of algorithmic systems (2020). https://search.coe.int/cm/pages/result_details.aspx?objectid=09000016809e1154. Accessed Mar 2023

7. Council of Europe. Convention for the Protection of Individuals with regard to Automatic Processing of Personal Data as it will be amended by its Protocol CETS No. 223 (2018). https://rm.coe.int/16808ade9d. Accessed Mar 2023

8. Council of Europe, European Convention on Human Rights (2013). https://www.echr.coe.int/Documents/Convention_ENG.pdf. Accessed Mar 2023

9. Zha, D., et al.: Data-centric artificial intelligence: a survey (2023). https://arxiv.org/abs/2303.10158. Accessed Mar 2023

10. Council of Europe. Convention for the Protection of Individuals with regard to Automatic Processing of Personal Data (1981). https://www.coe.int/en/web/conventions/full-list/-/conventions/treaty/108. Accessed Mar 2023

11. European Commission - High-Level Expert Group on Artificial Intelligence (AI HLEG). Assessment List for Trustworthy Artificial Intelligence (ALTAI) for self-assessment (2020). https://digital-strategy.ec.europa.eu/en/library/assessment-list-trustworthy-artificial-intelligence-altai-self-assessment. Accessed Mar 2023

12. European Commission - Ethics Guidelines for Trustworthy AI" by the High-Level Expert Group on Artificial Intelligence (AI HLEG) (2019). https://digital-strategy.ec.europa.eu/en/library/ethics-guidelines-trustworthy-ai. Accessed Mar 2023

13. European Commission's High-Level Expert Group on Artificial Intelligence (AI HLEG), Draft Ethics guidelines for trustworthy AI (2018). https://ec.europa.eu/digital-single-market/en/news/draft-ethics-guidelines-trustworthy-ai. Accessed Mar 2023

14. European Commission, Directorate-General for Research and Innovation, European Group on Ethics in Science and New Technologies, Statement on artificial intelligence, robotics and 'autonomous' systems: Brussels, 9 March 2018, Publications Office (2018). https://data.europa.eu/doi/10.2777/531856. Accessed Mar 2023

15. European Data Protection Supervisor (EDPS), Opinion 4/2015 - Towards a new digital ethics. Data dignity and technology (2015). https://edps.europa.eu/sites/edp/files/publication/15-09-11_data_ethics_en.pdf. Accessed Mar 2023

16. European Parliament - Think Thank, Artificial intelligence liability directive, Briefing (2023). https://www.europarl.europa.eu/thinktank/en/document/EPRS_BRI(2023)739342. Accessed Mar 2023

17. European Parliament - Think Thank, Artificial Intelligence and Civil Liability (2020). https://www.europarl.europa.eu/thinktank/en/document.html?reference=IPOL_STU(2020)621926. Accessed Mar 2023

18. European Parliament - Think Thank, Civil liability regime for artificial intelligence (2020). https://www.europarl.europa.eu/thinktank/en/document.html?reference=EPRS_STU(2020)654178. Accessed Mar 2023

19. European Parliament, Framework of ethical aspects of artificial intelligence, robotics and related technologies (2020). https://www.europarl.europa.eu/doceo/document/TA-9-2020-0275_EN.html. Accessed Mar 2023

20. European Union Agency For Fundamental Rights - FRA, Getting the future right - Artificial intelligence and fundamental rights (2020). https://fra.europa.eu/en/publication/2020/artificial-intelligence-and-fundamental-rights. Accessed Mar 2023

21. European Union Agency For Cybersecurity - ENISA, Artificial Intelligence Cybersecurity Challenges (2020). https://www.enisa.europa.eu/publications/artificial-intelligence-cybersecurity-challenges. Accessed Mar 2023

22. Buttarelli, G.: European Data Protection Supervisor (EDPS), Choose Humanity: Putting Dignity back into Digital (2018). https://www.privacyconference2018.org/system/files/2018-10/Choose%20Humanity%20speech_0.pdf. Accessed Mar 2023

23. Kunkel, R.: Artificial intelligence, automation, and proletarianization of the legal profession. Creighton Law Rev. **56** (2022). https://ssrn.com/abstract=4387638. Accessed Mar 2023
24. Lobel, O.: The Law of AI for Good, San Diego Legal Studies Paper No. 23-001 (2023). https://ssrn.com/abstract=4338862. Accessed Mar 2023
25. Fabiano, N.: GDPR & Privacy. Awareness and opportunities. The approach with the Data Protection and Privacy Relationships Model (DAPPREMO), goWare, Firenze (2020)
26. Fabiano, N.: Robotics, big data, ethics and data protection: a matter of approach. In: Aldinhas Ferreira, M., Silva Sequeira, J., Singh Virk, G., Tokhi, M., Kadar, E. (eds.) Robotics and Well-Being, vol. 95, pp. 79–87. Springer, Heidelberg (2019). https://doi.org/10.1007/978-3-030-12524-0_8
27. Fabiano, N.: European data protection regulation and the blockchain analysis of the critical issues and possible solution proposals (2018)
28. Fabiano, N.: Privacy and security in the internet of things. Cutter IT J. **26**(8) (2013)
29. Chatterjee, P., Benoist, E., Nath, A.: Applied approach to privacy and security for the internet of things. IGI Global (2020)
30. Proposal for a Regulation of the European Parliament and of the Council laying down harmonised rules on Artificial Intelligence (Artificial Intelligence Act) and amending certain Union legislative Acts - Annexes (2021). https://ec.europa.eu/newsroom/dae/items/709090 [retrieved: March 2023]
31. Regulation (EU) 2016/679 of the European Parliament and of the Council of 27 April 2016 on the protection of natural persons with regard to the processing of personal data and on the free movement of such data, and repealing Directive 95/46/EC (General Data Protection Regulation) (2016). https://eur-lex.europa.eu/legal-content/EN/TXT/PDF/?uri=CELEX:32016R0679&from=EN. Accessed Mar 2023
32. Rustad, M.L.: Global information technologies: ethics and the law (2d ed. West Academic 2023) co-authored with Thomas H. Koenig (2023). https://ssrn.com/abstract=. Accessed Mar 2023
33. The Treaty on the functioning of the European Union (2016/C 202/01) (2016). https://www.ecb.europa.eu/ecb/legal/pdf/oj_c_2016_202_full_en_txt.pdf. Accessed Mar 2023

Author Index

K. Rannenberg et al. (Eds.): APF 2023, LNCS 13888, p. 183, 2024.
https://doi.org/10.1007/978-3-031-61089-9

Printed in the United States
by Baker & Taylor Publisher Services